THE ROMAN
INVASION OF
BRITAIN

To the memory of
Donald Dudley

Graham Webster

THE ROMAN INVASION OF BRITAIN

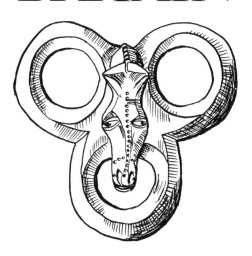

BARNES & NOBLE BOOKS
TOTOWA, NEW JERSEY

First published in the USA 1980 by
Barnes & Noble books
81 Adams Drive
Totowa, New Jersey, 07512

ISBN: 0–389–20107–3

First published 1980
© Graham Webster 1980

Photoset, printed and bound in Great Britain by
REDWOOD BURN LIMITED
Trowbridge & Esher

Contents

Preface

My interest in the Roman invasion and early campaigns in Britain was first aroused by an investigation of the legionary fortress at Lincoln, 1938 – 45 (*JRS* 39 (1949) 57 – 78). There was little opportunity for doing any serious research work until I was appointed as Senior Edward Cadbury Research Fellow at the University of Birmingham in 1953 – 57. This led to the publication of 'The Roman Military Advance under Octorius Scapula' (*Archaeol J* 115 (1960) 49 – 98), and subsequently, with the collaboration of Professor Donald Dudley, of a volume in the British Battle Series entitled *The Roman Conquest of Britain* in 1965. But new information continued to be collected and studied, so that constant revisions were necessary ('The Claudian Frontiers in Britain' *Studien zu der militärgrenzen Rome* 1967, 42 – 53 and 'The Military Situation in Britain AD 43 and 71' *Brit* 1 (1970) 179 – 197).

In 1972, my old friend and collaborator, Donald Dudley, died and I revised the Conquest book of 1965 for a new paperback edition by Pan in 1973. In the six years since much new evidence has come to light, mainly through aerial archaeology and major rescue excavations. Not only are there many new military sites but a radical reconsideration has been needed of the contacts of Rome with the tribes in south-eastern Britain in the period post-dating Caesar, as evidence of extensive trade has been discovered. It became evident as work proceeded on this book, that it was quite impossible to include all the events from AD 43 to 58, and the evidence for them into the space between the covers. So the publishers kindly agreed to allow me two volumes, the present one takes the conquest down to the end of the governorship of Aulus Plautius (AD 47/48) and a second volume will continue the study up to the short governorship of Q Veranius (AD 57/58).

I have been very fortunate in having the collaboration of A Barrett of University of British Columbia, who has been carrying out a careful study of the historical sources of this period and my gratitude to him will be evident from the footnotes. The only historical account of the invasion of AD 43 is that of Dio Cassius, and I acknowledge the help of two Cambridge scholars, Mary Beard and Neil Wright, for their entire reappraisal of this difficult text and new translation (Appendix 1). I must also thank Professor Antony Birley of Manchester University for his kind help with Roman personalities who came to Britain as *comites* with Claudius (and Barry Ecclestone for his skill and patience

7

in drawing his maps.

It will be abundantly clear from the text that I have had from many excacators, aerial photographers, museum curators and colleagues, a vast amount of help and information freely given, much of it before publication. To list them all would be difficult and I hope that full credit has been given in the text and footnotes. I am sorry for any omissions, due to carelessness or forgetfulness. To my wife, Diana, I owe a special word of thanks for improving the quality of the text and excising any over-fanciful ideas and humble gratitude to my secretary Mary Pinder, who has had to re-type so many pages so often. My thanks also to Peter Jennings and Tony Barrett for their careful proof reading. Mistakes and omissions are inevitable and I would be pleased to have any additions and corrections for any future edition, but it must be appreciated that this book can never be more than an interim statement. As more and more information comes to light, ideas are in a continuous state of change.

List of Illustrations

The Plates

Between pages 96 and 97.

Maps

Plans

Acknowledgments

The author and publisher wish to thank the following for permission to reproduce the photographs appearing in this book: the Trustees of the British Museum, 10. Committee for Aerial Photography, Cambridge University, 13 and 17. Colchester and Essex Museum, 1 and 19. Corinium Museum, 9. Professor S S Frere, 12. Curator of the Newark Museum, 12. Society of Antiquaries of London, 4, 6, 7, 8, and 18.

Introduction

To most people, Roman Britain is a distant memory of the early school years, as the teaching of the history of Britain before the Norman Conquest has been always considered suitable only for eight to ten year olds. Text books in the junior schools are expected to last and are so rarely kept up-to-date that youngsters are taught from knowledge and ideas current 20 or 30 years earlier. But these are the formative years and we tend to remember things learnt at this age throughout our life. It is then not surprising to find how difficult it is for adults to absorb and appreciate the results of discoveries and new ideas. It is as if people who still believed in magic to cure their ailments were suddenly asked to take little coloured pills without any mumbo-jumbo.

The span of time, when most of Britain was under Roman influence, stretched from 55 BC to c. AD 600, when control passed into the hands of Germanic peoples, many of whom had been living here already for over a century as troops or allies of the Roman army. Six and a half centuries is a considerable portion of our national history. If one counts back from today, it brings one to about 1330, well into the Middle Ages, a period totally remote from our present world. Yet in spite of this distance in time, the standards of living and the degree of civilization and of military and civil organization in Roman Britain were probably not reached again until the end of the eighteenth century. Admittedly, this applied only to the upper levels of society; the great mass of the people has rarely been affected by improvements at the top in any period.

Archaeology stands on the fringes of public interest and concern, and although there is a constant flow of new knowledge which may fundamentally change some ideas about the past, there is no need to know anything about it, unless it is one's work or hobby. So today, there remains a great and ever widening gulf between the popular images and the realities of our national past. This is as true of Roman Britain as any period. History, it has been said, repeats itself, but this is only because human beings have changed little during the last ten thousand years, and the circumstances in which they find themselves are bound to occur again and again, although with infinite variations.

The manipulations and manoeuvres in politics and government by unscrupulous men, and women, greedy for power and wealth, are a constant and fascinating theme throughout history, and in Roman times we find evidence of much which reminds us of the present. There

13

was a basic similarity in the complicated organizations which maintained a large empire supported by a crude but effective capitalist economy. Problems of currency, devaluation, inflation, heavy taxation and growth of bureauracy, were worrying to the people of the third and fourth centuries as they are to us today. We can study with sympathy and understanding the failure of the Roman government to enforce price controls, and the despair that galloping inflation brought to owners of businesses – and to those at the bottom of the heap, who always come off worse in the end.

One would like to hope that today's people would learn from the past how to emeliorate the effects of the follies of the present. But, alas, all the evidence points to the inescapable conclusion that very few, and certainly no politicians, ever learn from the mistakes of their forebears. Human nature makes us think we know so much better, and that we can always succeed, when so many failed. Yet it is perhaps as well that this over optimistic view of current events persists in the minds of the young, since it is the only way towards progress. If the lessons of history were too deeply absorbed, we might abandon the effort altogether.

Let us accept the story of the advent of Rome into the affairs of the Britons without offering any moral judgements, and allow these distant events to seize on our imagination. Then we may be drawn into a deeper understanding of the human frailities of our remote ancestors.

1 The Sources of Evidence

The ancient historians

The main task of the historian and the archaeologist is the collection and examination of evidence, the careful weighing and sifting of every scrap, to be quite sure it is accurate, or as near to the truth as possible. If not, then the precise degree of validity must be gauged. Some of the scraps have to be rejected, for although they may be genuine, they are irrelevant to the particular problem under study. Sometimes one has only a few tiny pieces, and naturally the utmost has to be squeezed out of them, but at other times, there is a confused mass of material which has to be sorted, graded and fitted into a coherent pattern. This is perhaps the most difficult task of all, and it imposes a serious mental discipline. It is all too easy to select or distort the evidence to make it fit one's current ideas, and to forget all the inconvenient details which could undermine them. This constant struggle to preserve a freshness of outlook which accepts the possibility of new interpretations is a losing battle as we grow older, for the more we know and understand, the more fixed and inhibited our minds become; we are reluctant to abandon theories arrived at by much toil and hard thinking. It becomes an affront to our established position when our authority is challenged, and we tend to fight back. But the true scholar and scientist is a humble person, quick to admit that he was wrong, or that his reasoning was faulty. In some professions one can fight for a lost cause for a long time, and still be respected by ones contemporaries, but there is little chance of this in archaeology, where the problem is that of keeping pace with the rapid expansion of knowledge, and the ever shifting pattern of ideas and theories.

There are, however, some facts which never change, and these survive in the work of the ancient historians. It is now most unlikely that any new writings will be found with any record of Britain, so we have to accept gratefully what has survived. The ancient texts themselves, have often been corrupted by the copyists, so that suggestions on improvements which may get back to the original wording are always helpful, and new interpretations of the text are then possible. The main difficulty with the ancient texts is their compression and selection of material, and it is necessary to try and understand why these historians wrote these histories, and for whom. Apart from the odd occasional statements by ancient writers, the conquest of Britain was described only by Tacitus and Cassius Dio, but there is little comparison between them. Cassius Dio, a Greek, was more of a compiler than an historian, and he accepted his material without any critical appraisal, while Tacitus, as a contemporary, is undoubtedly the main source for the first century. Unfortunately, Dio's work survives only as a collection of selected pieces, and a further difficulty is that he was writing in Greek of the early third century AD. He was, however, a senator at the time of Severus and at least had an understanding of contemporary events. Since it was the normal practice for readings to be given by professional speakers at select gatherings such as dinner parties, classical historians wrote for a small audience of listeners, although there were serious scholars who read in the solitude of their own libraries. The historians were, therefore, writing with these in mind and included, wherever possible, long rhetorical passages, which could be included in descriptions of debates in the Senate, or the law courts, and in their battle scenes, the carefully prepared orations put into the mouths of the protagonists were *de rigueur*, and more care was devoted to these passages than the battle itself. Tacitus developed a terse epigrammatic style of writing which makes him sometimes difficult to understand. He wrote as if each chapter ending was the end of a recitation, which had to be rounded off with a telling sentence to delight the audience and leave them in a state of suspense, eager for the next session. The passages of Dio selected by Xiphilinus for his epitome, were those which were considered most appealing to an audience, seeking entertainment, rather than for the enlightened reader. This is very unfortunate for the student of today, who wants the facts and not the trimmings. Tacitus had a great gift for compressing a series of complicated events and political relationships into a very small compass, and one grieves today for all the omissions, including most of all for the topographical and geographical details which would be so helpful to us. But one also has to appreciate that, although Tacitus was a true historian and astonishingly accurate with his facts, his writings were also affected by his passionate hatred of Domitian. But most of his working life was during the Emperor's lifetime, so he was forced to illustrate the ills and misfortunes of the contemporary scene with accounts of the misdeeds of earlier emperors, but even then he had to be careful and choose only those who had been officially condemned, and of these, Nero clearly offered the best material. Nero is portrayed as a paranoiac monster and the contemporary audiences were quick to appreciate the close parallel with Domitian, and could enjoy the savage comments of the historian, knowing that he wrote with Domitian in mind. But the Emperor could hardly persecute the historian for writing so scathingly about an Emperor who officially received the *damnatio* by the Senate, which, ironically perhaps, was also to be the fate of Domitian.

Archaeology

Casual finds, field work, excavations and aerial reconnaissance are all sources of evidence, but they usually need the experienced and specialist eye for their significance to become apparent. A simple example may suffice to illustrate the problems and the method. Museums are the repositories of archaeological finds made in their locality. This material is normally conserved to prevent any further deterioration, which happens quite rapidly to metal objects when they are suddenly taken out of the soil. The pottery and artefacts are carefully stored and a small proportion placed in cases for the public to see. Unfortunately, very few museums have the expertise and resources to publish the material they collect and store, and it is possible that there are objects wrongly described, or which may have escaped recognition altogether. Any student on the track of the Roman army should first visit all the museums in the area under consideration, and examine all the material. But this is of little use unless the student has sufficient knowledge to identify objects associated with the army. I once saw in a case in a museum in Lincolnshire, two small pieces of bronze which I recognized as fittings of the body armour of a legionary. The name of the place where they were found was stated on the label. There was no other evidence which connected this site with the army, so I had found a place where legionaries may have been established, and, as this site could well have fitted into the broad strategic pattern of the dispositions of units, it seemed to be a distinct possibilitiy as the site of a fort. The next step was to examine plans and aerial photographs of the area, and visit the site to see if there were any surface indications. These turned out to be negative, but one day, further chance discoveries may bring to light more objects, and so it was necessary to alert local archaeologists to the potential of the site, to make sure any road improvement, or development, was watched for traces of military occupation.

It may seem very tedious and time consuming to do all this thoroughly, but this is the only way the serious student can carry out research. Another line of approach is to examine those sites already identified as Roman forts. Sometimes there has been an assumption by our antiquarians of past generations based on the appearance of an earth-work or configuration of the ground. Some of these worthies thought every small defended enclosure had a Roman military origin, and even today, their identifications linger on Ordnance Survey maps as 'Roman Camps', one of their favourite terms. But they did not understand the difference between campaign camps and permanent forts, two quite different kinds of military sites; and often, too, this same label is attached to a small Roman town which happened to be surrounded with defences.

A much easier way of finding evidence of army military presence is by reading through archaeological periodicals. There was in the mid-nineteenth century a great enthusiasm generated for historical research, although most of it was directed towards the study of churches and the histories of landed families. Out of this grew the local archaeological and historical societies, until eventually almost every English county, and some of the major cities had their own societies. They still exist, although in these days of accelerating printing costs, it becomes more and more difficult for them to produce their annual volume of local studies. There exist, all the same, learned transactions covering about 150 years and occupying many yards of shelving in our academic libraries. Apart from these provincial publications, there are those of the national institutions, the premier of which is the Society of Antiquities of London, which has been publishing regularly since 1779. It is indeed a mammoth task which faces researchers looking for particular items of interest to them. It might be thought that the published indexes would make a detailed search unnecessary but, alas, it is rare to find that items of military equipment have been identified, or specifically classified, so one has to examine all the published drawings of small finds, to make sure such evidence is not overlooked. Others may already have trodden the same path, and their selections and comments have to be specially studied.

An example of a discovery made from looking at an old report is Broxtowe, near Nottingham. It started with the publication of the find of a bronze saucepan from the site in the *Antiquaries Journal* (XIX 1939 Pl lxxxvii); its striking likeness to another find on the site of the early legionary fortress at Gloucester, was noticed. When I made enquiries about the site from local archaeologists, they drew my attention to a publication which would normally have escaped my search. This was the annual Report of the Thoroton Society (the name of the county society of Nottinghamshire) Excavation Section for 1938, and which, as is the case with other similar reports, was not published in the *Transaction*, but as a separate leaflet. This included an account of excavations by G.F. Campion, with several illustrations of objects he recovered. To my great delight, I immediately identified many of them as military, and I subsequently found more which had escaped publication in the Castle Museum, Nottingham. There seemed little doubt this was the site of a Roman fort of the first century, although by then, most of the site had been covered by a council housing estate. Few excavators are specialists in this field, and quite often illustrate their finds without identification, or even get it wildly wrong. An amusing example of the latter is a bronze object in the 1972 *Verulamium Excavations* (Fig 32. No. 36) by that most distinguished excavator, Professor Sheppard Frere. The 'nodding Homer' identifies it as an earring, but it is actually part of a hook from a legionary cuirass!

The most positive evidence is in the form of tombstones. It was Roman practice, fortunately for us, to hold the dead in such respect that they provided elaborate ritual and costly memorials. This would, of course, only apply to those families and heirs who could afford them. Burial, even in those days, was an expensive matter, and prudent men took out an insurance by joining a burial club. The army made its own provisions with compulsary deduction from pay to cover the feast and all the rites, and anything left over could go towards the monument. To secure a good memorial, many soldiers, especially officers, made sure that there were beneficiaries. Usually these were the deceased's slaves, who often received their freedom on their master's death, and showed their gratitude in this way. Occasionally the heirs were instructed in the will to build a monument, and this fact is usually recorded on the inscription by the words *ex testamento*, (i.e. 'as directed under the will'). This is why we have, in Britain, quite a number of surviving stones, in spite of their excellence as building material, or in some cases, because of it. The remarkable collection of 98 tombstones, now in the Grosvenor Museum, Chester, owe their survival to their re-use as large blocks of stone for the rebuilding of the fortress wall, presumably in the late fourth century. There was actually a law passed at this period permitting local authorities to dismantle temples and tomb monuments if stone was urgently needed to provide and strengthen town defences. Similarly, the small but important collection at Bath was recovered from the enclosing wall there, and this is the case of many towns elsewhere, especially in the Rhineland. But some were still lying where they had fallen when ground was opened up for cultivation in the eighteenth century. This is how the Wroxeter tombstones came to light. The two remarkable stones at Colchester of the centurion Facilis (*RIB* 200) and the *duplicarius* Longinus (*RIB* 201) were found, lying face down where they had been overturned in their fury by the rebels under Queen Boudica. They had probably stood in the cemetery for only about 15 years, and the carving is very fresh, since the surface had been protected by a covering of thin gesso, the function of which was to provide a smooth surface for the paint, which helped to portray the figures in their natural colours. Sir Ian Richmond actually found on a close examination, a piece of gesso surviving behind the ear of the centurion. The importance of these tombstones is that they give, in full legal detail, the full name, rank and unit of the soldier, his age and years of service, and in many cases, his carefully detailed effigy in undress uniform. One can readily appreciate the enormous significance this has for students of military equipment and weapons.

To take these two fine examples (Pl 1), Marcus Favonius Facilis, was a centurion of *Legio XX* which indicates beyond any doubt, that this legion was stationed here before AD 60, probably immediately after the entry of Claudius into the British capital. The legion remained here until the foundation of the *colonia* by Ostorius Scapula in 48 or 49, when he needed it for protecting the lower Severn from the savage attacks of Caratacus. This is a reasonable inference of Tacitus in his *Annals* (xii 32), and another tombstone of a soldier of this legion was found at Gloucester, but unfortunately is lost (*RIB* 122). Excavations at both places, as will be seen below, have now produced legionary fortresses, and so the epigraphic, historical and archaeological evidence, all comes neatly together.

The cavalry tombstone (Pl 19) is equally fine and significant. It portrays the trooper, a *duplicarius* (i.e. he had double pay as an NCO), on his large horse somewhat shortened to squeeze it onto the stone. His face has been sliced away by a blow from one of Boudica's followers and his lance has vanished, but this could have been made of bronze and decayed in the soil. He wears a cuirass of large scales, a small hairy Celt crouches in terror beneath the towering horseman, symbolizing victory over death. The inscription tells us his name, Longinus Sdlapeze, and that of his father, Matygus. The trooper's name is half-Roman and half-Slav, difficult for the western tongue, but typical of Thrace, his country of origin, since his birthplace is given as Sardica, more commonly Serdica, which is now Sofia, capital of modern Bulgaria. His unit was the crack cavalry regiment *Ala I Thracum*. Aerial reconnaissance has recently revealed a fort of a size suitable for this type of unit, near the religious site at Gosbecks[1]. This may have been the first military post on the site of the British capital, to be replaced, or supplemented by the *Legio XX*, when all the initial resistance has been overcome.

There are other aspects of these tombstones which will be considered later; they are introduced here merely to exemplify the value of such evidence, and how it can be used to interpret the operations and dispositions of the Roman army units. Sometimes the evidence from other sources is tantalisingly limited, as with the two lead tags from Wall, on one of which is scratched the name of a centurion. It is not necessarily evidence of the presence of a legion, since auxiliary cohorts also had officers of that grade, but it does establish military presence there, and this has been confirmed by the discovery of a sequence of forts on the hilltop.

Evidence from coins

Yet another source of information comes from coins of the invasion period. The British tribal coins were in such variety of metal and weight, that they were unsuitable for a ready currency required by the Roman troopers when they arrived and wished to purchase goods from the Britons. The supply of Imperial coins was inadequate, perhaps because it was a problem not foreseen by the authorities. The result was that the army had to strike its own bronze coins for small change. The models were the current issues of Claudius, and Britain produced a large quantity of these imitations of varying competence. Dr C.V.H. Sutherland has recognized four grades from reasonable copies to very bad ones[2]. Although these coins are clear indications of the Roman army in Britain, the find-spots do not necessarily indicate the site of a fort, since the Britons would also possess them through trade. It is, however, always worthwhile examining this evidence, since many have been found on military establishments. Unfortunately, there is a snag in their continued use up to *c*. 65, as Nero was reluctant to issue his base metal coins until he found Greek designers and die-cutters who would provide him with a satisfactory artistic product. So the Claudian provincial imitation issues continued to circulate all through this period, many coins becoming so worn that they had to be over-struck with a countermark to make them legal tender. This means that they could be found on many military or civil sites up to *c*. 65, so their archaeological value is thereby limited.

Evidence from pottery

Far more plentiful and universal are pottery sherds, but as signposts to military occupation they present problems and difficulties, which can only be overcome by much careful study. Fortunately, after a period of stagnation in this important field of research, there has been a resurgence of interest, especially among the young professionals, and if this continues we will be in a much better position in the years ahead to come to terms with this difficult material than we are at present. The main problem is the sheer quantity of pottery and the many and diverse sources of supply. There is also the difficulty of distinguishing between the pre-conquest and post-conquest products. In the south-east there was a growing importation of pottery from Italy, Gaul and the Rhineland, between the periods of Caesar and Plautius and this was a continuing process[3]. While the imports of say from 50 to 1 BC can be readily distinguished, there are problems in dating sherds of the first half of the first century. At one time it was thought that this only applied to the area around the Thames Estuary, which had been opened to Roman trade by Caesar, but a recent study by Professor Cunliffe of the material recovered from Hengistbury Head[4], has shown the extent of the trade which had developed with north-west Gaul. This, however, was abruptly terminated by Caesar's devastating attack on the Veneti and the destruction of their fleet. The pattern of trade and distribution of imports changed considerably as Gaul became a Roman province, with the ending of tribal feuds and development of an overall capital economy. At present it would seem that the hinterland of ports like Hengistbury Head were virtually cut off from trade with the Continent, but it is difficult to accept this in its entirety unless there was also a strong political element. The deep anti-Roman feeling demonstrated by the Durotriges and southern

Dobunni, could have started with the appalling fate which had overtaken their Gallic allies and trading partners under the hands of Caesar's legionaries. They probably received refugees whose tales of horror, magnified in the telling, may have caused the British rulers to decide on a policy of the total extinction of all things Roman from their territories. Should this have been the case, it will make pottery studies in this area that much easier, but one cannot accept such a speculation as offering a firm base on which to build further conclusions. In any event, such considerations do not hold good from the coast-line and hinterland east of the Solent.

The next problem is the material in our museums found by past generations of antiquarians. There are many pottery vessels and other artefacts in our collections for which there is no firm provenance. Many were presented by collectors who had a local pride in the place where they had been born and lived much of their lives. This caused some of them to indulge in what must have seemed at the time, to have been a piece of innocent subterfuge. Pottery vessels they had purchased abroad or through the auction rooms were labelled as being found locally. This seems to have been a common practice, especially in London, where many objects bear this information, often with some precision as with – 'found in Lombard Street', sometimes even with a date added. Unfortunately, this applies to some key pieces of pottery of the period under our consideration, especially the so-called 'Arretine' wares[5]. Some of these are undoubtedly early pieces and if the alleged provenances are correct must indicate a pre-conquest origin for London – one for which there is no other evidence. This casts serious doubt on the old labels. Geoffrey March has done a recent careful study of this material and his conclusions for the London pieces could also affect similar labels on pieces in old collections[6]. This means that one cannot rely on the early labels in museums elsewhere and evidence for these sources cannot be accepted unless it is soundly supported by other means.

Another problem is the practice of the army in buying and storing pottery, which obviously varied from time to time. Where pottery was readily available in the quantities and quality demanded, it was purchased in bulk under contract and when consignments reached forts, the quarter-masters would put them into store for withdrawal by centuries when needed. Normally, the pottery supplied to newly established fortresses would have been made specially, but crates could have remained in the store for some time, dependent on the rate of demand and the whims of the issuing officers. When crates were received, the task of shifting all the older consignments to the front and replacing them with the new stock now put at the back, might have been considered too great. One assumes a natural tendency for old crates to remain in the deeper recesses of the store for a long time if the replacements were made on a regular basis[7]. In these circumstances, old stock could have been brought out of store 20 or 30 years after it had been received. There were specific occasions when this was likely to happen, the most obvious being due to the movement of a unit. There is archaeological evidence[8] of the disposal of pottery when the unit was ordered to dismantle its fort – unused and complete vessels have been found tipped into a ditch or pit. Presumably this could only have applied to small batches in which the quartermaster could not be bothered to involve himself with all the paperwork needed for transfer. Small quantities would have been left in the store-houses and taken out and disposed of by the demolition parties, which were only concerned with rapid clearance. The quartermaster could have written off such trifling losses and indented for new goods. The invasion of Britain moved four legions from their well-established stations on the Continent. They came to a country where there was no pottery industry organized to produce the quantity and quality of wares they would need as they settled into their permanent fortresses. Any sensible quartermaster, knowing this in advance, would have made quite sure his stores were up-to-date and he would have arranged to tranship everything. This would have been an occasion when crates of old pottery were dragged out of the backs of the stores and brought to Britain for immediate distribution. This all seems to offer a possible answer to what otherwise is an intractable problem and one example may suffice to illustrate it.

The waste heap at Oare in Wiltshire[9] produced a fair amount of imported pottery presumably for the use of those operating the works. These include a fragment of *terra rubra*[10] stamped by Attissu, a well known potter whose output lasted about 25 years. The accepted date of Attissu has been based on the find of one of his stamped vessels at the fort at Haltern on the Lippe and which was destroyed in the Varian disaster in AD 9[11]. It is possible from a close study of the different dies used for these stamps to arrange them in chronological order and this particular stamp from Haltern was one used early in his career. This would suggest that he was still producing pottery up to *c*. AD 25 but the stamp from Oare is also an early one in the series[12]. This is not, however, the whole story, as stamps of Attissu have also been found at Fishbourne, Casterly Camp, two at Camulodunum and another at Puckeridge in Hertfordshire. In the last two places it might be possible to argue that these vessels came to Britain prior to the conquest, except that much of the pottery from the Sheepen site at Camulodunum is now thought to be later. Fishbourne could have had a native occupation, but this is in doubt; Casterly Camp is, however, another problem. The suggestion that most of the Attissu pieces could have been brought here by the conquest army means that all these vessels would have been at least 20 years old when they arrived, and such an anomaly cannot be accepted. The only satisfactory explanation is that far more imported wares were reaching the south-west in the first decades of the first century than has been realized, and the proof of this may well emerge from the excavations at Hengistbury Head, started by Professor Cunliffe in 1979.

Nevertheless, there remains the problem of the uneven nature of the pottery production in Britain at the time of the conquest. The introduction of superior wares and greater variety of types of vessel into south-east Britain in post-Caesarian times would undoubtedly have encouraged the local potters to extend their range and to improve their techniques. Many potters would have come to Britain as refugees fleeing from Caesar, bringing with them their knowledge and techniques. When the army arrived in Britain and began rapidly to spread across the Lowland zone to occupy and hold down the new province, the quartermasters soon discovered that the local sources of pottery were quite inadequate for their needs. Only on the Thames Estuary were they likely to find the right standard of quality and variety of types, but even here, hardly in the large quantities they needed; elsewhere the native cooking pots and hand-made bowls and jars were usable only for cooking and storage, but in some cases their crudity would have meant they were rejected instantly. The matter was further complicated by the differences in demand between the legions and the auxiliary units. The former had a higher standard of living and pay, and also the unit strength was ten times that of the auxiliaries, so that pottery and other commodities were normally acquired by large-scale contracts with the ensuing quality control. Whether these are the real reasons or not, the fact remains that there is a great distinction not only between the pottery of legions and auxiliaries, but also between each legion. The inescapable conclusion is that the pottery was either made by the soldiers themselves, or by contractors working in close proximity to the fortresses[13]. On the other hand, the auxiliary units depended on local production supplemented with imports for their table-ware and unless some sherds of the latter are found, the pottery assemblage in the absence of any other evidence would not distinguish the site from a normal native settlement of the period. In areas where there was very little suitable pottery from local sources, as in much of the Midlands, potters from the south-east had to be induced to follow the army and establish themselves at suitable points to service several forts[14]. It is even possible that some potters followed a unit across the Channel from their homeland. This would help to explain the strange exotic types found in unexpected places[15] but the main effect on the native potters was to force them to compete or go out of business; so the anomalies rapidly disappear, and by the 60s, the crude hand-made wares only survive in the frontier districts[16].

The Island of Britain

The most important physical fact about Britain is that it is an island;

one accepts this from birth without question but it conditions our attitude towards our Continental neighbours. To most of us they are distant and alien, and this is why so many find it difficult to accept our full partnership in the European Economic Community. The sea has kept us safe from invasion even into this century. There have only been two successful invasions, the Roman and Norman. The remarkable ease of modern communication does little to dispel the armour of invulnerability in the hearts of the modern Britons. Viewed from the mainland of Europe, it was always the terror of the sea which outweighed fears of resistance to landing; even the hardened and disciplined troops of the Roman army hesitated before committing themselves to the will of Oceanus, and it was the victory over this savage and capricious deity which was regarded in Rome as a greater glory than that over the Britons.

Pressure of land hunger and large-scale folk movement in earlier prehistoric times after the loss of a land-bridge, caused a constant stream of refugees to seek landfalls along the coast of Britain. The starting point usually determined the area of landing. Those moving from Spain and Portugal made for the north-west and, rounding Lands End, sailed or paddled up the Bristol Channel or Irish Sea. Those from the Baltic countries had to cross the North Sea, and, dependent on wind and tide, cast up at some point along the north-east coast – from the mouth of the old Rhine, the Wash or East Anglia offer the likely points of contact. The physical shape of Britain is of great advantage to the invader, since the lowlands, with their wide estuaries and deep access into the hinterland, face Europe, while the more difficult landfalls are on the Atlantic coast.

So those who were determined or resolute enough to leave the European mainland found easy landfalls. But they had to move inland to find a suitable area for settlement. As the population grew, resistance to the newcomers stiffened, as can be judged from the construction of defences. These were fairly slight until the early Iron Age (*c.* 800 BC), but they became progressively larger and more complex. The new settlers probably had superior weapons as the techniques of making them developed, and some may also have had better social organization. Archaeology is gradually helping to piece together the sequence of these landings. The tribes with poorer weapons and organization were forced further and further inland, driven away from the rich lands of the south-east into the hills and wastes of the north-west; but it was by no means as simple as that. The greatest concentration of defended sites of the Iron Age is on the Welsh Marshes, and this may reflect great pressure of peoples moving up the Severn Valley; or it could equally signify the lawless character of those already there, and their constant inter-tribal wars and cattle raids. The peoples in the north and west, by the very nature of the barren hilly terraces, were pastoralists, tending their flocks and herds and supplementing their diet with hunting. Taking a broad view of the country, one could say that the most backward peoples were living in the hill country of the north and west, while the most sophisticated, in terms of social organization and knowledge of the crafts, especially in metallurgy, occupied the lowlands of the south and east, and in those parts nearest the Continent dwelt the very latest newcomers.

But such statements should be treated with caution. As more detailed studies are made, the pattern of settlement is seen to have been very complicated, and there is still a great deal to be discovered and understood. The growth of archaeological knowledge is so rapid that every year brings new facts to light which entail a continuous revision of ideas. Indeed, the prospect of any view being out-of-date by the time it is published makes most archaeologists over-cautious in their statements, and to draw any far-reaching conclusions is considered foolhardy, especially among the young whose careers may be at risk.

The cultural divisions and invasion theories[17]

The old broad cultural divisions of prehistory were classified by the basic materials used, i.e. stone, bronze and iron. The introduction of new materials and the tools and weapons made with them does not necessarily mean invasion and subjection by waves of migrant peoples. Artefacts were carried by traders from the earliest period of settlement. There is a deal of evidence of the distribution of stone axes, many of which have travelled a long way from their factories near the quarries which produced suitable types of rock. It has been possible to identify the sources of most of the axes by cutting out and polishing thin slices and identifying the minerals present. The development of metallurgy was of great importance since it provided better tools for chopping down trees, hoeing the ground, and for making weapons. Copper and bronze axes and smaller tools appear in Britain well before 2000 BC, to be bartered for and used by the Neolithic farmers, who had begun to settle in Britain *c.* 4000 BC. Newcomers crossing the North Sea can be identified by their pottery in the form of beakers, stone axes with shaft-holes and evidence of archery. They also had a different method of burial by inhumation in small round barrows. There are sufficient differences to be certain that they indicate the appearance of newcomers, rather than the distribution of artefacts in the course of trade; but, at the same time, the earlier settlers would have continued to occupy their old sites, slowly changing their ways as the new tools and weapons became available to them. It is not always easy for the archaeologist to determine whether the pattern of distribution of pottery and tools is entirely due to those brought in by trade, or whether it indicates that new peoples were settling in the area. It is complicated by the wanderings of the bronze and iron-smiths themselves. There is plenty of evidence to show that the craftsmen moved about collecting scrap material, melting it down in the case of bronze, and fashioning new tools and weapons on the spot, people in the low-lands built in timber, whereas in hill country, if suitable stone was available, this would have been used; likewise, one has to consider materials like clay, turf and reeds for walls and roofs. Already much work has been done in recent years on late prehistoric sites. It is doubtful, however, whether there is a sufficient body of evidence yet to enable clear distinctions to be made between the cultural divisions and the waves of invaders from across the sea. Recent new discoveries have drastically altered many old ideas, and they indicate an urgent need for radical reassessment of all the evidence, old and new and, to some extent, this has already started[18] but some of the conflicting views clearly indicate the present uncertainty.

The Iron Age comes to Britain

The first Iron Age culture to make inroads in Britain is known as the Hallstatt, from the name of a type-site in Austria, where a rich cemetery was excavated in the mid-nineteenth century[19]. The earliest finds in Britain are not of iron objects, but the bronze swords and daggers which came by way of trade, though some may have belonged to explorers prospecting for sources of iron. The long bronze sword typical of this culture would indicate the use of the horse and has given rise to the idea of small bands of warrior horsemen sweeping across Europe from the East, looting and conquering everywhere they went. But this is too simple and romantic a view. The detailed study of the shapes and decoration of pottery can be more telling than that of the distribution of pieces of exotic metal-work. New styles were being introduced along the east and south coast and up the large rivers, especially the Thames, in the eighth and seventh centuries BC and possibly earlier. As soon as the sources of iron were located and exploited the blacksmiths were able to produce weapons, tools and horse and chariot-gear, not only for the use of the new settlers, but to trade with the older peoples, thus producing a very complicated cultural pattern. So great had been the influx of new settlers, that there are signs of land hunger and a struggle for possession.

This is seen in the growth of defended enclosures in strong positions, the first hill-forts. They were of fairly simple construction, mainly forms of the box-rampart, with a timber revetment at front and back, held together with horizontal beams and the space between filled in with spoil from the ditches. In stone areas, the backs and fronts of the banks were protected with dry-stone walling, a technique which had developed in Britain centuries earlier. The entrances were also of simple plan with double gates, small guard chambers and a bridge across the top linking the parapets on each side. Even so, this would involve quite sophisticated carpentry techniques, and it shows familiarity with the use of timber for heavy construction work. It is often difficult to date these early defences with precision, but it would seem that by *c.* 700 BC the newcomers had spread across Britain, taking possession of lands and setting up their hill-forts to protect themselves from others coming along in their wake or, of course, against the people whose lands had been taken over. But as Sir Cyril Fox[20] demonstrated in 1938, the distribution of the Hallstatt type of defences and artefacts was confined to the south and east of a line from the Bristol Channel to the Humber, apart from settlements in east Yorkshire. This important geological division was to remain, as we shall see, a cultural divide in the organization of the Province of Roman Britain.

But this is only the beginning of the building of hill-forts. In the centuries which followed they were to become more plentiful, with larger ramparts, more ditches and, in many of them, extremely complicated entrances, which in plan-view look almost like mazes. All this must have involved political fusion and integration, the small family units cohering into larger groupings, until the tribal areas of Caesar's day came into being. It is beyond the scope of this study to review this fascinating story in detail, but it is necessary for us to understand the differing attitudes of each tribe towards Caesar and, a century later, to Claudius.

Britain was open to other cultural influences from the Continent than those associated with Hallstatt. The use of type-site names for cultures has led to serious over-simplification, and this became evident as soon as the term La Tène was introduced. This is another type-site derived from a lake-side settlement on the shores of Lake Neuchâtel, excavated in 1858. For a long time the British Iron Age was polarised along the Hallstatt – La Tène axis, as if there were two kinds of people battling it out for the possession of the lowlands of Britain[21]. But a glance at the distribution patterns in Europe shows how false this is: there are many variations in the development of style of design and decoration on metal wares and in the techniques of metallurgy. In this period too, there is an increasing influence from the classical world beyond the Alps and the Danube. There are many threads interwoven into a rich tapestry some of them stretching out from Gaul and the Rhineland to Britain.

There is in east Yorkshire the only area in Britain where there is definite evidence of new settlers with La Tène affinities. The evidence comes from a large cemetery which must have consisted at one time of as many as 500 small barrows and similar but smaller cemeteries have been found in the area. Many of these were excavated in the last century by Canon Greenwall[22] and J.R. Mortimer[23]. From a study of the artefacts, it can be deduced that the most productive graves had been the cart-burials, where the body was placed in a cart, sometimes with fully equipped horses. A third type of barrow to be recognized is the one inside a small square-ditched enclosure, a type well known in north-west France and west Germany. The presence of this type in Yorkshire has only come to light through aerial photography, and some have been excavated with modern techniques. Valuable studies of these burials and their artefacts have been made by Dr Ian Stead[24]. His careful analysis does not lead to any positive conclusions, but it is clear that there are two different cultural entities present. The parallels for burial rites seem to indicate an area of origin in north-west France, but apparently the migration was not directly from that area, but was part of the general folk-movement towards and into it. In other words, there were people entering the Humber and settling in the lands of east Yorkshire about the same time as their kindred were moving into the Marne area during the fourth and third centuries BC. Moreover, this may not have been confined to a single group. Although a counter argument could be based on the name, the Parisi, by which this tribe was known in Roman times, and which may indicate a link with the people settled in the area of Lutetia (modern Paris) in Caesar's day[25], Dr Stead does not like the idea of a warrior aristocracy carving out for itself a slice of rich countryside; they were, he thinks, 'peaceful herdsmen with interesting burial rites like those of their Continental ancestors'.

The question which immediately arises is the possibility of similar invasions, or infiltrations along the rest of the eastern coastline of Britain. Finds of exotic metalware in Lincolnshire, especially at crossings of the River Witham, led at one time to the theory that they were lost by people crossing the area on the way to settle in Yorkshire. But such finds may not always be accidental losses, but rather the result of the widespread Celtic practice of casting valuable objects into rivers and lakes as sacrificial appeasement to the gods. There has recently been a swing away from the invasion theory[26] which is considered by some to be still inhibited by ideas of Victorian colonial imperialism.

At present, the pendulum is swinging back, but it will take some time to settle into a position which satisfies all the evidence. The fine pieces of metalwork found in Lincolnshire are now hailed as masterpieces of British art, and there are good reasons for thinking they are the products of local craftsmen. Nevertheless, many of the decorated motifs are clearly derived from continental sources. How they came here and were so readily absorbed by the natives is a difficult question, which only more archaeological evidence of burial customs could determine.

It is important for an understanding of the peoples of East Anglia and those round the Thames Estuary, that their origins be considered. When Rainbird Clark wrote *East Anglia* in 1960, he was in no doubt about the arrival of aristocratic warriors rudely shattering the peaceful development of a peasant society of an earlier Iron Age culture. There are no cart-burials matching those of Arras, although there are a few rich and interesting graves. One of these, found at Newnham, Cambridge in 1903,[27] was the burial of a middle-aged man wearing a most elaborate brooch which had pieces of shell attached to it with bronze rivets, and covered with an incised decoration. He also had a jointed bronze bracelet with a beautiful curvilinear design; there were, too, pieces of harness in the grave. Of this rich assemblage, the metalwork is thought to have been British, but with strong continental affinities. Another man was found buried at Mildenhall, Suffolk, with two ponies, and there are other undated warrior graves of this period, but these are scattered finds and they vary greatly. What is lacking is a cemetery with distinctive kinds of metalwork or burial customs. Until one is found, all the brooches, swords and horse-trappings could have been made here by local craftsmen copying imported examples.

The wealth of East Anglia can be measured in the finds of gold torcs, many of which have been turned up by the plough. Their owners were people of status, chiefs or kings controlling a large peasant population, whose hard work provided the means of acquiring these symbols of wealth and authority, as well as swords and horse-gear. The horse had become an important factor in warfare, for both riding and chariots. Contact with Europe was close, but this could have been solely by trade. The theory of migrating bands of warriors remains only a faint possibility.

The Iron Age is a period of at least 500 years, during which many changes took place, due mainly to gradual growth and development. There are clear indications of this in the great variety in the forms of pottery and metalwork. Archaeologists so often concentrate their attention on artefacts, their distribution and affinities, that they overlook the people who used them. They would naturally argue that it is only through their remains that the people can be understood, but at some point the artefact research became the main quest and its original purpose was forgotten. Yet we can get some notion of the kinds of people living in Britain at the time of Caesar from classical sources, since fortunately, several Greek and Roman historians were fascinated by the Celts.

2 The Celts and Julius Caesar

In the first century BC there is evidence from historical sources, mainly in the *Commentaries* of Julius Caesar, although the glimpses he gives are limited and often create more problems than they solve. Perhaps a more important source of evidence are the coins minted by the kings of the British tribes of the south-east. They often bear the names of the rulers, and sometimes even the place where the coins were minted. Their distribution patterns give useful indications of the territories of the tribes. To these must be added a great increase in the goods being imported into south-east Britain from this time onward. All these factors form a considerable body of evidence which is continually increasing. Even so, this offers a very imbalanced view of the state of Britain, since it only applies to a restricted area of the south-east, much of it comprising what are now the counties of Essex, Herts, the greater London area, Kent and Sussex. For the rest of the country, one has still to rely on the evidence gleaned from pottery, metalware, burial customs and building techniques, to distinguish one tribe or group of tribes from another.

The Celts in Europe

It should now be evident that the people of Britain, at the time of the Roman conquest, were an amalgam of those who had been here for thousands of years and of the spasmodic succession of migrants more recently from Europe seeking refuge and lands for settlement. The most important ethnic groups which came to dominate much of Britain were the Celts. These peoples originated in central Europe in the valleys of the Upper Danube and Rhine. Quite suddenly they began to move outwards in a dramatic explosion. Folk movements like this in the history of a people are difficult to explain. There is an excellent later example in the Northmen, who became Vikings and Normans. These small fierce and determined groups, sailing from their deep fiords of Scandinavia, were to have a profound effect on the early Middle Ages from Britain to Palestine, and their leaders established dynasties all over the Mediterranean and north-west Europe. The usual, explanations for these ethnic movements are over-population, land-hunger and pressure on the borders by other and more powerful neighbours. In the case of the Celts, it may have been the movements of the Nordic peoples southwards from the areas

Map I The extent of Gallo-Belgic influence at the time of Caesar

around the Baltic, which eventually created modern Germany. The Celts looked naturally to the rich lands of the south, which they knew through trading contacts over the centuries. In that direction lay the wealth of the classical world.

But other factors must be considered, such as the great advance in metallurgy, with the discovery of the technique in making wrought-iron. This was to have an enormous effect on warfare, for it provided heavy swords and axes with fine cutting edges, which did not bend or break. Once the blacksmiths had spread over Europe, the new weapons were plentiful, and therefore not too expensive. Iron could also be used for horse-gear, giving more control of the animal for riding, and in chariot warfare; the more effective use of the horse spread into Europe from the great plains of Russia. Iron weapons and horses combined to create warrior aristocracies with heroic ideas about warfare, and with the advantage of speed of movement. Soon bands of young warriors were on the warpath, raiding the wealthy peoples on the fringes of the ancient world round the Mediterranean. At the risk of an over-simplified picture of events over a wide area and covering a long period, from *c*. 500 BC, the Celts were apparently on the move, both as raiding parties and as settlers, the one often following the other. By *c*. 500 BC they had settled in Gaul and the Iberian peninsula and, about the same time, they appeared in Britain, spreading westwards rapidly. They poured over the Alps a century later, and quite suddenly appeared in Rome and sacked it in 390 BC and just as rapidly seemed to vanish, but, in reality, were settling in the fertile lands of the Po Valley. The effect on the Romans of the sudden appearance of these wild men from the north was traumatic. It has been argued that it turned the tide of history, for the Romans were determined that this must never happen again. Their defensive strategy from that time was planned to prevent any more barbarians from approaching their city, they did not feel safe until the whole of Italy was under their control.

The Celts were later spreading into the middle Danube, and soon appeared in Greek records as mercenaries. But one tribe, taking independent action invaded Thessaly and tried to force the Pass of Thermopylae. They might have posed a serious threat to the city states of Greece – at that time so often at odds with one another, until one of the Celtic groups attacked the sanctuary at Delphi in 279 BC. This action so aroused the ire of the Greeks that they took rapid joint action to drive the would-be plunderers away, with the aid of a snowstorm sent by Apollo to save the famous shrine. Another group managed to cross the Dardanelles and spread panic in Asia Minor through tales of their ferocity and cruelty. Eventually, these Celts were offered the barren lands of Galatia. They settled here and found it a convenient base for their raiding parties and mercenary services, while retaining their ethnic integrity for centuries.[1]

Julius Caesar

Had it not been for Caesar, Britain might not have become a province of the Roman Empire. His decision to cross the Channel was to have profound consequences on at least six centuries of our history and with some effects such as the siting of many of our towns and the road system, which have lasted to the present day. The reasons for it are thus worthy of consideration, although it stemmed from events far removed from Britain and its peoples. Caesar's motive was an integral part of his dynastic struggle for power. He had had himself allocated to the governorship of Cisalpine Gaul and Illyricum. The addition of Transalpine Gaul was a fortunate accident following the sudden death of the governor in office. His enemies may have thought that his reputation would be buried in the barbarous territories beyond the Alps, and he would in any case be removed from the central arena. But Caesar saw his appointment as a great opportunity for advancement for it gave him the power not only to raise troops and gain victories which might rival Pompey, but also to amass a fortune, which he badly needed to avoid dependence on Crassus. Caesar felt it necessary to write an account of his remarkable nine years in this office. This was not prompted so much by the desire for glory but as a justification of his actions, since he lost no opportunity of extending the war by adroit manipulation and provocation. Looking to the future, he evidently sensed the need to appear before the Romans as a statesman carrying out the will of Rome in a just and legal manner. There is no doubt that his account was intended for wide attention, although he probably made extensive use of the despatches which he sent regularly to the Senate, and which were available later to Suetonius when he wrote his biographies.

In assessing the accuracy of the information Caesar gives us, one has to take into account the calculated propaganda he skilfully wove into it. He gives the reason for his invasion in 55, as the help the tribes of Britain had been giving to the Gauls (iv 20). This information would have come as no surprise to his readers as, in an earlier passage, he had stated that Divitiacus, who had been in his day the most powerful king king in Gaul, had exercised sovereignty over Britain (ii 4) and also that chiefs of the Bellovaci had fled to Britain when Caesar had advanced towards their territory (ii 14). Some Britons in the south-west may have come to the aid of their allies, the Veneti of Brittany (iii 9).

Caesar's motives

It might seem that Caesar was curious about Britain and sought glory in the conquest of a remote, almost romantic island beyond the ocean. But this is hardly credible, Caesar was too realistic to give way to such fantasies. He is careful to phrase his motive in politico–military terms, i.e. that he wanted to stop aid from reaching the Gauls from their kinsmen and allies in Britain. This is certainly a justification, but his real motive was probably the seizure of plunder to add to his capital to finance his political plans on his return to Rome. Possibly he had heard of the wealth of Britain in gold and silver, and he could be certain of captives, who gave a valuable return when sold as slaves. He may have imagined an easy conquest following his enormous successes in Gaul: so he would acquire the glory of extending his Province and of adding more lands to Rome.

It had been through his governorship that he had realized his great talents as a field commander, although before this in the political struggles in Rome, he had been able to attract loyalty and to manipulate men. But Gaul gave him quite new experience. Caesar did not invent new tactics or weapons, but seemed to appreciate instinctively the value of the unexpected, which could be gained by speed of movement, combined with a brilliant military unorthodoxy. He gained great advantages by suddenly appearing with his troops when the Gauls thought he was a hundred miles away. On one occasion his troops carved a path across mountain snows, and crossed much sooner than the natives thought possible. Caesar also had that rare gift of winning the hearts of those around him, which today is called 'charisma'. Many of his troops, especially in his favourite legions like the Tenth and V *Alaudae* would have died for him. Like Alexander the Great they must have thought him invincible, and when superstitious people believe a leader has divine powers, it gives them complete confidence in him. So it was with Caesar, and he exploited it to the full.

Folk movements in Europe

Whatever may be the truth of the Marnian invasions it is certain that eastern Britain was subject to a movement of goods and people from the Continent, both of which are difficult to evaluate in quantitative terms. It would have been surprising if there had been no migration in the last four centuries BC, since there were large folk movements taking place all over Europe, and it was, after all, the wandering of the Helvetii that brought Caesar into Gaul and gave him the pretext he needed for starting a war. Caesar tells us later that the Treveri were alarmed by the Suebi, a Germanic people, a 100 cantons of whom had settled on the east bank of the Rhine and were trying to get across. But the worst fears of the Gauls were directed against the Germans, led by Ariovistus, who was pressing heavily into their territories. It was Caesar's great victory over these Germans that gave him the foundation on which he was able to build tribal alliances which led to the subjection of Gaul. The continuous movement of people to the west and south must have precipitated many minor disturbances in the Low Countries, and the open coastline of eastern Britain could hardly have been immune.

These migratory movements are recorded by Caesar himself, who specifically stated that the maritime area of Britain was inhabited by tribes which had migrated from Belgica in earlier times, but suggests that they had to take their lands by force. He adds that most of these tribes still carried the name of that from which they had sprung (v 12). The migration of the Bellovaci may have been on a small scale, but it is the only one for which there is direct historical authority. The evidence for Caesar is clear enough, although he may deliberately have over-emphasized the strong connections between Britain and Gaul, to justify his invasion. There had been sporadic movements of peoples from Belgica and north-west Gaul into Britain within living memory and during his Gallic campaigns.

But what was Caesar's real reason for what, in the event, turned out to be a very hazardous and foolhardy venture? The first crossing was purely a rapid reconnaissance late in the season. It is evident that the traders were not prepared to give Caesar any helpful information (iv 20), and may have seen his action as damaging to their relationships with the Britons. He especially needed to know something of the coastline and more particularly of any safe harbours, but he had, in the end, to send a warship under Gaius Volusenus to sail along the coast and report back what he saw, and this in itself is clearly indicative of the traders' silence. His speed and dash must have had a demoralizing effect on his Gallic tribes but it also led him sometimes into serious difficulties. Yet, even when outnumbered and cornered, he could fight back with great courage and determination, and inspire his men to the same heights. It almost seems as if he had such a firm belief in his destiny that he felt instinctively that he could not possibly be killed in a skirmish in the woods and marshes of Gaul, to be dismissed by Rome with a shrug and soon forgotten. Yet, of course, we have only his own version of the events, no doubt carefully organized to impart the maximum effect. Where there are glimpses of his military logistics, as in the preparation of the second expedition to Britain, it is evident that he could rapidly organize and coordinate vast resources. Some of his exploits may not have been so casual and foolhardy as they sometimes appear and his occasional 'throw-away' style may also have been calculated.

The British Expeditions

The first expedition in 55 BC was a reconnaissance raid late in the season and its purpose was to gain information about the harbours on the south-east coast of Britain, in preparation for the real assault the following year – in this sense it failed. He made a land-fall below the chalk cliffs, and sailed round the coast in a north-easterly direction, until he found a suitable beach. The legionaries were quite unnerved at having to make a forced landing in deep water, but in a confused battle drove the Britons off the beach. They immediately sued for peace, handing over Commius, the Atrebatian, whom Caesar had sent on as an envoy to win over the tribes to Rome. Commius had failed in his task and had been taken prisoner.

On the fourth day of the raid, the power and hostility of the ocean became manifest. Eighteen transport vessels bringing the cavalry came within sight, but were driven back by a sudden storm, and the same night was the equinox, a regular tidal phenomenon, about which the seafaring traders had kept curiously quiet. So, without warning, the waves rolled up the beach and destroyed or damaged most of the ships lying there. With prodigious efforts, the Romans made all but 12 of their ships seaworthy again. At the same time, the Britons on seeing what had happened began to prepare a fresh attack. They surprised the Seventh Legion out foraging and Caesar rescued them with difficulty and it was here that the Romans encountered the British chariots and were thrown into confusion by a tactic unknown to them. Caesar was so fascinated by this method of fighting that he gives us a detailed description (iv 33). It was new to him and his troops since chariots had long since gone out of fashion in Gaul, as is clear from their absence on the Arch at Orange. The problem arises as to which of the British tribes used them in battle. It seems unlikely that they belonged to the Gallo-Belgic peoples who had recently come to Britain, so it must have been those who had settled here in earlier times, and the open downlands of the south are better suited to chariots than the dense woodlands and marshes on the north bank of the Thames. This is borne out by the next phase of the fighting. The Britons now saw a real hope of success and despatched messages in all directions calling for assistance. Caesar soon realized that he was opposed by a considerable body and he was still deprived of his cavalry. Although the legions put the Britons to flight they could not follow up their victory. As soon as the weather abated, he sailed back to Gaul.

His despatch to the Senate would have made interesting reading, doubtless he dwelt on the terrible power of Nature rather than his lucky escape. The Senate was much impressed and ordered a thanksgiving of 20 days. This was an extraordinary, if not extravagant gesture and the prestige of Caesar was greatly enhanced. The reasons for the raid and inadequate preparations were forgotten and the unhappy incident turned into a great victory. This may have been more than Caesar expected, but was the Senate vote of confidence inspired by his friends or his enemies? By the seal of approval, the Senate committed Caesar to a full-scale expedition the following year and his enemies could reflect on the real possibility of literally shipwrecking his career. The concern of Caesar's friends in Rome is seen in the letter Cicero wrote to Atticus (iv 16) the following year. 'The outcome of his expedition to Britain', he wrote, 'is worrying, for the approaches to the shores are notorious for the ramparts and sheer cliffs, and also it is now known that there is not a penny-weight of silver in the island, and there is no hope of loot except for slaves, and it is hardly likely that there would be secretaries or musicians', i.e. people who would command a high price in the market. This must have been dispiriting to Caesar, coupled with the obvious fact that the Gallic merchants had managed to feed him with misleading information, and the implication that there were powerful interests at work to keep the Romans out of Britain. The Gallic sea-captains and merchants must have realized that once Britain came under the mantle of Rome, they would lose out to the larger business interests of Italy, and this is what seems to have happened.

Before he left to spend the winter on his usual judicial and administrative business in Cisalpine Gaul, Caesar left detailed instructions for his requirements for the expedition in the spring. The 600 transports were to be of shallow draft, and thus easier to load and beach, but to contain stores and animals they had to be broader. The vessels were thus rather ungainly and difficult to manage; but to compensate for this Caesar was probably advised to equip them with sails and oars. The fighting force he assembled was a large one consisting of five legions and 2000 cavalry; although it was a major expedition it is difficult to appreciate whether Caesar was intent on conquest or merely punishing the hostile tribes or opening Britain up to trade. It was by now evident that there were no suitable havens on the south-east coast of Kent, only the gently shelving beaches. But this time, in the face of such a formidable armada, the Britons did not oppose the landing, so that the Roman forces were able to disembark without difficulty. This time the ships were not beached, but left riding at anchor.

With typical audacity, Caesar marched his legions 12 miles inland, in the dark of the early morning, to a river, which may have been the River Stour near Canterbury. The Britons must have been taken aback at the sudden appearance of the Romans and they retired to a fortified position. Caesar then gives us a brief description of a British hill-fort. 'A place well fortified by nature and strengthened by artifice, built doubtless for their own tribal wars, all the entrances were blocked by felled trees packed closely together' (v 9). There is a hill-fort which may have been the one he attacked three miles west of Canterbury in Bigbury Wood at Hambledown. It is a roughly rectangular enclosure constructed round the 200-foot contour. The site has been much disturbed by old gravel workings, during the course of which many iron objects, mainly tools and farm implements, have been found[2], as one might expect from a peasant community. While these modest defences were quite adequate to keep out raiding bands from nearby tribes, they presented no problem for the disciplined professional legionaries trained in such storming attacks. The Seventh Legion quickly built a ramp against the rampart and formed a *testudo* (tortoise) by holding their shields over their heads to protect themselves from missiles, and hacked their way into the fortress, driving the Britons out and through the woods. The whole action had taken the best part of a day, and Caesar needed time to build his own fortified camp, so he did not take up the pursuit until the following morning. But he was forced to abandon any thought of a speedy advance which would have found the Britons in a state of disarray, with the news of a storm which had wrecked his fleet. So, once more, he had underrated the fearful and sudden powers of the elements.

His army worked day and night for ten days to repair the damage and drag the boats high up the beach into a fortified encampment. This loss of time, and above all initiative, cost Caesar a resounding conquest, for he could in this time have been sweeping across the Thames and struck deeply into the lands beyond, before the Britons had time to organize any resistance. Now some of the tribes had formed an alliance and forgotten their differences in the face of the common danger. They had even appointed a supreme commander, Cassivellaunus, a chief of lands bounded by the north bank of the Thames and who had hitherto been continuously at war with other tribes. There followed some brief but desultory engagements, until the main British force was routed by a charge of three legions followed by cavalry. By now the Britons had seen enough of the organized ferocity of the legionaries and they decided to avoid further encounters in open battle, so they withdrew to the woodlands of the heavy clay-lands north of the Thames, where the river crossing was to be resisted. The Britons, however, relied too much on their underwater defences, which consisted of sharp pointed stakes fixed at an angle to impale a swimmer. Once more the Roman troops showed their discipline and training. Units of cavalry were specially trained for this type of action, but the legions were so keen that they crossed at the same time and put the Britons to flight.

Cassivellaunus must have been bitterly disappointed that his forces had not even held the Thames. Giving up the prospect of any type of a major engagement, he disbanded the levies, and kept only 4000 charioteers to harass the flanks and rear of the advancing Romans. He also removed all the inhabitants and their cattle from the area of advance, to prevent any Britons being taken as slaves, and food becoming available. This produced a kind of stalemate.

But Caesar held a trump card. A young prince of the Trinovantes had come to Caesar in Gaul to seek his protection, after his father had been slain by Cassivellaunus. Caesar had thus a valuable ally in the Colne peninsula of Essex, and this tribe not only supplied his army with food, but persuaded others to join them in submitting to Rome. These are listed as the Cenimagni, the Segontiaci, the Ancalites, the

Bibroci and the Cassi. These people must have belonged to small tribes[3] on the boundaries of the kingdom of Cassivellaunus, and had reason to fear him, but we know nothing of them, except the first, who are presumably the Iceni. The political implications of this are discussed elsewhere, but its effect on Caesar's advance was dramatic, since the allies were able to tell him where to find the stronghold of Cassivellaunus in the thick woodlands and marshes (v 21). This was promptly and effectively attacked. Many Britons were killed, the rest fled and a great store of cattle, which had been driven into the British stronghold for safety, was captured.

As a last throw, the British commander ordered the Kentish tribes to attack the Roman naval base in a desperate effort to cut Caesar off from Gaul. But when their forces appeared, the Romans did not wait behind their defences but moved out and attacked, putting the Britons to flight. Cassivellaunus now had little option but to sue for peace, Commius acting as negotiator. Any plans Caesar may have had for staying in Britain and developing his victory had to be abandoned on receiving news from Gaul of serious trouble which demanded his immediate return. He collected hostages, levied an annual tribute on the hostile tribes, and ordered Cassivellaunus to leave the Trinovantes alone. He waited in vain for ships from Gaul to ferry his army across the Channel and which clearly indicates that his decision was sudden and had been made before full preparations could be made. In the event he packed everyone into the ships he had and crossed in calm seas, just before the autumn equinox.

This brief account of the expedition omits many points relating to the tribes and geography of south-east Britain, and their fighting tactics, both of which will be considered in detail later. Caesar's grand plan of adding Britain to his conquests had failed through the agencies of the capricious weather and tides of the English Channel. Had there been an adequate harbour in the south-east there would have been a different ending. But Gaul remained far from vanquished; Caesar's greatest trial of strength was yet to come against Vercingetorix. With the advantage of hindsight, it is easy to argue that Caesar overreached himself, yet he had crossed the Rhine and frightened the Germans. Where Caesar failed was in misapplying his maxim of getting to know the enemy, which turned out to be, the ocean and not the Britons.

3 The Tribes of South-East Britain and their Rulers

The next problem is to consider where these recent migrants had settled in Britain. Fortunately, there is a means of determining this by the coins which the tribes of south-eastern Britain began to mint. Caesar stated that the Britons used bronze and gold coins or tallies of a standard weight (v 12). The iron tallies can be identified with currency bars which were rough-cuts in wrought-iron of long swords and which had a real intrinsic value. It is interesting to note, however, that these bars are found mainly in Wessex and Gloucestershire, and very few have turned up in the south-east[1]. Caesar was never in contact with the tribes using them, and must have heard about them from the British allies.

The Celtic coins of Gaul were copies from gold staters of Macedon (c. 350 BC) and it may seem strange that coins of such age and remoteness should be so used 100 years after they had ceased being in circulation. One theory has been suggested that these coins were included in the vast booty Rome collected as spoils of war and tribute at the end of the Macedonian wars early in the second century BC. The practical Romans, so the theory proceeds, saw no reason why such coins should not be available as currency, and so they came into Gaul via the Greek colony at Massilia (Marseilles), the main entrepôt through which goods entered Gaul from the classical lands. There is another and more likely theory, which has now gained acceptance[2], that these coins were given to Celtic mercenaries as payment by the Greeks. They were copied by tribes along the Danube and the idea slowly spread westwards eventually into Gaul, to be copied by the tribes of north Gaul and Belgica. The tribes in southern Gaul had, much earlier than this, been copying Greek silver coins for their trade with the Mediterranean. The coin mostly selected for copying was a stater of Phillip II. A beautiful example of Greek art and craftsmanship, with the head of Apollo on one side and a two-horse chariot on the reverse, symbolizing the god's daily journey across the heavens, as the sun-god. The local copying of these coins apparently began in Roumania, at a time when the original was in circulation there through the Celtic migrations into Thrace. By c. 200 BC the peoples in the northern Alps

The tribes of south-eastern Britain

Events in Britain	Atrebates	Catuvellavni	Trinovantes	E. Kent	Iceni	Events in Rome and Gaul	Dates
Gallo-Belgic migrations – pre-Caesar				↑		Caesar in Gaul	BC 58
CASSIVELLAVNVS Commander of the anti-Roman forces			MANDVBRACIVS			Caesar in Britain	55 and 54
	COMMIVS					Commius fled from Gaul	c.50
Polarization of the tribes	anti-Rome	pro-Rome	pro-Rome	anti-Rome	pro-Rome	AVGVSTVS	27 BC – 14 AD
	TINCOMMIVS	ADDEDOMAROS				Augustus in Gaul	27
		TASCIOVANVS					c.20
TINCOMMIVS became an ally of Rome		ANDOCO[. . . SEGO[. . . DIAS[. . .	DVBNOVELLAVNOS				c.15
				VOSENIOS?			c.5
						Revolt in Pannonia	AD 1
	EPPILVS		CVNOBELINE	↑		Tincommius and Dubvellaunos in Rome as suppliants	Before 7
	VERICA			↑			
					ANTED[	Loss of three legions under Varus	9
				VODENOS in Canterbury	AESV[. . .	Death of Augustus	14
		EPATICCVS			SAEMV[. . .	TIBERIVS	14–37
c.25 EPATICCVS expelled	VERICA			ADMINIVS		GAIVS (CALIGVLA)	37–41
		TOGODVBNVS				Adminivs flees to Rome	c.40
Death of CUNOBELINE c.40		CARATACVS		↑		CLAVDIVS	41–54
						Verica fled to Rome	c.42
Roman invasion	COGIDVBNVS also king of the Regni, succeeding A[. . .				PRASVTAGVS		43

——— indicates movement of tribes

·········· indicates establishment of control over

were copying the copies circulating from the east. It was not until *c.* 150 – 100 BC that the Gallic tribes began to continue this process. This slow westward drift and persistent copying of copies produced an extraordinary degeneration of the original design, and even its main elements have become virtually unrecognizable. Of the head of Apollo, all that survived was the laurel wreath as two straight bands and parallel with them a line of crescents derived from the god's ear; likewise, the charioteer, his chariot and two horses became a scatter of circles and pellets and a few sticks with knobs at each end are all that was left of the horses' legs. It makes a fascinating sequence of change by copying spread over a long period of time, but it could hardly have happened like this if some of the originals had been circulating in southern Gaul.

Eventually, *c.* 100 BC, the Gallic copies reached Britain, first perhaps as trade and later by immigrants. Some of the tribes of north Gaul were still striking gold staters, based on the Greek model, at the time of Caesar's invasion, which, as we have seen above, in turn precipitated a flight of refugees into Britain. These people brought their portable wealth with them, and it should be possible to trace their points of entry and areas of settlement, with a study of the particular coins they carried. Derek Allen identified nine different Gallo-Belgic coin types found in Britain[3], but only four of them have any real significance, and the problem is to place them in a chronological order. It is now, however, the view of Dr Scheers that the coins were all minted within a short period of 58 – 50 BC.[4] Allen's type 'A' seems to originate from an area of the Somme Valley and might be associated with the Ambiani, who gave their name to Amiens. The main concentration of this type in Britain is in north Kent, but there is another spread on the Essex coast and a scatter north of the Thames. Allen distinguished two sub-types of this series, and if one is later than the other, it is possible to detect spreads from two original settlements, one on the Medway Estuary, and one other in the Colne peninsula in Essex, and also into a new area north of the Thames in Hertfordshire[5] (p 32). What is of interest here is the blank area immediately to the north of the Thames, which must have been occupied by a tribe which resisted any entry by the migrants into their lands. Allen's type 'B' is a very odd one, as the obverse of the dies has been deliberately defaced, and no specimens struck from untouched dies have been found. One naturally wonders if such a strange way of treating coin dies had anything to do with the migration, and if so, why are there no undamaged examples in Gaul? The distribution pattern does not indicate an area of settlement very distinct from that of type 'A', except a small group to the west of the north Kent area and another round a Thames crossing, which overlaps with type 'A'. If this represents a separate invasion it is very small. Allen regarded this type as the earliest one, and if this is a correct assessment the distribution shows the areas of first Gallo-Belgic settlements.

Gallo-Belgic 'C' has close affinities with 'A', and seems to indicate a group entering Britain by the Thames Estuary. But there is a marked difference in distribution since they are more numerous in Gaul than in Britain, and they spread up the Somme areas into the Oise Valley, almost reaching the Marne. The British concentration is on the Medway in north Kent almost coincident with that of the early 'A' type. If these people moved after the 'A' group, they joined them to share their lands. Dr Scheers considers that this was one of the types minted in 58 – 57 BC but, if so, it shows that only a small section of the tribe migrated to Britain. Are types 'A' and 'C' variations produced by the same tribe? If so, 'C' would seem to be the earlier. On the other hand, it is this type which provides the model for the Britons when they started to make their own coins, and the logical implication of this would be to place type 'C' late, if not last in the series. The question which has never been satisfactorily solved is the relationship between the distribution patterns in Britain and Gaul of the different types, and how it is that coins considered to have been minted in Gaul should be so much more numerous in Britain? The answer to this may simply be that the finds in Gaul have not been so well recorded, and the imbalance has much to do with the difference in archaeological activities and interests on the two sides of the Channel.

Gallo-Belgic 'E', a uniface stater, (i.e. with one blank face; the other side shows a horse), originating with the Ambiani and the Suessiones, is the commonest type found in Britain, as well as Gaul. It is spread evenly over the earlier settlement areas with two additional ones on the Sussex coast and in south Lincolnshire, but this latter may be part of the peripheral scatter. This type can hardly belong to any particular tribe, but may represent general trade in Britain and with Gaul. Another explanation advanced by Dr Scheers and supported by Dr Kent[6] is that type 'E' was minted *c* 58 to pay for British mercenaries to go to the aid of the Gauls against Caesar[7]. Its distribution pattern gives an indication of the presence of coin-using peoples in Britain and with whom it may be possible to equate the Gallo-Belgic migrants at the time of Caesar. This pattern, as with the others, shows a large blank area north of the Thames, which presumably represents the territory of the kingdom of Cassivellaunus, but the name of the tribe has not survived.

The coin evidence can be summarized thus accepting that type 'B' is the earliest, this could represent the first Gallo-Belgic migrants. Types 'A' and 'C' represent the second invasion which according to Dr Scheers, cannot be earlier than 58 BC, while 'E' is common to many tribes, but the significance of this is far from clear. It now seems that coins did not come to Britain until the first century BC and most of their subsequent development, including all those minted in Britain, must post-date Caesar.

There remains yet one more point about coins raised by Dr Warwick Rodwell, and that is the distribution of hoards of Gallo-Belgic coins in Britain (1976, 198, 203 and Fig 8). It is often assumed that people buried their wealth as an emergency in times of unrest. It so happens that a number of these have been found near the coast, and this has suggested to Dr Rodwell that they were deposited by goldsmiths, traders or men of wealth fleeing from the advance of Caesar in Kent. But a simpler explanation would be that the coast is a dangerous place anyway, always subject to the sudden appearance of raiders or migrant bands, and there would have been many occasions for alarm, causing anyone with a quantity of valuable metal to bury it hastily, until the danger passed. The hoards vary considerably in content and are not necessarily of the same date, and Dr Rodwell has to admit, that they are only 'roughly contemporary'.

The three main tribal groups in south-east Britain at the time of Caesar's invasion can be identified as

1. the tribes of east and north Kent, which were throughout hostile to Caesar, who gives us the names of four of their kings – Cingetorix, Carvilius, Taximagulus and Segovax – but he does not add the names of their territories. This part of Kent was evidently divided into at least four regions, and most of these people had migrated, possibly at different times, from northern Gaul.

2. the tribe occupying the Colne peninsula, named by Caesar as the Trinovantes. The coins indicate that their leaders had been part of the migration associated with type 'A'. A prince, Mandubracius, had been suppliant to Caesar before the invasion of 55 BC, and we are further informed that he had fled after his father had been killed by Cassivellaunus. One might infer from this that the Gallo-Belgic migrants had been at war with a neighbouring tribe and suffered a defeat. This hostility may have involved other migrant tribes, and they may be included in the list which Caesar gives us, the Cenimagni, Segontiaci, Ancalites, Bibroci and the Cassi (v 21). None of these people are otherwise known,[8] except the first, which, it has been assumed, refers to the Iceni or a group of tribes subject to them, although Caesar states that the migrant tribes were named after the areas from which they originated (v 12), it is not certain if these five tribes were Gallo-Belgic, but they must have had sufficient reason for fearing Cassivellaunus, to seek the help of Rome, and it is probable that they lived on the borders of their hostile neighbours. These areas would have been on the north and west sides of the kingdom of Cassivellaunus, and the distribution of coins could be held to demonstrate that these were the lands of the Gallo-Belgic migrants.

3. The kingdom of Cassivellaunus comprises the third group. It has been a long standing assumption that this was the Catuvellauni, presumably since it was this tribe which faced the army of Claudius in 43. This tribe linked under Cunobeline and the Trinovantes occupied

Hertfordshire and Essex, the main area of the Gallo-Belgic settlement. The finds from Welwyn, Braughing and Camulodunon clearly show a close trading contact with the Roman world. It follows that the Catuvellauni can hardly be the tribe which suffered such a humiliating defeat under Caesar. The only area left in which to place the kingdom of Cassivellaunus is the blank space on the map where there are no Gallo-Belgic coins, this is a small area of about 20 by 30 miles, bounded by the north bank of the Thames. Within it are only four known fortified sites of this date, and, of these, Uphall Camp is too near the Thames to have avoided being found by Caesar. It may have been one of the other three, or an unknown site which he eventually attacked – Laughton Camp, Weald Park Camp or Ambresbury Banks, all rather small sites. There is, however, a larger and better defended site about 30 miles to the north of these, known as Wallbury, just to the south of Bishops Stortford, which seems a more likely prospect. Of course, Wheathampstead, the choice of Sir Mortimer Wheeler[9], cannot be ruled out entirely, although this site seems unlikely if the Gallo-Belgic migrants had moved into this area via the Lea Valley by this time, or the Catuvellauni may have helped themselves to part of the lands on the northern border of their defeated enemy. This unknown tribe was of an older stock, but just when it had come to Britain, or how much it had been influenced by continental migration, it is impossible to say on present evidence. One thing is clear; its peoples were hostile towards the Gallo-Belgic migrants in Essex and effected an anti-Roman alliance with the tribes of Kent. It is this basic polarization of the tribes on each side of the Thames Estuary which is a key factor to an understanding of subsequent events.

Caesar's impact on Britain

The most important effect of Caesar's appearance on the British scene was to divide the south-eastern tribes into pro- and anti-Roman groups. Those who had suffered defeat, i.e. the tribes on the north bank of the Thames and in Kent were forced to pay an annual tribute which sustained a festering hatred of Rome. Those who benefited, the Trinovantes, the Catuvellauni if as logic demands are the people of the Verulamon and Braughing areas and their allies, would have been rewarded by political alliances and access to trade with Rome, and for which there is archaeological support, as will be seen below. As far as Rome was concerned, south-eastern Britain had been conquered and treaty relationships had been established with a powerful group of tribes. The next stage would have been to allow the effects of trade and cultural contacts to prepare the way for full occupation with all the apparatus of government and law. But any immediate plans were put aside by the great Gallic rebellion which was to be followed immediately by the civil war splitting Rome itself into two great warring factions, until Caesar's nephew Octavian emerged the victor. He slowly brought the empire back to normality, and in 27 BC assumed the title *princeps* (first among Romans) and took the name Augustus. From Caesar's departure from Britain to this moment, Britain was almost forgotten, except by the traders who gradually introduced some of the 'delights' of the civilized world to the Britons. But the polarization of the tribes remained and a fascinating pattern of shifting inter-tribal relationships can be dimly perceived through a study of the coinage now being minted by the Britons for themselves.

The Coinage of the Britons

The 97 years between the two Roman invasions can thus be divided into two parts; the first, when Rome was preoccupied by her own internal troubles and when there are no historical references to Britain; the second, when Augustus began to consider the problems of his Empire, and Britain was placed on the diplomatic agenda and references begin to appear. One has to rely heavily on the archaeological evidence to supply the missing parts in the story of these changes. They were of two kinds; the pottery, metalwork and glassware now being imported, and the British coins.

Thanks to the devoted work of that great scholar Derek Allen, we know a great deal about the coins of the British tribes and what they tell us about the ruling dynasties of south-east Britain. It must, however, be admitted that this leaves great areas of Britain for which there is no such evidence, our knowledge about the peoples who lived there rests almost entirely on a study of their hill-forts, habitations, tools, pottery and artefacts traded from elsewhere. If one draws a line from the Humber to the Bristol Channel, it more or less makes a division between the tribes in the south and east for which there is evidence from coins and imported wares and those beyond for which there are no such guide-lines. Derek Allen recognized no less than 17 different types (A–Q) of British minted coin-copies from the Gallo-Belgic series, but not all of their distribution patterns are helpful in determining the boundaries of the British tribal territories. Most of these British minted coins appear to be outside the area of the Gallo-Belgic migrant settlements. This can only mean that the older British tribes began to imitate the newcomers who continued to use the earlier Gallo-Belgic types[10], although if this is so, it places a question over Allen's opinion that all these coins were, in fact, minted in Gaul.

British types 'A' and 'B' are common in Wiltshire, and are clearly the first coins of the Durotriges. To the north of this group is type 'Q', with its triple-tailed horse in a tight distribution pattern in the Upper Thames Valley, and must indicate the territory of the Dobunni at this period. But there is another group of these coins on the coast, which causes Allen to postulate that it could have belonged to the Atrebates.

There is, however, a great concentration of coins of many types spread along the coast from the Solent to Bosham Harbour, and it would be reasonable to assume that they represent trade at the ports of entry, where imported goods were being docked, traded and loaded onto carts and pack-animals for the inland journey. British type 'L' is the exception in having a Hertfordshire distribution and so must belong to one of the Gallo-Belgic tribes (Catuvellauni?) settled there, now beginning to mint its own coins. Types 'J' and 'N' consist of small numbers of Icenian coins, while 'H' and 'K' represent the first efforts of the Coritani in north Lincs, to provide for themselves. The rest of the Allen series are either too small in number and too widespread in distribution to offer any suggestions of origin. All these coins are copies of the old Gallo-Belgic types, which derived from the Macedonian staters but they would seem to offer clear evidence of the tribes of south-east Britain adjusting themselves to the realities of trade now possible with the Roman world.

The next stage in the development was for rulers to follow the Gallic practice of placing their names on the coins, but, apart from Commius, this does not include any names listed by Caesar. This would suggest that it was a generation before this practice started, for not even Mandubracius, the young king of the Trinovantes, recorded his name in this way. Perhaps the first to do so in Britain was Commius, but the quantity is so small that he may not have started to do it until late in his reign. His successor was Tincommius, a son, or more probably grandson. His coins, however, are not plentiful enough to be used to define the area of his tribe, but they are confined to the lands south of the Thames. His contemporary was Addedomaros, whose coins spread over a wide area of the Gallo-Belgic territories north of the Thames. The distribution spread across the Colne peninsula, but the thickest concentration is west of Verulamon, spreading into Oxfordshire. All the coins of Addedomaros are gold, but there are silver and bronze issues which Allen classified under Type L[11] and their function was probably to supplement the gold. They are thickest in the areas around Braughing and Colchester. Dr Rodwell thinks that one of them bears the letters CAMV, which would indicate the place of minting, concluding on this evidence and that of the distribution pattern that Addedomaros was King of the Trinovantes, but this remains speculative, and one is only justified in claiming him as a ruler of one, or a combination of the Gallo-Belgic groups *c* 20 BC.

What is certain is that coins were now being used on an increasing scale, although by whom, and for what purpose remains uncertain. There has been much speculation on the function of these coins[12]. Dr Scheers has suggested that the Celts continued the practice of the Greeks in paying for mercenary services in staters, others have mentioned bride-price or dowries or regal gifts. What is quite certain is that one cannot think of them in terms of modern currency, but when commodities were insufficient to pay for the expensive wine and other imports, gold would have been acceptable to the traders. The Roman merchants and government officials may have seen it as a softening up process before the full introduction of the crude but effective form of capitalism practised in Italy and the Roman provinces. But there is one incontrovertible fact, that when the British tribal coinage became distinctive enough, the distribution pattern remained very strictly within the tribal boundaries up to the end *c* AD 10, showing that the coins were not used for intertribal trade. A development which may have some bearing on the problem of payment for Roman goods are the large-scale field patterns in Trinovantian territory. These have been studied by Warwick Rodwell[13] and he has been able to demonstrate that in some areas, the Chelmer Valley and the system south of Braintree, in particular, ante-date the Roman roads, and this suggests a pre-conquest origin. The scale and degree of organization implied in these systems may demonstrate a powerful drive by the tribal chiefs towards increasing cereal production, now needed in exchange for the luxury imports.

Tasciovanus

Addedomaros was the first Briton north of the Thames to put his name on coins, the next to appear on the British scene is Tasciovanus who minted a large number of different coin types, Allen lists 43, and they have a very wide distribution. In spite of this, the site of his capital and the area over which he reigned is still in doubt. He used the Celtic word *riconos* (or *rigonos*) equivalent, one presumes, to the Latin *rex*, and the two mints are named CAMV(LUDVNON) and VER(VLAMION). Either these two mints operated at the same time, or one replaced the other during his reign since both mint-marks are on his early series, the former seems the most likely. The implication of the two mints and the wide distribution of his coins, is that Tasciovanus was able to bring the two powerful tribes, the Catuvellauni and the Trinovantes together to create one large kingdom to pass on to his son Cunobeline. But the wealth at this period seems to be in the Lea Valley, rather than the Colne peninsula, which suggests that the King belonged to the house of the Catuvellauni, and this explains why this tribe became the more dominant of the two under Cunobeline. Such an alliance could have been achieved by conquest or by dynastic marriage. The former could have evoked a Roman reaction at this period and a link between the royal households would have been simpler, and just as effective.

Tasciovanus extended his range of currency to include both silver and bronze, as well as gold. Other coins circulating freely during this period were those of a strange base metal known from the French word for them 'potin'[14]. They were actually chill-cast bronze with a high tin content, made in clay moulds joined together in a line. The

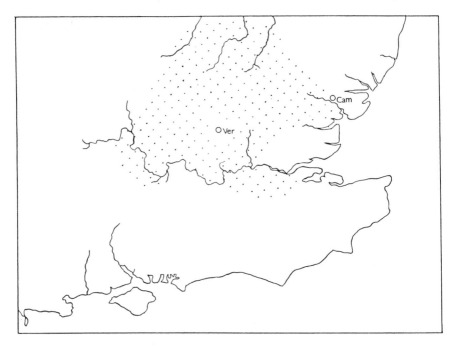

The approximate distribution area of the coins of TASCIOVANUS

coins were then separated with a chisel, but with a projecting tang being left on each side. There is an even odder fact about one particular series: the moulds were lined with strips of papyrus. The designs were derived from Gallic copies of the bronze coinage of Massilia of the second century BC, which had the head of Apollo on one side and a bull on the other. But, by the time they were made in Britain these motifs had been degraded to sketches outline-drawn with a stylus. Apollo looks like a diver in his helmet, or even a space-man, and all that survived of the bull are legs and horns, making a kind of abstract design. The only clue to the date is that some have been found on Roman sites in Kent, so that they overlap into the conquest period. Logically, they have to be seen as small change in a rudimentary currency system based on the gold, silver and bronze issues starting with Tasciovanus. This can only mean that by this time trade had developed within and beyond the Gallo-Belgic areas, and with Rome.

The early gold issues of Tasciovanus are the first coins to be found in the territory suggested for the Kingdom of Cassivellaunus, but silver and bronze are absent[15]. Another point of interest is the striking concentration of silver and bronze in the Braughing area. It is impossible to be sure of the site of the Tasciovanian capital. Oddly enough his coins are sparse at the mints, but the indications suggest that he ruled from somewhere in the Braughing area and there is other evidence, as

The approximate distribution area of the coins of ADDEDOMAROS

we shall see below, which seems to support this. There are four other names on his coins, SEGO, DIAS, RVES and ANDO. Of these only DIAS is linked with a mint-name – VER which suggests that this is the name of a local ruler at Verulamion. ANDO can be expanded to ANDOCO [. . . the name of a local ruler contemporary with Tasciovanus, and the coins of whom spread north and west of Braughing, but there are none at all in the Camulodunum area. It is not certain if the other names are those of people or the places where the coins were minted. Allen lists only three coins of SEGO, one from Tring, Herts., and the other two, possibly with another[16] from Kent, but RVES has a definite concentration in the Braughing area, and could be either a local ruler or the mint-name[17]. These rulers have all to be placed in the last quarter of the first century BC in order to fit their reigns into the chronology of the following century which is securely based on historical dates.

Imports from the Roman world

As seen above, a case could be made for the proliferation of coins to indicate a crude currency system, and one naturally asks what kind of commodities were being marketed in these areas. A few years ago, there would have been no answer to this except to point to a few imported silver and bronze vessels and burials with imported *amphorae*

The find-spots of the coins of ANDOCO [. . .
VER = VERULAMION

(large wine containers). Recent research and excavations have continued to produce new evidence, in particular, the valuable work of Dr David Peacock, of Southampton University, on the Roman *amphorae* in pre-Roman Britain[18]. These large cylindrical containers were mainly used for transporting wine from the vineyards in different parts of the Roman world, but they were also used for olive oil, a kind of Mediterranean fish sauce (*garum*), and more solid foods packed in salt for preservation[19]. They are very common in all Roman sites in Britain, and the difference in their shapes has been recognized, the early ones are long cylinders, while the later tend to be globular. The first classification of the vessels types was by a German scholar H. Dressel in 1894[20] and the type which concerns us most is the Dressel 1, which came from the wine-producing areas between Terracina and Capua in the Campanian region of Central Italy, and which also produced the famous Falernian wine, extolled by the poet Horace. It is possible to date these *amphorae* from examples found on cargoes recovered from shipwrecks in the Mediterranean, from which it seems that this trade had ceased by the end of the first century BC (i.e. by *c.* 1 BC). Thus, the discovery of any of these *amphorae* in Britain helps to assess the amount of trade with the Roman world and where it was concentrated. Dr Peacock plotted the find-spots of these vessels and his map has been supplemented by Dr Rodwell[21] (p 32). The area of distribution is precisely that of the British coins discussed above, a broad band from Camulodunon stretching west to Verulamion. There are a few outliers, two in Cambridge, which could be a little later, and a few from the North Thames Estuary shore. Significant also is the fact that only three fragments have turned up in Kent, two of them at Canterbury.

The inference is clear enough, the alliance made by Caesar with the Catuvellauni, the Trinovantes and the other Gallo-Belgic peoples had opened up their territories to Roman traders. Wine was imported in bulk from Central Italy in the last two or three decades of the first century BC, during the reign of Addedomaros, Tasciovanus and Andoco [. . . But this luxury trade was denied to the elements hostile to Caesar and Rome, the kingdom of Cassivellaunus and the tribes of Kent. There is, however, another small group of these vessels, as Dr Peacock has shown (his Fig 36 and p 173), on the south coast from the Isle of Wight to Portland Bill, including the important site on Hengistbury Head, which had widespread trading contacts over a considerable period[22]. The tribe here was that of the Durotriges, and there is no indication at present that this trade reached the lands of the Commian Atrebates. Dr Peacock's map reveals another fascinating aspect of this trade; there are very few examples of Dressel 1 in north and central Gaul. The shipments were coming either direct by sea from Massilia, or by boat up the Rhône and its tributary the Saône, crossing by an overland route to the Moselle and the Rhine, thence across the North Sea. This would seem to be a very cumbersome and expensive way of transporting these heavy and awkward vessels, hardly compensated by the possible losses on the sea route, but the archaeological evidence seems indisputable. Dr Peacock advances the reasonable suggestion that it was a well-established route for goods pouring into the rich Rhineland market, following Caesar's Gallic conquests and the passage across the North Sea to Britain, on what has become the Hook–Harwich route, was a natural extension[23].

This will not, however, account for the discoveries on the south coast and at Hengistbury Head, where there is a mixed assemblage of imports with an earlier starting date. An obvious route for this is the Rhône–Seine, although north-western Gaul may not have been fully pacified at this date the tribes in this area were probably trading with Rome and Britain.

With the high-quality Italian wine flowing into Britain, one might also expect fine silver flagons, strainers and drinking cups to grace the tables of the wealthy tribal rulers. Objects of gold and silver have always been treasured, when an article was damaged or went out of fashion, it had good scrap value. This is why objects of precious metal are rarely found except under special conditions, one of the more likely of which is the burial custom when important people are interred with their personal jewellery and tableware. This has been, throughout all ages, a universal way of providing for the dead in the after-life, giving them the comfort of their own things. Moreover, they were also imbued with the *persona* of their owner and it was considered unlucky for anyone else to use them. There was a tale told not so long ago of a fond widow in Dorset insisting her husband being buried with his favourite beer mug. For examples of such signs of wealth, one should find and study burials of this period, especially in the area of the early *amphorae*. Fortunately this has already been done by Dr Ian Stead, but, alas, he found only eight[24], and half of them seem to be too late for this period; the earlier four have all been discovered in the Welwyn area. It was unfortunate that the first of these important burials was found by chance during road works in 1906, and the vessels was indiscriminately pulled out of the trenches by workmen. It happened again in 1965, when trenches on a housing estate cut through more graves and workmen burrowed into the sides of the trench for complete *amphorae*. A sub-contractor had the happy idea that he could sell them as garden ornaments! One was then identified by a knowledgeable resident, but it took two months for action to be taken to carry out a proper investigation of the site. The pipe-trench was re-opened and found to have bisected the grave. Apart from five *amphorae*, no less than 36 other vessels were found, most of them fine grey well-burnished jars and cups, many with pedestals and obviously for wine. They appeared to be the products of local potters with one or two possible exceptions, where the fabrics are quite different. An outstanding item in the grave group was a complete set of 24 glass counters in sets of four colours, white, blue, yellow and green, six of each colour. As they were all found in a tight cluster, it is assumed that they were originally in a bag of textile or leather which has not survived. Another compact little group, consisted of six glass pieces, segments of three perforated beads and three short lengths of glass bracelets. It was assumed by the excavator that all these glass pieces made a set for some kind of game played on a board, and the function of the six beads and bangle fragments was to act as a kind of dice, since when thrown on to the surface they came to rest in one or two positions with the flat or rounded side uppermost. One could thus move the sets of counters about the board, as we do today in many variations of race-games, such as Snakes and Ladders. It was the opinion of Dr Harden, one of our most foremost authorities on Roman glass, that they had probably come from north Italy. Among the pieces of iron were four clamps, two lengths of frame with a projecting hinge and an odd kind of oval boss with nail holes in each corner. Dr Stead made the attractive suggestion that these fragments represent the remains of the actual gaming board; the four clamps being a repair and the oval boss a sunken area in the middle where the glass pieces were kept.

There were also metal vessels, including a fine bronze wine-strainer in the form of a shallow bowl with a loop handle opposite a spout, the strainer itself, a thin piece of bronze with perforation in a crude curvilinear design was fixed vertically across the bowl which was partly covered by a lid. There was also a fine bronze oval dish with a flat projecting flange rim of attractive design. There was a scatter of bronze domed studs which had been attached to a piece of furniture or screen, and it was clear from other fragments that there had been several other wood objects in the grave, which were impossible to reconstruct. Another iron object was a triangular razor with a handle in the form of a duck's head. Part of the grave had been covered with a straw mat, identified by small fragments preserved by the salts produced by oxidizing bronze. But the finest item was a silver double-handled cup, with a pedestalled foot, with bands of decoration including the familiar classical 'egg and tongue' round the rim; the elegantly shaped handles with an attachment to the body in the form of leaves. It had been badly crushed in the grave, but enough remains to allow an accurate reconstruction which showed it to be typical of the late Roman Republican period, dateable to *c.* 25 – 0 BC and very similar to another cup found with the 1906 discoveries[25].

There are probably more of these exotic objects of Italian origin to be found, while others have doubtless been lost or ill-recorded in the past, as is usually the fate of gold and silver which touches the cupidity of the treasure hunter. One can reasonably assume that a trading connection had been well established by *c.* 10 BC following the wine route. Fine Roman wines needed fine vessels to grace the tables of the richer Britons of this area. But thanks to the recent work of Mr Clive Partridge in Hertfordshire we know now that the trade extended far beyond this range of goods. A rescue excavation at Skeleton Green, not far from Braughing, has produced a large assemblage of pottery, which included nearly a hundred vessels from the well-known factory at modern Arezzo, halfway between Florence and Perugia. The red-slipped Arretine wares made here were the precursors of the Gallic samian wares which copied them and captured the western market by the end of the reign of Augustus. There were also a large number of mica-dusted jars with a lid-seating for a sealing lid, which also seem to have been made in north Italy, and may have been containers. But the most significant vessels found by Mr Partridge are *mortaria* – heavy bowls with a pouring spout used for pulverising food in the kitchen – since it is hardly likely that the Britons, however sophisticated their drinking habits, would have acquired Roman kitchen techniques by this time. These vessels seem to indicate that there were traders from the Roman world actually established here in a depôt. It seems, however, peculiar that these imported wares would not have been found before in this area, the explanation may be the limited amount of investigation until quite recently. Nor is this likely to be the only trading post; one would surely expect another in the vicinity of Camulodunon.

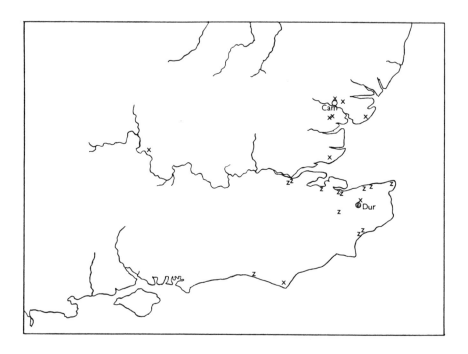

The find-spots of the two coin types of DUBNOVELLAVNOS
  x Essex types
  z Kent types (excluding six for Durovernon)
  CAM = CAMULUDUNON
  DVR = DUROVERNON

Dubnovellaunos

On the death of Tasciovanus, or towards the end of his reign when his power may have weakened, the throne of the Trinovantes was taken by Dubnovellaunus, who may have been the rightful heir. His centre was certainly Camulodunon, since the main concentration of his coins is there, but others have been found in the Lea Valley. The designs of these coins suggest that he succeeded Tasciovanus and was in turn followed by Cunobeline; they do not, however, indicate his affiliation. From this we may conclude that he belonged to the royal house of the Trinovantes, and managed to hold together the two tribes for a short time, although ANDOCO [. . . may have established his independence on behalf of the Catuvellauni. If this was a period of central weakness and uncertainty, it would explain the seizure of power by Cunobeline, who claimed to be the son of Tasciovanus, and who, to maintain the alliance of the two tribes, established himself at Camulodunon. Another possibility is that, if Tasciovanus had created the alliance by means of a dynastic marriage, Cunobeline may have been brought up in his mother's house with Dubnovellaunos, who could thus have been his cousin. Instead of elimination, Cunobeline offered him an alternative kingdom in north-east Kent, where another and different series of his coins is found, again with no affiliation, but distinctly based on issues of Tasciovanus. These two areas of coins bearing the same name have created much discussion, and it has been argued that he was a Kentish king, who seized the throne of Tasciovanus. The problem is that no one is prepared to say which of the two series is the earlier, but perhaps this crux can be resolved by considering another important fact about him. His name appears with that of Tincommius on the *Res Gestae* of Augustus. This is a document prepared by the Emperor, listing his main achievements which survives in the form of fragments of monumental inscriptions, in the various parts of the Empire where they were set up. The most complete version has been found at Ankara, and this became known as the *Monumentum Ancyranum*.[26] The two British kings are listed here as suppliants before Augustus. As the generally accepted date of this inscription is AD 7, these kings must have been refugees in Rome sometime before this date. To understand this and to see the whole sequence in its historical background from the Roman viewpoint, one must consider the changing political scene south of the Thames in the kingdom of Commius, under Tincommius and his successors.

Commius and the Atrebates

There is one more historical incident associated with Caesar and Britain which must not be overlooked. Commius had been a good friend and colleague of Caesar, who had made him King of the Atrebates. He had acted as Caesar's diplomatic emissary in Britain and had been given similar tasks in Gaul. For reasons which Caesar fails to give us, Commius turned against him at the time of the great Gallic revolt and threw in his lot with Vercingetorix, raising troops for him from neighbouring tribes and even persuaded the Germans to help. He escaped from the first battle, evading a special search party sent after him, and, although severely wounded, managed to set sail for Britain. Frontinus relates, as one of his *Strategems* (ii 13, 11), how Commius, although becalmed, hoisted his sail to give the impression that he was under way and so deceived his pursuers. He knew enough about the people of Britain to avoid capture by either the pro-Roman elements north of the Thames, or the anti-Roman in Kent, both of whom had good reasons either to dislike or mistrust him. He landed on the Sussex coast and established himself and his small band of followers on the western edge of the Weald, to found the Kingdom of the Atrebates, the capital of which was eventually to be established at Silchester (Calleva). It was a considerable achievement, even for such a strong personality with great qualities of leadership, and shows him to have been an outstanding example of a warrior aristocrat taking lands for himself.

The find-spots of the coins of COMMIUS
CAL = CALLEVA

Since the Regni occupied the Sussex coast, either Commius must have persuaded them to allow his small band to pass through their territory and establish his authority over their neighbours on the north, or, of course, his landfall may have been further to the west, possibly up the Solent. Professor Cunliffe has a different account for this episode, assuming that the Atrebates were already here and that Commius merely joined them and was accepted as their king.[27] He goes on to show the territory of the tribe (his Fig 7:2) covering an enormous area, a hundred miles from east to west. This is not supported by the archaeological evidence; there are virtually no Gallo-Belgic coins except on the coast, nor any Gallo-Belgic inspired pottery. The latter, in fact, shows two quite distinctive types which he calls Northern and Southern Atrebates, producing further evidence that this division was maintained up to the Roman Conquest, with suggestions of pro- and anti-Roman groups. The coins of Commius seem to be concentrated in a very small area south of the Thames round Silchester, whereas those of Tincommius, his son or grandson, spread to the south as if to suggest that the kingdom was steadily enlarged.

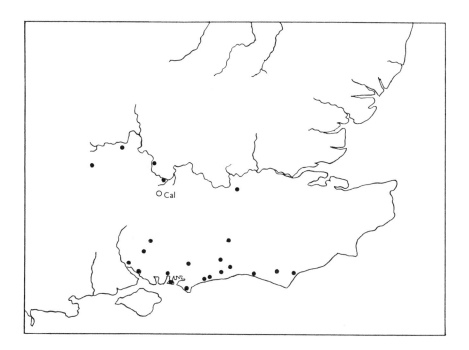

The find-spots of the coins of TINCOMMIVS
CAL = CALLEVA

The Regni[28]

These people play no known part in the subsequent dynastic struggles. Although they may have been allies or subject to the Atrebates, their tribal integrity was kept intact. This fact is clear from the presence of their own tribal capital Noviomagus – though, as its name implies, it was a new foundation replacing the older centre at Selsey Bill, which was being lost by coastal erosion. After the conquest, as will be seen later, the territories of the two tribes jointly became the kingdom of Tiberius Claudius Cogidubnus. The pre-conquest history of this coastal area has yet to be studied in detail, but there is no doubt as to the importance of the site as the tribal centre in its relationship to the key point-of entry, Bosham Harbour. This can be demonstrated by the elaborate system of dykes which virtually cut off the harbour and the Selsey peninsula[29] from the northern approaches – a vast scheme comparable to that at Camulodunum. There were powerful influences at work here, but the political relationship to Rome and names of the rulers remain unknown. There is, however, a small silver coin bearing the letter A in the centre of two interlaced arcs (Mack 316). At one time this coin was linked with Adminius of Kent but Derek Allen became doubtful of this, although he knew of only two examples, one found in 1938 on the Sussex Downs and the other in 1967 on the early Roman fort at Waddon Hill, Dorset.[30] Since then three more have been found, one on the temple site on Hayling Island and two in excavations at Chichester.[31] Some of them also bear the letters AM on the reverse and this could be a mint name. All five coins have been found on the south coast, and so it offers the possibility of a ruler of the Regni and by a strange coincidence, as Derek Allen pointed out, the name AMMINVS actually occurs on a tombstone at Chichester (*RIB* 90).

The Dobunni

The Dobunni occupied the upper Thames Valley to the west of the Goring Gap, but had spread into Gloucester up the Bristol Channel and lower Severn, to form a compact bloc north of their neighbours the Durotriges, as their coin distribution clearly indicates.[32] They minted coins with a very distinctive motif, a triple-tailed horse, and early in the first century AD names of rulers in an abbreviated form appear: ANTED [.... EISU [.... CATTI [.... COMVX [.... INAM [.... CORIO [.... and BODVOC [...., more or less in that chronological order. They seem to be in pairs, as if the tribe was divided into two parts. This especially applies to the last two names; the Corio [.... examples are found in the southern area, i.e. Somerset and north Wiltshire, and Bodvoc [.... in Gloucestershire, and the coins of the latter show definite Roman influence.

Two useful pieces of information come from Dio, who tells us that the tribe was subject to the Catuvellauni (lx 20). Cunobeline may have had an alliance with Bodvoc, the northern ruler, which could explain the help he obtained in cutting the dies for his coins. Dio also records that a section of the Dobunni surrendered to Rome in the very early stages of the conquest, and this could imply a direct link with Rome, established with the help of Cunobeline, and which remained firm after his death, in spite of Caratacus. Another result of such an arrangement should have been the presence of Roman trade in the area, but so far, there is very little evidence of this. The reason may be the limited amount of excavation of late Iron Age sites in Gloucestershire. The most significant discoveries have been made at Bagendon, about five miles north of Cirencester, excavated by Mrs Elsie Clifford, from 1954 to 1965, but on a minute scale in the enormous 200-acre site.[33] The excavation did, however, produce a large quantity of artefacts and pottery, probably since it was sited near the main entrance. The dating of the imported pottery was largely based on the finds from the Sheepen site at Camulodunum, which is now considered to be almost entirely of the conquest period. The Bagendon pottery has recently been re-examined by Mr Geoffrey Dannell.[34] Since the publication of the excavation report, a study of the wares produced in central and southern Gaul, have shown that there were many variations of the pottery formerly known as Arretine, from Arretium (the modern Arezzo). This important factory was in a state of decline towards the end of the reign of Augustus, but it was still producing pottery, although of an inferior quality, under Tiberius. Some of the potters had moved to Gaul to be near the new provincial markets, and their products have been described as 'provincial' or 'Gallic' Arretine. The tracing of these products to their centres of manufacture and their close dating is still a matter of debate. A small amount of pottery of this type was recovered from Bagendon, but Mr Dannell cannot place any piece earlier than AD 20–30 and there is no indication that occupation extended much beyond the conquest period.

The most striking evidence of Gallo-Belgic influence in the area is the system of dykes which appear to enclose very large areas at Bagendon and Minchinhampton.[35] This is clear and unequivocal evidence of the presence in Gloucestershire of people with definite ideas derived from the Gallo-Belgic migrants. All this would seem to confirm that a ruler, who could be identified as Bodvoc, had trading and political contacts with the people to the east *c.* AD 20–40. This could only have been through the agency of Cunobeline, who sought to strengthen his frontiers with alliances, much in the Roman manner, and so protected his power from interference from the north and the west, and from the south too, through Verica and his own son Adminius in north-east Kent.

The Durotriges

According to its coin distribution, this tribe occupied a very compact area[36] of Wiltshire and Dorset, defined on the east by the rivers Avon and Wylye, and on the west, by a line roughly between Lyme Regis and Taunton, while the northern limit was the Valley of the Wylye and the west edge of the Mendips. There is also a scatter of British copies of Gallo-Belgic type B and this has been accounted for by Dr Kent as payment for mercenary services. If this suggestion is valid it would indicate that their hostility to Rome went back to Caesar and may even have been associated with his destruction of the Veneti, their trading partners on the other side of the Channel. The coinage remains British without any classical influences, and totally uninscribed except for the few bearing the enigmatic letters CRAB (Mack 371 and 372), but this type most probably belongs to the people to the east. Durotrigian hostility to Rome is evident from the campaign of Vespasian and further evidence suggests that it continued unabated up to AD 60. Their black burnished pottery is quite distinctive and was eventually to become one of the main sources of kitchen wares for the army and much of the province.[37]

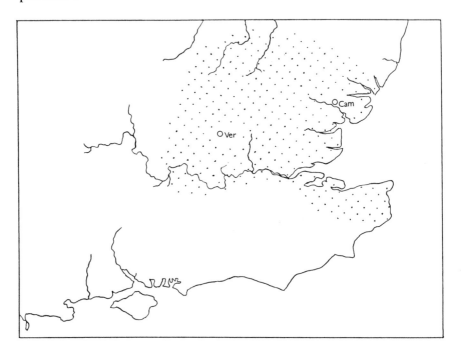

The approximate distribution area of the coins of CUNOBELINE
VER = VERULAMION
CAM = CAMULUDUNON

Cunobeline

This remarkable man, the greatest of all the British kings, was a son of Tasciovanus, and extended his kingdom and influence on the basis of his father's alliance between the two powerful tribes, possibly by a dynastic marriage. The centre of power, however, shifted from the Lea to the Colne Valley, and this can only be explained by assuming that Camulodunon, the seat of the royal house of the Trinovantes, was now absorbed into the greater kingdom. Cunobeline decided at the outset of his reign, as his early gold coins show[38], to make his capital at Camulodunon, and, although this evidence is at present rather thin, there is from this time a decline in the wealth of the Braughing–Verulamium area, and a rise of that in the Colne peninsula. It is almost as if the Roman traders had moved their depôts to the glittering prospects of the new court. The coinage of Tasciovanus had included the names of local dynasts, which suggests that he was prepared to accept autonomy among sections of the Catuvellauni. This is certainly not so with Cunobeline, who established his presence over the whole area of his alliance, with no other names on his coins. He began his reign at Camulodunon. Of the earliest gold staters (Mack 201 and 202), five of the six known examples have all been found nearby, and one of the series has the mint name CAMVL [... His second series has an ear of barley on the reverse, reflecting the wealth of his lands, and these coins are spread widely over the whole territory of the alliance, which shows that Cunobeline was quickly in control. When all his coins are plotted on a map (p 62), the final extent of the kingdom and influence is seen, spreading up to the Ouse in the north, and as far up the Thames as the Goring Gap, while his boundary with the Iceni seems to be the Rivers Lark and Gipping, which flows into the Orwell. The only blank space is the thick woodland north of the Thames, but the concentration along the Lea Valley shows this to be the main route to the Catuvellaunian heartland. If the idea which has been put forward, that the old kingdom of Cassivellaunus was on the northn t bank the Thames, as Caesar informs us, it must have been absorbed, possibly by Cunobeline, and the tribe then lost its identity.

Cunobeline probably gained his throne in the very first few years of the first century AD as a young man in his twenties or early thirties, and his power and wealth grew throughout his long reign. It must be assumed that he continued to follow the pro-Roman tradition of his people, although this does not show on his coins until the very end of his reign, with the so-called 'Classic' series, the issues of which are the products of a skilled die-cutter from Greece or Rome. In view of events south of the Thames involving the expulsion of the pro-Roman rulers Tincommius and Dubnovellaunos, it is probable that Cunobeline had to be careful throughout most of his reign, not to show undue bias towards Rome. There were strong anti-Roman elements, kept active by the Druids in the royal household, as became obvious at the moment of his decline or death. But during his lifetime, he maintained a careful balance and was successful in satisfying his own people with their growing prospects, as well as persuading Rome of his loyalty, and, at the same time, keeping the power of the Druids in check.

Augustus and Britain

While the civil war, which followed the assassination of Caesar, continued on its devastating and bloody course, Britain had been forgotten. But as soon as Augustus established himself as the first *princeps* in 27 BC, he realized that this unfinished business needed attention. There is an indication that he was thinking about Britain in the autumn of that year, when he was in southern Gaul reorganizing the Province. But any serious plans for an expedition the following year were swept aside by trouble in north-west Spain, where he mounted a campaign against the Cantabrians and the Asturians, the rigours of which seriously affected his health, always precarious. Augustus was quite a different kind of person to Caesar, who had a brilliant incisive mind, preferred an intensely physical life of continuous movement (sometimes very rapid), making instant decisions. Augustus was essentially an intellectual, whose great mental abilities were dedicated to the perfection of the state organization which he gradually established. He was a quiet man, often withdrawn, living modestly on plain fare, but never permitted by his strong sense of duty, the luxury of a family life. His decisions were usually reached after a careful consideration of all the factors, but he held in his mind almost a total grasp of the complexities of his great Empire. He was by nature cautious, preferring the compromise solution, and had little of the dashing brilliance of Caesar. Yet Augustus attracted men of action like Agrippa, to him, and they served him loyally. Such a man, trying to balance the needs of a large sprawling Empire, was unlikely to launch a punitive campaign against Britain when there would have been pressing military problems elsewhere. Yet he would not have neglected the problem, but maintained the Roman influence by diplomatic means. Providing Rome had strong allies in Britain, and they controlled the main points of entry from Gaul, there was no need for further action. This seems to have been the thinking behind the Augustan plan for Britain. Thus, Rome kept a wary eye on Britain since dynastic changes could upset the balance of power and might even allow coastal areas, important for trade and as potential landing points, to fall into hostile hands. Augustus was reluctant to interfere with British politics, but there were times when this became necessary. It is this use of skilful diplomacy which may account for events in Britain at the death of Tasciovanus.

If Augustus was in close touch with Britain through his agents, he could have used his influence to avoid a clash between Cunobeline and Dubnovellaunos, both of whom may have had a legitimate claim to the Trinovantian throne. A civil war, north of the Thames, could only weaken the two great tribes, and Rome would certainly lose trade, but the worst danger would have been the anti-Roman forces gaining control. It was, therefore, very much in the Roman interests to help to bring about an amicable arrangement which would maintain the balance of power. We have no means of knowing what was the political situation in Kent at this time, but Roman control over the coastline remained the main objective. This is, of course, very speculative, but on the basis of these background factors, a likely solution would have been for an amicable exchange of thrones across the Thames, with suitable compensation for Dubnovellaunos, no doubt from Rome.

The rise of anti-Roman forces in Britain

The political balance in Sussex and Kent suffered a severe upset with the overthrow of the Roman ally Tincommius, King of the Atrebates, by Eppillius, another son or grandson of Commius. This must have been regarded by Augustus as a serious set-back for Rome. Although there is, as yet, no evidence of luxury trade with the Atrebates similar to that of the north of the Thames, the alliance was marked by the coins of Tincommius, some of which were copies of Roman *denarii*, and the products of a Roman die-cutter (Mack 96, 105 and 106). C. E. Stevens dated the alliance to 27 BC when Augustus was in Gaul but it is probably somewhat later. Augustus visited Gaul again in 17 BC to ameliorate the disastrous effects on the Rhineland of the *clades Lolliana*[39] and to complete the pacification of Gaul by improving the administration. It was a good time to reconsider his policy towards Britain. Eppillus may have made his move in the last decade of the first century BC when Augustus was a sick man, overwhelmed with the affairs of state and lacking the aid of Tiberius,[40] who had retired to Rhodes. Eppillus could not have lasted very long at Calleva, his capital, since his coin series is of only four types, and we next find him in East Kent, where he minted at least 18 different types, signifying a longer reign (Mack 300–311). His move to Kent must be connected with the expulsion of Dubnovellaunos, and it is an odd coincidence that he was responsible for ousting two pro-Roman rulers. It may seem a fanciful suggestion, but there is a parallel here in the Cunobeline-Dubnovellaunos relationship. Could it have been that the anti-Roman forces, inspired by the Druids, finding Cunobeline too powerful for them had become active south of the Thames and succeeded in removing two pro-Roman rulers? Or was Eppillus turned out by another palace revolt and took a new kingdom for himself in Kent? Pure chance, or the operations of powerful internal forces? Verica who succeeded Eppillus, also claimed to be COMMI F(ILIVS), but was probably a younger man, as he was still alive in AD 42.

Whatever may be the truth behind these moves, they occurred early in the reign of Cunobeline when he was in no position to challenge them, since he was absorbed in the consolidation of his power. He was probably under great family and priestly pressure in those years to withdraw contact with Rome, for this was a time when once more Augustus was beset with a series of appalling disasters, and Britain was far from his thoughts. In AD 9, there was the great Pannonian revolt, which was put down, with difficulty, by Tiberius, but at great cost to Rome. It was soon to be followed by an even greater blow – the loss of three legions under Quinctilius Varus in the forests of Germany. The effect on Augustus was traumatic, and its impact deepened by his realization that he had totally misjudged the political situation there. He had assumed that Germany had been pacified, and his policy of incorporating the area, west of the Rhine, into the Empire was based on an alliance with Arminius, King of the Cherusci.[41] But this man was playing a double game, and, after entertaining Varus and

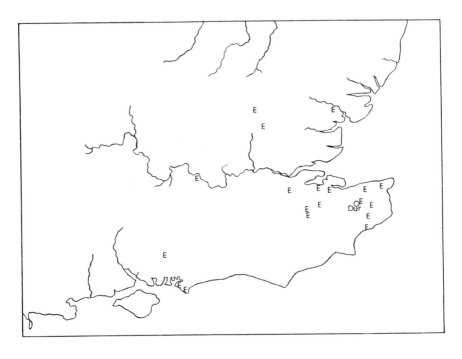

The find-spots of the coins of EPPILLUS
DVR = DUROVERNON

his troops, he ambushed them on their return journey to their winter quarters. Germany was lost to Rome, and the loss in military manpower was so great that Augustus lost interest in any further extensions to his Empire. News from Britain revealing the deterioration of Roman influence fell on unresponsive ears: the saddened and ageing Emperor was not to be drawn into any further imperial ventures. In spite of this disinterest, no further changes took place in Britain, Cunobeline was now in firm control, able to keep the forces hostile to Rome at bay, and to encourage the development of trade.

Augustus died in AD 14, and was succeeded by Tiberius, now an elderly and disillusioned man, but with a firm sense of duty. He accepted the injunction of Augustus to allow things to stay as they were and concentrated on sound administration, until he allowed control to slip into the hands of his praetorian prefect, Sejanus. There is, however, evidence of a renewal of diplomatic activity towards Britain. Verica of the Atrebates became an ally of Rome, and adopted the title REX on his coins, some of which are the work of Roman die-cutters including one issue bearing a head which has been identified as that of Tiberius himself (Mack 127, 131 and 132). Verica also used the motif of the vine-leaf which may reflect the trade then established with Rome. In

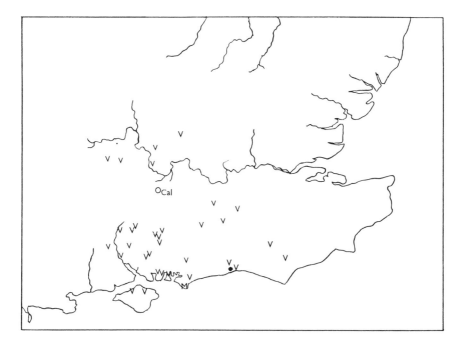

The find-spots of the coins of VERICA
CAL = CALLEVA   M = the Selsey mint

contrast, Cunobeline takes the tile REX only on a single bronze issue (Mack 246), but he felt strong enough to reverse the slight of his cousin's removal from the throne of east Kent, by placing his own son, Adminius there at the very end of his reign. As there are only five of his coins known, his reign must have been very short,[42] for he appears as a refugee before Gaius (Caligula) when he was in Germany in AD 39 or 40. This caused that unbalanced Emperor to have thoughts about an invasion of Britain, but such is the garbled version of his preparations that it is difficult to decide how serious they were.[43] But the death of Cunobeline had by then entirely changed the political scene in Britain.

Camulodunon[44] – the capital of Cunobeline

A king as wealthy and powerful as Cunobeline would be expected to live in style, if not splendour, but the precise whereabouts of his palace and settlement named after the Celtic god of war, Camulos, is not certain. This is all the more surprising when one considers the number and scale of excavations carried out at Colchester and its environs over the years. The problem to be faced is the sheer size of the territory in which the British capital could be situated. It can be roughly defined by a system of defensive dykes, embracing an area of just over 20 square miles with the River Colne flowing through the centre. The northern boundary is marked by two small streams, the Salary Brook and the Black Brook and the south side by the Roman River. The dates and sequence of dykes have been a problem for many years, but they have been recognized as Gallo-Belgic, enclosing a typical *oppidum*. The latest study by Dr Warwick Rodwell[45] arranges them in seven phases and the last of these, the triple-ditch system on the west side, has since been shown, by material found in it, to be of second century date, and therefore belongs to the Roman *colonia*. Phase VI is also late in the series and is difficult to fit into the pattern since its alignment has no regard for any known centre, but appears to be protecting the junction of the Colne with the Roman River, and extends beyond the south of the latter.

The site of Colchester has been shown by extensive excavations to have been entirely Roman. The Sheepen site about a mile to the north-west was investigated in advance of a by-pass road in 1930 – 1939, in what must have been one of the earliest large-scale rescue excavations in Britain. Its avowed purpose was to investigate 'the ancient British capital'. The results were disappointing, but the excavators felt that they had succeeded in locating the site of Camulodunon concluding that, 'it was not a city in the organic sense of a concentrated inhabitation-area, peopled by a compactly dwelling body of citizens'[46]. With the advantage of hindsight, it can now be said that it was almost certainly not the site of the capital, and the scattered pre-Conquest remains represent no more than scant occupation peripheral to the main centre.

The earliest ditched enclosure of the dyke system is that around the site at Gosbecks which contains a very large religious site of the Roman period. This can reasonably be assumed to have been built over an older Belgic one. Whether this would have been the principal Druidic sanctuary is impossible to say without evidence. The dykes which surrounded the early nucleus are the most likely to enclose the earliest native settlement to which Gosbecks was an adjacent sacred area. This area has been subject to intensive study by Philip Crummy with the aid of aerial photographs.[47] The resulting plan (p 131) shows about 70 hectares (173.9 acres) covered with small land units with their boundary ditches, probably representing a field system. The later religious site with its temple and theatre in close association with a spring, occupies part of the northern area and seems to include on the west side a sub-rectangular enclosure which, as Mr Crummy has pointed out, may have been the nucleus of the settlement, maybe the palace area. The Roman fort had been carefully sited within the dyke system, but clearly on the north-western perimeter of the British settlement, but only 300 metres from the central 'enclosure'. One cannot be certain without extensive excavation that this is an outline plan of Camulodunon, but it seems a strong possibility.

The Belgic cemetery and the Lexden Tumulus

Another factor is the site of a Gallo-Belgic cemetery about a mile and a half to the north. It includes a number of burial mounds (tumuli), the largest and most interesting of which is the Lexden Tumulus. The area has been much disturbed by modern housing and the opportunity for further discoveries or investigation now seems remote. The most interesting fact about this is its size – 80 feet in diameter, although it has been eroded down to a height of nine feet. It was excavated in 1924, in advance of housing development, by local antiquarians, the two Laver brothers[48]. Such a prominent burial mound, well known to eighteenth-century antiquarians, is not likely to have escaped the attention of tomb-robbers in earlier centuries. There is an ominous note in the records of the Ordnance Survey stating that 'In 1860 Roman remains were found in this tumulus consisting of an *amphora*, the neck and handle being broken two feet, nine inches high, together with a quantity of fragments of Roman pottery'. The excavators noticed in 1924 a large hole in the centre of the mound, 20 feet across and four feet deep, 'full of black soil' which may represent the 1860 intrusion. But the discovery of broken pottery at this time strongly suggests an earlier disturbance, for had the burial been intact, there would have been a number of complete *amphorae* stacked in the grave. The 1924 excavation produced a large quantity of broken *amphorae* fragments, representing all that remains of at least 15 vessels.[49] As Dr Rodwell has pointed out, the very fine bronze griffin mount must be the only survivor of several such decorations attached to a large wine crater which the tomb-robbers removed.[50] The almost total absence of human remains, and objects of precious metal are sure indications of a considerable disturbance of the original grave. The Laver excavation removed most of the oval burial-pit, as indicated in their plan (Fig 2 in the report) so there is very little left for any further enquiry to test the relationship between the different disturbances. The presence of a large tree (a Wellingtonia) on the mound and its considerable root disturbance made it difficult for the Lavers to recognize the precise extent of the earlier digging, although this is marked on their plan (Fig 3 in the report). In spite of all this, a vast amount of material was recovered by them and this is now stored in the Colchester and Essex Museum. Although the published report is only reasonably comprehensive for its time it includes items only considered by the excavators to be of interest.

This is not the occasion to review this collection in detail, but there are some items crucial to the date of the grave and the identity of the person it contained. It is a thoroughly Romanized assemblage, almost all of it imported; even the Celtic bronze boar has been considered by Miss Jennifer Foster as 'possibly an import'[51]. The fragment of a mail cuirass, clearly indicating the presence of a man, could be Gallic, but the hinges and silver studs are classical. Even the enamel discs lack the typical Celtic assymmetry. But the most astonishing Roman artefacts are the small white marble *tesserae* not mentioned in the report. These must have come from the inlay in a table-top, similar to those found in the early palace of Cogidubnus at Fishbourne[52]. The date of this remarkable burial is a difficult problem, although one of the objects, a medallion of Augustus, would seem to give a direct answer. On examination by H. Mattingley, it was found to be a *denarius* minted in 17 BC, the bust of his Emperor having been cut out and mounted on a silver disc and placed on a moulded frame. It seems unlikely that the Emperor would have given such a cheap gift to anyone of importance, but it is possible that this kind of commemorative object was distributed to junior officers, or to young children of royal households in distant places. As Mattingley indicated, it is similar to medallions mounted on ceremonial swords, like the one of Tiberius in the British Museum.[53] Roman officers are not likely to have been buried in Britain at this time, and therefore one has to consider the second possibility. It could have been a modest Imperial gift to a young noble visiting Rome as part of an embassy, or perhaps being educated there.[54] In such a case, the medallion would have belonged to the early years of a man buried here, but kept as a valuable memento and buried with him 40 or 50 years later. A closer date may come with a detailed study of the pottery which includes some tiny scraps of Arretine. The *amphorae* include Dressel 1 type, but also some from Rhodes, which were being imported as late as AD 40 – 50. It would be unwise at present to narrow the bracket much beyond 10 BC – AD 40, and it is not easy to identify the man in the grave. He was a person of wealth and importance and with thoroughly Romanized customs. The earlier searchers may have removed any gold or silver objects, and if this fact is considered it is not impossible that it could have been Cunobeline himself, although this might stretch the date unreasonably. If it is not the great king, it must be a member of his house, as it is too late for Tasciovanus or Addedomaros.

The people of Kent

It seems remarkable that the people of the rich lands of east and north Kent appear to play such an insignificant role in the events which have so far been discussed. Even the names of kings that appear on coins there are not from this area. Dubnovellaunos may have come from Essex, Eppillus was certainly an Atrebatian and Adminius a son of Cunobeline. Apart from these intruders, there are no other names or series of coins specifically belonging to Kent, apart from eight examples of gold and silver bearing the name VOSE [NIOS, and a unique coin from Canterbury with the name VODENOS[55] while SA [. . . . appears on a bronze coin and could be a mint-name. These coins have slight Atrebatian characteristics (Mack p 88), while on the others the *bucranium* (ox-skull) is a link with Dubnovellaunos. Vosenios may have been a ruler of the area to the south and west of the kingdom of the other two kings on the tip of north-east Kent. Apart from these coins, the people of Kent continued to use the earlier uninscribed staters, which often bear signs of wear and clipping.

It has been noted above that very little imported wine reached Kent, nor is there evidence of any imported metalwares or pottery, although the extensive excavations at Canterbury have not yet been published. Kent has, however, made a distinctive contribution with the pottery from the Aylesford/Swarling cemeteries. Aylesford, in the Medway Valley near Maidstone, was excavated by Arthur Evans in 1908[56] and Swarling, 25 miles to the east in the valley of the Great Stour, by J. P. Bushe-Fox in 1921.[57] The most striking vessels from these cemeteries are the finer wares with their elegance and sophistication. They consist of tall pear-shaped jars and conical beakers with well-formed feet or with raised pedestals, the surfaces smoothed and burnished with well cut grooves and cordons, and in some cases the whole of the side of the vessel is corrugated. They are the earliest vessels in Britain to be made on a turn-table and one could almost say, by the first professional potters. They are not, however, peculiar to Kent, many similar vessels having been found north of the Thames. The Kent cemeteries, or urn fields, are 'flat graves' which means that they have no mounds over them. The burial rite was cremation, and in several there were bronze fittings of wood buckets. A close study of the pottery from both cemeteries by Dr Ann Birchall[58] has convincingly shown that the two assemblages are very similar and probably contemporary; the problem of the date is, however, a difficult one. Two British coins were found in the Evans' excavation, but the precise findspots are not certain, and in any case it is evident that these coins had a long life and could have been lost or deposited in the grave at any time from *c*. 55 BC until the end of the century. Dr Birchall gives a long and careful analysis of the chronological possibilities, but there seems very little that is certain except Derek Allen's coin dating, which is now suspect; her conclusions are that the date bracket is probably 50–10 BC for the earliest pottery. We now have the 1965 discovery of a grave group at Welwyn, Herts dated by silver-ware to *c*. 25–1 BC (p 54). The elegant pedestalled jar in the Welwyn grave (Fig 7 No 1 – 6) compares reasonably well with the Swarling series, although the rims are wider here. Another range of Welwyn vessels is the bowl, with and without a pedestal, but all having a sharp carination which produced a considerable concave effect on the side of the vessel (Welwyn Fig 7 Nos 8 – 13); this vessel is called a tazza by prehistorians, but unfortunately is somewhat different from a bowl given this name by Roman archaeologists[59]. There are no bowls of this type from the two cemeteries, nor from any other sites in Kent, so it seems to be peculiar to the area north of the Thames. Welwyn produced other unusual types, a small pedestal bowl, or perhaps a lid with a large and flattened everted rim (Welwyn Fig 8 Nos 14 – 17). The only parallel Dr Stead could produce was from northern Italy, and an even odder box-like vessel with tripod feet and decoration all over the outer surface (Welwyn Fig 8 No 25). It should be evident from this example that the Kent group bears very little relationship to those from Welwyn, but most of them appear to be more devolved, and therefore, later forms. The pottery from the Kent cemeteries seems to bear out the evidence, or lack of it, in the absence of early *amphorae* and the very small quantity of fine metalware, all of which points to the lands south of the Thames being in a cultural backwater. The date of the earliest of the vessels would also seem to be rather later than that suggested by Dr Birchall.

The poverty of Kent, compared to Hertfordshire and Essex, can only be partly due to the heavy defeats suffered under Caesar; one could reasonably expect people to recover in two or three generations, but the area was not receiving Roman trade on the scale of the northern shores of the estuary. Caesar, in listing the names of four kings, may have given us another reason for the divisions of these peoples. If there had been only petty kingdoms with no strong ruler comparable to Tasciovanus or Cunobeline, they would have lacked political power, and thus been unable to develop the economy to create the wealth needed for imports. The kings of Kent could not expand to the west, the only possible direction, while the Atrebates were under strong rule; so they were oddly isolated and much of the area belonged to the heavy clays of the Weald. One must conclude that Kent had little to contribute to the political struggle of the period, except as a region passing alternatively from pro- to anti-Roman control.

Epaticcus

A ruler who is difficult to fit into the dynastic struggle considered so far is Epaticcus. This man claimed to be the son of Tasciovanus, and was, therefore a brother of Cunobeline. The most complete version of the name is EPATICCV, it may be that adding the final S normally to give the Latin ending is incorrect. The coins are rather barbaric and the motif of the corn-ear was derived from the coins of his brother, which Derek Allen considered to be issued almost in the middle of his reign. Other motifs seem more akin to these on the coins of the Atrebates; he was only able to list 12 coins[60] to which Colin Haselgrove has added another nine,[61] and they have a very wide distribution, from Oxfordshire to the south coast (p 73). Perhaps the most significant fact is that it was a coin of Epaticcus that Caratacus copied, which seems to

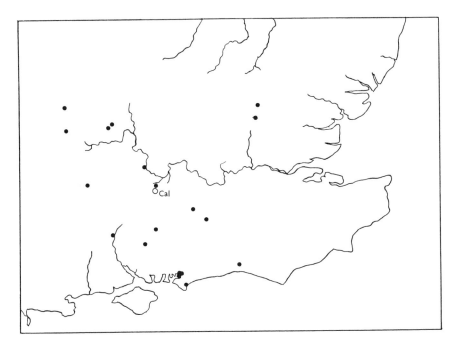

The find-spots of the coins of EPATICCUS
CAL = CALLEVA

indicate that he felt some affinity with his uncle. In the light of this, it could be argued that Epaticcus was hostile to Rome and, with the support of the Druids, managed to establish himself over the Atrebates at a time when Rome was preoccupied with her own troubles, i.e. *c* AD 10. But Verica recovered and fought back to regain his throne, and the usurper was thrown out and killed. This may not seem to be a very satisfactory explanation, but it seems to fit the meagre scraps of evidence.

The new power lords in Britain

The death or sudden enfeeblement of Cunobeline led to a very sudden shift in the balance of political power. It is almost as if the two sons Togodumnus and Caratacus had been waiting for this very moment and had planned their joint strategy, such was the rapidity of the change. Almost all of this activity was, however, due to Caratacus, while his elder brother was taking over and consolidating his authority north of the Thames, he seems to have achieved control of much of the land south of the Thames possibly with the help and connivance of the Durotriges. As a result of this two pro-Roman kings were forced off their thrones and fled to seek the help of Rome. First was Adminius, who tried to persuade Caligula to invade Britain, and secondly Verica of the Atrebates appears before Claudius *c* 41 AD. Since the two Catu-vellaunian brothers, Caratacus and Togodumnus, led their forces against the Roman invasion army, it is clear that they were the leaders of the new hostile element. It could be argued that it was Caratacus who created the disturbances south of the Thames by seizing the north-east tip of Kent from his brother, Adminius, who may have been the eldest of the sons of Cunobeline. From subsequent events, it is evident that Caratacus was not only a man of decision but had a fair grasp of strategy and an ability to plan ahead. If Cunobeline can be said to have been the first British statesman, Caratacus was certainly the first great British commander. But evidence of his presence south of the Thames consists of no more than six coins only three of which have a provenance, one from Guildford, another from the Savernake hoard, Wiltshire[62] and the third from Calleva. If, therefore, he deposed Verica[63] and gained control of the Atrebates, his reign was very short for so little trace to survive. Even stranger may be the total absence of any coins of Togodumnus, but the reason for this could have been that Cunobeline was still alive when his sons seized power, but that he was in too feeble a state to be in effective control; his death could have been as late as AD 42. The sudden upheaval certainly produced a hardening of the pro-Roman elements, which was to be helpful to the invading army. The Iceni, the Atrebates and the northern section of the Dubunni, welcomed the advent of Rome and this may partially have been due to a reaction against the zealous, even fanatical efforts of the two rebellious sons of Cunobeline, in their efforts to create an anti-Roman state in the south-east.

The influence of the Druids

The old antipathy towards Rome caused by Caesar's victories and the heavy retribution he exacted against the defeated tribes must have continued to rankle. In the light of subsequent events, it could be argued that it was the Druids who had reason to maintain and foster a permanent hostility to Rome. This body of priests, recruited largely from the Celtic nobility, had seen their religious beliefs and practices seriously threatened by the Roman conquest of Gaul. While the Romans were always very tolerant of local religions, they were not prepared to accept Druidism, since it was such a strong political force uniting the tribes against them, and the Druids were also responsible for maintaining their own laws and legal system, which it was virtually impossible to integrate into those introduced by the conquerors. Nor did Rome look favourably on human sacrifice (which the Druids practised on suitable occasions), but this was doubtless a useful propaganda weapon to be exploited by Rome, when an excuse was needed for punitive action. The Druids realized that they could not possibly continue to maintain their powerful grasp on Celtic society under the

Roman State. It is likely that some of the Gallic Druids fled to Britain to seek refuge here, and they would have strengthened the anti-Roman feeling. The continuing presence in Britain of such a powerful element, aimed at keeping the tribes free of any Romanizing influence and control, was probably a dominating factor in the politics of the tribes of the south-east, and is the only satisfactory explanation of the sequence of events set in train by Caesar. By capturing the minds and hearts of some of the young nobles of the royal households, the Druids were able to split tribal loyalties and exploit their power by organizing palace revolts to secure thrones for their protegées. The Druid leadership had intellectual ability, infinite patience and a communication link with all the Celtic tribes of Britain and Europe, thus they could plan for long-term objectives.

With this kind of background, it is not difficult to understand how two of the main Roman allies in Britain, Tincommius and Dubnovellaunos, were deposed and forced to flee to Rome. But clearly the Druids were not able to manipulate all the tribes. Cunobeline maintained an independent line and it may have been with his help that Verica was able to seize the throne of the Atrebates. It was only with the death or weakening of Cunobeline that the Druids could have expanded their power and achieved their most striking success. Their control of two other sons Togodumnus and Caratacus, created a great reversal of the British relationship with Rome, for within a very short time the whole of the south-east was in the hands of the anti-Roman faction. Togodumnus was presumably the elder of the two and so took over his father's kingdom and this left Caratacus to seek one for himself. Unfortunately, the evidence for this dramatic coup is very slight and only has significance in the light of the political background and all that followed.

4 The Opposing Forces

The Britons at war

The Celts regarded warfare as part of life, and, as in many societies the world over, it offered the young men an opportunity for initiation into manhood. Some primitive peoples had very elaborate and sometimes repugnant rites, but the process of growing up involved the selection of the fittest into the ranks of the mature warriors. The weak, the puny and the physically uncoordinated did not survive and so, by this ruthless selection, the tribes remained strong and healthy. This did not eliminate the highly intelligent, who were often lacking in physical strength, for there was a place for them among the priests and any child showing this aptitude would have been placed under their care. So warfare was essential to preserve the continuity of the tribe and for the youth to demonstrate their prowess and fitness to breed. Nature attempts to work in the same way today on the football terraces, as social anthropologists have recently discovered, but the elaborate rites are branded by an unsympathetic older generation as hooliganism. Now that war is not so common, means have been found by the young to prove themselves by open display. It is a pity perhaps the rival gangs of fans cannot be allowed to do it properly and battle it out on the football pitch before a match, thus providing entertainment for the older elements in the stands, who otherwise have to satisfy their natural instincts through viewing violence on film and television. An alternative is available in joining an extreme political faction, but public opinion is on the whole against physical clashes, on the unfortunate assumption that we are now a civilized society. The human creature changes very slowly and the thin veneer of sophistication merely covers the basic animal nature in us all.

The ultimate in Celtic battle was not so much a victory but the taking of enemy heads. There was almost an obsessive interest in the head, based on the belief that the whole nature and soul of the individual rested there, and in slaying a warrior and removing his head, the victor imagined he took over all the heroic qualities of his victim. Heads were thus highly prized and dedicated to temples, or kept in the family possession as trophies. To bring back a head from the wars was for a youth a qualification of manhood and acceptance as a full member of his tribe. There was thus no concept of war and peace as being philosophically undesirable or abhorrent, they were necessary states of existence. The tribes went to war every year as a matter of course, maybe for a full-scale campaign over real differences, or merely for cattle raiding and stealing of women. In the long winter nights, the tribes were regaled with long and much embroidered sagas of the heroes of the past and their exploits.

Methods of fighting and types of weapons and equipment developed as part of this concept of warfare elevated to a heroic level, fully supported by the tribal gods. The warrior was equipped in the panoply of bright and glittering accoutrements for himself, his horse and his chariot by the work of the superb Celtic metal workers and enamellers. Caesar gives an eye-witness description of the British chariots in action (iv 33). They appear suddenly and drive all over the place, the warriors in them hurling their javelins. He stated that the noise of the wheels spread terror and confusion, but he says nothing about scythes being fixed to the axles and there is in fact no supporting archaeological evidence.[1] Yet this remains a very popular view of a British chariot. It was certainly an eastern custom and it would have been practical in an open desert for demonstration only, to demoralize an enemy unused to such a sight. In a well vegetated landscape like Britain they would seem to be more of a hindrance than use. After their sudden and terrifying appearance, the chariots withdrew, and the warriors they had carried sprang from them to join in the battle at points where they could be most effective, but when under pressure and tiring, they could leap on to the chariot and be driven away to recuperate. So the best fighters could be suddenly brought to a point of danger and as rapidly taken away. These tactics were used to some effect in the second expedition (v 15 and 16) when Caesar realized that his legionaries could not deal with such fluid and elusive units and that his cavalry were also at risk in dashing after the retreating Britons, only to find themselves cut off and surrounded. Presumably the Britons also used the German method of warriors springing off their small horses and fighting on foot, which would have given valuable support to the swordsmen from the chariots. Unfortunately for the Britons, these tactics could not be sustained since they are so tiring on men and horses, nor had they the resources for continuous replacements. It is like a boxer in the ring who relies on his speed and surprise to outwit his opponent, but if he fails in the early rounds, the other man by sheer dogged slogging will eventually wear him down.

The victories of Rome over the Celts are depicted on several monuments with sculptures showing arms and equipment piled up as trophies, the most famous being the Triumphal Arch at Orange, which has survived the centuries with very little serious loss or damage.[2] The surface of this fine monument is covered with reliefs of Celtic war-gear, and gives us splendid details, except for the lack of colour. There are two different battle scenes, the one on the friezes on the south and east faces show the Gauls in single combat with Romans, one warrior is completely nude with a long oval shield, which suggests some truth in Caesar's statement that the Celts relied on the magic of the symbols painted on their bodies in blue woad (v, 14). But the fine armour and equipment may have been worn only by the warrior class, and that the poor levies had no protection and preferred to fight unencumbered. In the two great friezes on the south and north faces, the battle is an assorted melée of men pressed tightly together. That on the south face is a cavalry engagement and the three helmeted Gallic horsemen; most of them have sword belts, some loin-cloths and long flowing cloaks attached to the shoulders. It is possible, however, that they are also wearing tight fitting mail and leather trousers, which would originally have been picked out in colour. On the other scene, the Gauls are on foot and the Romans mounted, and here one has the impression that the Gauls are clothed, since the anatomical detail given to them on the individual combat scene is lacking; on the other hand, the sculptor may have wished to bring out the heroic quality associated with the gods themselves, a common feature of classical art.

The piles of trophies are seen on the spaces above the arches and the entablature. The fine detail of these scenes makes them worthy of close study. The shields are long and kite-shaped, some with rounded ends and the decorative patterns are all different, but whether any is meaningful is not certain. One shield has two cranes, which may have had a tribal totemic significance. There are also ten names on ansate panels and four instances of a verb indicating 'made by'[3]. Professor P. M. Duval considers that this refers to the armourers rather than the sculptors[4]; but it seems strange that the makers' names should occupy such a prominent position on the shields. Very few Celtic shields have actually survived, and those found in rivers may not have been for combat, but made as votive objects for appeasing the gods, as is clearly apparent in the case of the famous Battersea Shield[5] in the British Museum.

The finest British shield is undoubtedly that found in the River Witham near Lincoln in 1826 and now in the British Museum. What has survived in the river is the thin bronze facing sheet over the wooden shield, but the superb decoration on the umbo and spine is as, Professor Jope has written, 'a *tour de force* in beaten bronze-work'[6]. On the face of the sheeting is the faint outline of a Celtic boar which had been presumably also in beaten bronze, but had become detached.

The Roman army

The army sent to Britain by Claudius could look back on centuries of growth and development, crowned by a succession of glorious victories. Hannibal had two centuries earlier almost reduced Rome to submission, but for her streak of obstinate stubbornness which refused, against all the odds, to surrender or even to consider making terms. But these painful days could be forgotten, expunged by the glorious memories of Scipio in Spain and North Africa or Marius against the Germans and, almost within living memory, the great figures of Caesar and Pompey. With such traditions as these, the Roman soldiers regarded themselves as well-nigh invincible. But, as with most successful armies, there was also that rigidity which fossilized them into impotence against new weapons and tactics. The enormous success of Rome through so many centuries was based on an ability to adapt to change. Whenever Rome found an enemy using a superior weapon, it would inevitably be copied, and it was common for whole tribes, which had been difficult enemies, to be recruited into the army after a campaign. This happened with the heavily armoured Sarmatian cavalry which had so impressed Trajan in the Dacian Wars of the first decade of the second century, – numbers of them were absorbed into the Roman army; later they became an embarrassment under Marcus Aurelius and a large contingent were sent to Britain, where their headquarters were at Ribchester in Lancashire.

Thus, the Roman army was rarely allowed to get stale or out-of-date, although there were of course, always periods of inactivity on some parts of the frontier, which caused units to get relatively slack and run-down. This was how Corbulo found the legions in Syria when sent out by Nero to deal with the problem of Armenia. He rounded up the troops in the winter, and marched them up into the high Erzerum plateau near Lake Van, and kept the whole army under canvas through the winter in such severe conditions that sentries froze to death at their posts.[7]

The organization of the army
The legions
The legions were the main fighting force of the army. Although the number varied there were usually about 30 stationed along the frontiers at any one time. It was also possible to assess the degree of threat on any particular section, as considered by Roman high command, by the number of legions stationed there or in adjacent areas. Recruitment into the legions was originally restricted to those to whom Rome had granted citizenship, often with reluctance, and one of the 'privileges' of which was liability for annual service from the age of 16. These proud citizen armies of basic farming stock developed into some of the toughest fighting men of the ancient world. They fought on foot and, by their mobility and tactical skill based on a thoroughly pragmatic view of warfare, were able to out-fight the solid Greek phalanx which had held the field as the best form of infantry for centuries. Although citizenship expanded with the Empire, until it became no longer an honourable status, recruitment into the legions continued to be restricted to citizens, although the *delectus* (levy) was rarely enforced. It is clear from a study of tombstones that by the middle of the first

century, enrolment came mainly from the frontier areas, and young barbarians were drafted into the legions receiving the franchise in the process. These youths were nevertheless carefully selected for fitness and physique and underwent hard training to fit them for the required discipline and professional fighting skills.

A legion consisted of ten cohorts, each divided into six centuries of 80 men (i.e. each cohort had 480 men) except the first cohort, which consisted of five double centuries ($160 \times 5 = 800$ men), and could be used as an independent tactical unit. The men were equipped with body armour, but the mail cuirass of Caesar's day had been replaced in the early first century, by the strip armour (*lorica segmentata*). This remarkable suit of horizontal curved strips of steel encircling the torso, was hinged at the back and fastened with hooks and laces at the front. The strips overlapped and were held together by vertical leather strips on the inside, and this enabled the soldier to bend his body, the strips sliding over one another. The armour was strengthened with back and front plates below the neck, and a pair of curved shoulder pieces of attached strips of varying length to fit. These parts were buckled together so that the cuirass could be easily and quickly donned, and removed. The torso of the legionary was thus well protected from sword blows and thrusts.

The helmet, adapted from the Celts, had been carefully designed to provide against sword-cuts from above on the skull, and there were also large cheek pieces for the sides of the face, projecting ear pieces and a brow-ridge to stop a sword from slicing off the nose. The only weakness of the early Imperial helmet was at the back of the neck, where the horizontal projection stopped down-strokes, but not horizontal or upward sweeps which could penetrate the neck below the strip. A modification was introduced at the time of Claudius when this 'jockey-cap' was replaced by one with a guard fitting more snugly over the back of the neck. A metal studded apron hung from the belt and afforded protection for stomach and genitals, but the legionaries wore no greaves on their shins, since the weight would have affected their marching ability. The *caligae* on the feet were a heavy type of sandal with several thicknesses of leather sole, studded with conical hobnails. This footwear had to take very hard service, not only for marching over rough ground, but stamping over the fallen enemy and grinding them into the earth. But their best protection was from the shields (*scuta*), large and semi-cylindrical in shape, they reached from the chin to the knees, and when held tightly to the body, covered half of it. Yet they had to be light enough to be held continually in battle, and the main component was several thin layers of wood glued together so that the grain in attached layers was at an angle one to the other, in other words, it was a primitive kind of plywood. The edge was bound with light sheet bronze, but the central boss (*umbo*) was heavy bronze with a hand grip on the inside; one presumes that an inner strap allowed the weight of the shield to be taken on the forearm, but as no complete fighting shield has ever been found, it is not possible to be certain about such important details.

The legions had two different weapons, the javelin (*pilum*) and the sword (*gladius*). They carried two of the former, and these were seven feet long and cunningly designed; the tip of elongated pyramidal shape was hardened, but its long thin shank left in softer metal opened out into a socket at its lower end to fit over the wooden shaft. The tactic for the use of this weapon was quite simple but very effective. The troops were drawn up in a carefully selected position at the top of a rise, where they would wait for the army to attack forcing them to rush up the slope. As soon as the first ranks were about 30 yards away, at a blast of the trumpet, the legionaries hurled one of their javelins and the second followed immediately. The visual effect of several thousand long javelins in the air at one time must have been terrifying, and many would pause, crouch on the ground and attempt to protect themselves with their shields, but this was difficult, as they were being forced by the pressure of the ranks behind them. When the javelins landed, their sharp points pierced bodies and shields, but the soft shanks bent under the weight of the shaft. This had two effects, the shields became useless with such a large and unwieldly encumbrance wedged in it, and there was no time or room to pull it out, the shield was discarded, but the bent javelins created a kind of hedge, obstructing the enemy pressing forward. At this critical point of confusion, the ranks of the legionaries closed up, each man had slid his sword out of its scabbard, pulled his shield close to his body, lowered his head and the first ranks suddenly leapt into the enemy in tight wedged-shaped formations. The sword was designed for the kind of work which followed, the blade usually 18 to 19 inches long and slightly more than two inches wide and waisted in the centre, (in appearance similar to the much earlier leaf-shaped bronze sword of the Bronze Age). It was a fine piece of steel with a sharp point and honed down razor-sharp edges; it had a comfortable bone handle grooved to fit the fingers, and a large terminal knob to help with counter-balance. This light rapier-like thrusting weapon was used for rapid execution, as the Romans drove into the enemy mass, they continually thrust their swords into the soft parts with an ease and skill born of long training and practice, at the same time, leaning forward with the shields to push the bodies to one side and stamp them down with their heavy boots. The impetus alone drove them into the opposing mass and forced their opponents so tightly together, that they were unable to use their long Celtic swords effectively. The legion was designed as a highly organized killing machine.

But legionaries were not pursuit troops; once the enemy lines were broken and they began to flee, it was not the task of these weary men to follow. This was the task of the cavalry waiting in the flanks for this moment, then riding in with their long swords and lances cutting the foe down before they could escape. The killing had to be complete, for it was Roman military policy to destroy the enemy's fighting power. A victory was never considered complete until their opponents lay dead in the field of battle, or had been rounded up as prisoners. If too many escaped they could live to fight again, and to the logical Roman mind, this was wasteful of effort and man-power.

The auxilia

As the name implies, these troops assist the main citizen body, the legions. The sturdy Roman peasant farmers had no traditional skill with horses and had to depend for the cavalry on their allies, who were mainly Celts, and, after Caesar's time, Germans. When they became part of the regular army they were organized in units of about 500 men, although later under Hadrian some were doubled. The fighting methods and equipment of the original ethnic group was maintained, although the national identity of each unit was lost as recruits were drafted regardless of origin; so that a recruit into the *auxilia* might expect to join any kind of unit and have to learn its methods. One has to appreciate that the stirrup had not yet reached Europe and fighting on a horse required quite a different technique to that of later periods after its introduction. The horse in classical times and earlier, was controlled with the knees and the bit, there was no solid fixed seat and the rider could not stand up to wield his sword or throw his spear; nor could cavalry be used as shock troops in a charge. Nevertheless, there was no lack of skill and fighting ability, much of which depended on the mobility of the rider on the horse. It also meant that there was a much closer relationship between the horseman and the foot-soldier. This is well illustrated by Caesar in his description of the tactics of the Germans.[8] Each horseman had a companion on foot, when one of the former was wounded, the infantry would rally round and protect him. The men on foot were trained to move rapidly with the horses by clinging on to their manes.

The functions of auxiliary cavalry varied. When the legions were on the march, they acted as a screen at the front and sides, clearing the ground and woods of any enemy lurking there, chasing off small parties and giving warning of any large body advancing or lying in wait. In a set battle they were stationed on the flanks protecting the legions in the centre from sudden attack from the sides and from the rear, but their most important contribution came when the legions broke the enemy line and their warriors began to retreat and to turn and run. This was the moment when the horsemen rode in from the flanks to cut them down from behind with their long swords and lances.

The *auxilia* was organized in three different kinds of unit. That with the highest status was the *ala* – a crack cavalry regiment with the finest horses and equipment. Then came the infantry *cohort*, these were of many different kinds since they were originally allies recruited from different nations, and allowed to continue to fight in their own manner. Thus, there were heavy and light spearmen, javelin throwers, archers, slingers and even bargemen from the Tigris, who specialized in ferrying troops across shallow estuaries. They could thus provide all specialist services the legions may have required. The third kind of unit, and of the lowest status, was the *cohort equitata*, about a third consisting of mounted men and the rest infantry. The difference between the two mounted units becomes clear when one studies the daily duty lists, which have survived on scraps of papyrus in the East. The *alae* were crack fighting regiments while the *cohortes* preferred all kinds of general duties, such as patrolling, reconnaissance and acting as escorts; this is also reflected in the standards of pay and equipment.

There are other important sections of the Roman Army which had special functions, such as the Praetorian Guard, which is the Emperor's personal corps and accompanied him on campaigns. They were hand-picked men and their presence in Rome gave them a very powerful political influence, sometimes even in creating emperors. A lesser, but also necessary arm, was the fleet, which kept the seas clear of pirates and moved supplies and troops across them for large campaigns. There were fleets on the main rivers too, acting as a kind of police and generally assisting the army. The British fleet the *classis Britannica* had a specially significant role throughout its history, in keeping the sea-lanes free and transporting men and material in the campaigns against the Caledonian tribes, from Agricola to Severus.

The supporting services
Some of the most important, but unknown aspects of the Army, are those in the shadowy background for which there is little record. Historians tend to concentrate on the battles and campaigns, but like all frontier armies, the troops spent most of the time in readiness or preparation for war, and, in Britain, in the second century, one could have served out one's whole period without being confronted with the enemy. But there are also the essential services and facilities which keep the fighting men in the field, and it is the logistics of the army which are so fascinating, yet so difficult to appreciate. These consist of problems of communication and supplying of food, armaments and equipment, behind the warrior was a vast organization to keep him fit, healthy, and in constant readiness for rapid movement and lengthy periods away from base. When contemplating the invasion of Britain, one should spare a thought for all the careful planning which would have been behind such a vast enterprise, not only with the ships, but all the provisions for men and horses and the necessary equipment, such as tents, pontoons for bridges, and so on and so on. Behind the

legions was a vast organization to maintain them in constant fighting trim.

A summary of the causes of the invasion

It will already have become clear from the earlier chapters that the Roman invasion was precipitated by the sudden change in the political climate in south-east Britain. The rise of the anti-Roman forces, following the death of Cunobeline, totally changed the balance of power; Rome had now either to abandon any hope of maintaining useful political and trading relationships, or seize the country by force of arms. It could not have been difficult for Claudius and his advisors to reach a decision. To the Emperor, the reversal was a direct affront to the name of his great forbear, Julius Caesar, and from his own point of view, he badly needed to draw public attention away from Rome where he was still at odds with the Senate – and to win the support of his army, and what better way than to lead them to a great victory? The Empire was in one of its rare peaceful intervals, and troops could be spared. But an important underlying motive could well have been economic. Trade with Britain was now bringing a good return and investment to the wine growers, the pottery factories and those dealing in general merchandise. More important perhaps, was the serious state of the Spanish silver mines, on which Rome depended heavily for her coinage, since the deeper the shafts and galleries were sunk to extract the ore, the more difficult and expensive it became, in spite of elaborate sets of wheels to raise water which continually poured into the mines. Information must have been acquired by Rome of extensive surface deposits of argentiferous lead ore (galena) in south-western Britain. According to Pliny the Elder, such was this quantity, that a law was passed restricting extraction of lead[9]; since, presumably, the news from Britain created consternation among the lessees of the Spanish mines, who were quick to see the danger of being priced out of the market, for they realized too late that there was little chance of them being able to obtain leases of any British ventures, as the State would take over conquered territory, and any extraction of a precious metal like silver, would be by government enterprise. The significance of lead was that it was the waste product of silver extraction. The lessees of the Spanish mines now managed to persuade the Senate to restrict the output of British lead, no doubt hoping to reduce the quantity of silver being extracted.

Iron was also available in Britain over a wide area, it would have been surprising if Caesar had not known about the Wealden source,[10] since he was desperate for materials to repair his ships, stricken in the equinoctial gales in 55 and 54. One wonders if even the Kentish tribes were obliged to pay their tribute in this metal – it was certainly being extracted at this period, but, as noted above, there is no evidence of any great wealth being accumulated in their territories.

The Roman forces taking part in the invasion

When Caesar invaded Britain for the second time in 54 BC there is little doubt that he intended a conquest of the south-east. He brought with him five legions and 2000 horses, which represented an army of about 27,000. But this assumes that his legions were up to full strength, although on another occasion, when Caesar hastened to the relief of the beleaguered Cicero, he gives the number of his force of two legions and some cavalry as 7000.[11] The army of Claudius would certainly have been up to strength and fitness. For such an important enterprise, all units would have retired their elderly and unfit, replacing them with younger men in the customary manner. The army, assembled on the Gallic coast, consisted of four legions, some 20,000 crack troops and, unlike Caesar's army, as many auxiliaries, so the total, excluding the fleet, could have been as many as 40,000.

The legions

The four chosen legions were *II Augusta, IX Hispana, XIV Gemina* and *XX Valeria*.[12] There are inconsistencies in the numbering of Roman legions, dating from Republican times, when new ones were created as occasion demanded, and this tended to persist into the Empire. The consequence is that some legions have the same number, and are defined only by their additional name, which is often derived from its origin. Thus *II Augusta*, one of five legions bearing that number, was raised by Augustus, *IX Hispana* must have been stationed in Spain for some years in the late Republic, *XIV Gemina* had been created by Augustus by the amalgamation of two other legions, and *XX Valeria* was raised by Augustus[13] or Tiberius, to crush the great Pannonian revolt in AD 6. The governor at that time was Valerius Messallinus, (*cos* in 3 BC) who campaigned successfully with Tiberius, and according to Dio (lv 29) it was his imposition of the military levy that caused the revolt, and he may have given his name to the legion in consequence. But an alternative explanation may be that it was given by Claudius as a mark of distinction for its service in the invasion of Britain, in honour of his wife, Valeria Messalina.[14]

Each legion made its way separately to the port of embarkation. *II Augusta* from Argentoratum (Strasburg), *XIV Gemina* from Mainz, *XX Valeria* from Neuss, both on the Rhine; thus three of the four legions came from the Rhine garrison, clearly indicating the strong connection which was to exist between Britain and the Rhineland throughout the Roman period.[15] *IX Hispana* had the longest journey from Pannonia, where it may have had its fortress at Siscia (Sisak).[16] It is possible that detachments of other legions were drafted into the invasion army, which was quite usual in large expeditionary forces.

These troops would either be sent back to their bases when the main fighting was over, or some of them remained as replacements for the battle casualties in the permanent legionary establishment. The only other legion for which there appears to be evidence of its presence in Britain is *VIII Augusta* stationed at Poetovio in Pannonia, the same province which supplied *IX Hisp* and whose governor Aulus Plautius, became the officer in command of the invasion. The idea first arose on the basis of a stamped tile from Leicester.[17] But it now seems unlikely that any legion was making and stamping tiles in Britain as early as this, and, in any case, such work indicates the presence of a permanent establishment of *Legio VIII*, hardly likely if a detachment sent over merely to reinforce the invasion force. A stronger piece of evidence appears to come from an inscription from Turin[18] of a *primus pilus* of this legion who was heavily decorated in the Claudian war in Britain. Dr Lawrence Keppie, has, however, clearly demonstrated that this man could not have held this post at the time of the invasion, so it must belong to an earlier and unrecorded part of his career with one of the four invasion legions.[19] The same paper also deals with another officer, who had been a tribune of *VIII Aug.* who had also received decorations from Claudius, but the circumstances are not given.[20] Finally, there are two more tribunes, one of the famous *V Alaudae*, but again there is no direct connection with Britain,[21] and yet another of *III Macedonica*, but clearly when the officer had been an *evocatus*[22] serving in Britain. So the question of detachments from other legions taking part in the invasion, remains an open one.

The auxiliary units

The identification of auxiliary units is a more difficult matter, since the names of units are very rarely given by the ancient historians. One has to rely on inscriptions, of which there are very few of this early period. It is possible to draw up extensive lists of units in Britain during the second century from the discharge certificates, known as *diplomata*, in the form of bronze plates,[23] but the earliest one from Britain is dated to AD 98, and by then many changes in unit dispositions had taken place.

Assuming that the auxiliary strength was kept in reasonable balance with that of the legions, there may have been at least 40 units of quingenary size (i.e. 500 men) allocated for the garrison of Britain, but in the early years of the conquest there were probably more. Fortunately, one can make an excellent start in identifying particular units if one accepts Mark Hassall's well-considered argument[24] for eight Batavian cohorts being included in the initial force. The later attachments of these units to *XIV Gem* suggests that they may have accompanied this legion from the Rhineland, and as will be seen presently, made the vital breakthrough in the great two-day battle of the Medway, by forcing a crossing of the river, as they were trained to do. The evidence from the tombstones is limited to the monuments from Colchester, (*RIB* 201) and Gloucester (*RIB* 121), both are Thracian units, *Ala I Thracum* and *Coh VI Thracum* respectively, since both appear to belong to an early phase of the occupation. The use of these Thracian troops at the invasion period may seem strange, in view of the serious trouble in Thrace in AD 26 when some of the tribesmen revolted against the introduction of the military levy. Their main grievances were that their clan system would be disrupted, with the young men forced to serve in distant places far away from home.[25] Seventeen years after Poppaeus Sabinus had so crushingly reduced the rebels, regular Thracian troops were part of the Roman army for some years. Longinus, the *duplicarus* at Colchester, had served 15 years at the time of his death, which must have been a year or so after AD 43. An auxiliary of a Thracian cohort also died at Wroxeter (*RIB* 291) presumably between *c.* AD 50 and 56, but the number of the unit has been lost in damage to the edge of the stone, so it could have been the Gloucester unit moved from here when *Legio XX* was transferred from Colchester in AD 48.

The only other possible invasion units are those on the two stones at Cirencester, and one at Bath. The former two record the presence of the *Ala Indiana* and *Ala Thracum* (*RIB* 108 and 109), either brigaded together as a large mobile task-force, or one succeeding the other, the Thracian unit could be that from Colchester, moved forward by Scapula. The Bath stone (*RIB* 159) records a serving trooper of the *Ala Vettonum*, the unit later to occupy Brecon Gaer in Wales, but the granting of citizenship signified by the letters CR (*civium Romanorum*) after the man's name seems to show that this stone cannot be earlier than Vespasian.[26]

The Roman personalities associated with the invasion[27]

The man chosen to lead the invasion and become the first governor of Britain was Aulus Plautius Silvanus. It may not have been an exciting choice, but it was sound, and above all, at a time when Claudius faced hostility from a number of senatorial families, it was safe,[28] since Plautius was a distant member of the Imperial family, a daughter of his father's cousin, Plautia Urguanilla, was the first wife of the Emperor[29] by whom she had two children, Drusus and Claudia. Furthermore, the mother of Urguanilla had been a close friend of Livia, the wife of Augustus, so the Plautii were closely linked with the Imperial dynasty. The wife of Plautius, Pomponia Graecina, was rather more interesting, and was descended from a distinguished line, starting with a knight, Pomponius Atticus, whose grand-daughter was Vipsania Agrippina, who became the first wife of Tiberius and mother of Drusus, but who is not to be confused with the two other women also called Agrippina, one the mother of Nero and the other her daughter[30]. Pomponia Graecina, in spite of her aristocratic background, was accused in AD 57 of serious misconduct, as related by Tacitus.[31] She was said to have succumbed to a foreign superstition, thought by some historians to have been Christianity, but on no firmer grounds than that it was the period of St Paul's Epistle to the Romans, and a similar name has been found in the Roman catacombs. It could equally well have been an Egyptian cult considered too outlandish for a member of the higher ranks of Rome society. It was a period in Rome of gradual adjustment to the acceptance of these new ideas, many of which were totally repugnant to the older generation.[32] According to ancient Roman tradition, Pomponia, was tried for her offence by a family council headed by Plautius and found innocent. This practice was normally used in cases of infidelity, which seems unlikely in this case. Pomponia maintained her dignity and austerity during a long period of 40 years mourning 'lost in perpetual sorrow', which drew from Tacitus a typically ironic epigram.[33]

While Plautius is only referred to as 'distinguished or renowned', his younger nephew, Lateranus,[34] became involved with that voracious nymphomaniac, Messalina, wife of Claudius, and only escaped the death penalty through the relationship to his revered uncle. But this did not save him from a rapid and undignified execution when the Pisonian plot against Nero was uncovered in AD 65.[35]

The *comites*

Included in the large group of advisors Claudius brought with him, were some distinguished senators, who could well have formed a war council and helped to determine the future of Britain, but there were others who had exposed their strong republican sympathies in AD 41, and Claudius could hardly risk leaving them behind. The Emperor was lavish in his rewards, he granted the *ornamenta triumphalia*, according to Dio, to all these senators and not just the ex-consuls, as was customary.[36] He brought with him part of his Praetorian Guard and its commander Rufrius Pollio, received the unusual distinction of having a seat in the Senate whenever he attended in the company of his Emperor. He was also granted as a *statua triumphalis* which, as seen in the case of Sentius, indicated the award of the *ornamenta* – both most exceptional gifts to an equestrian. His colleague Catonius Justus who had been left behind in Rome was not so fortunate; he was despatched by Messalina before he could report her scandalous activities to the Emperor on his return.[37] Pollio did not have long to enjoy his special privileges, for he was executed before AD 47 in circumstances not recorded.[38] Dio also mentioned a certain Laco who had been the *praefectus* of the *vigiles*[39] of Rome and who had had similar honours.[40] At the time of the invasion he was a *procurator* of the Gauls,[41] presumably ably associated with the area of embarkation, and could have been of material assistance to Plautius.

Among the senators in the party was *D. Valerius Asiaticus* (cos suff 35 and ord 46), the first Gaul to become a Consul. He was immensely wealthy and moved in high circles in Rome, marrying the sister of Lollia Paullina, the wife of Caligula, who forced her into an adulterous relationship with him. For this reason, it was supposed that Asiaticus was one of the chief plotters in bringing about that Emperor's assassination and he was too powerful for Claudius to remove and may have been one of the men too dangerous to leave behind. On the other hand he could have been helpful in Gaul with his local associations. In spite of all this, Messalina managed to poison the Emperor's mind against him and he was condemned to death in 47, after retiring early from his second consulship.[42]

Another senator was *M. Vinicius* (cos ord 30 and 43), a distinguished man to whom Velleius Paterculus dedicated his history. He had married into the Imperial family through Julia Livilla, the youngest daughter of Germanicus. Unfortunately, she was also the sister of Caligula, who developed an unnatural fondness for her. Like Asiaticus, Vinicius had good reason to hate this dreadful madman, and they were both involved in the plot of 41, furthermore, he was actually nominated to fill the vacant 'throne'. Claudius must have viewed these two with the utmost apprehension and so took them with him to Britain. Again, as with Asiaticus, Vinicius fell foul of the greed and jealousy of Messalina.[43]

The person accompanying Magnus as bearer of the tidings of victory to Rome was *L. Junius Silanus* then a boy of about 16, in spite of this he also was given the *ornamenta triumphalia*. His distinguished family connections – his mother was a great grand-daughter of Augustus – as with Magnus, brought him into the Imperial family, with his betrothal to Octavia, the Emperor's daughter. However, this did not suit the ambitions of Agrippina, who wanted Octavia for her son Nero, to secure his succession. She organized a false accusation against Junius that he had had a relationship with his sister, which went beyond the fraternal.[44] This carefully worded charge was enough to sow serious doubts in the mind of Claudius about his suitability as a husband for Octavia. The innocent and unsuspecting Junius, who was a praetor at the time, suddenly found himself actually removed from the Senate by the censor Vitellius who was the main agent in Agrippina's plot, her main objective being Claudius himself whom she secured by marriage in 48.[45] The unfortunate Junius felt obliged to commit suicide.

Another name to be considered, that of *A. Didius Gallus* (cos suff 36), later to become a governor of Britain and who had been associated with the invasion force. This idea is based on fragments of an inscription from Olympia (*ILS* 970) on which he is described as a *praefectus equitatus*. This unusual post could have been held at any time during his early career, as there is no connection on the inscription with a campaign or a province.[46]

It is an interesting thought that every single one of the known *comites* of Claudius was removed by Messalina, which meant that knowledge and experience of Britain was lacking in the top échelon of the Senate in the critical days of decision to come.

L. Sulpicius Galba (cos ord AD 33)

This man, who became emperor in AD 68, took part in the invasion, but precisely in what capacity is not known. The expedition, Suetonius informs us, was delayed by Galba's indisposition; although considered 'not all that serious'[47], yet his presence was regarded by Claudius to be essential. One of the most respected commanders of his time, although a stern disciplinarian,[48] he had just served as Governor of Upper Germany, and so would have a personal interest in the invasion force, as two of its legions had been taken from his command. Plautius had been consul in 29 and would have been senior to Galba and whose presence in Britain could therefore have presented difficulties in protocol, unless he came with Claudius as one of his *comites*. Had Galba been here during the serious fighting and duly been decorated, there would have been comment from Suetonius.

M. Licinius Crassus Frugi (cos ord 27)

This man came from a long and distinguished line[49] although Seneca considered him stupid enough to be an emperor, and 'as like Claudius as two eggs in a basket'[50]. Nevertheless, he had conducted a successful campaign in Mauritania and earned the *ornamenta triumphalia*.[51] Thus, when Claudius celebrated his triumph in Rome all the *comites* marched in procession wearing their purple-bordered *togae*, except Crassus, who sported a palm-embroidered one and rode a gaily decked charger.[52] His wife Scribonia was the descendant of Pompey, and her eldest son took the name of *Cn Pompeius Magnus* after his famous forbear, but this caused trouble with Caligula.[53] Claudius brought him into the family with the gift of Antonia, his eldest daughter as a bride, an alliance the Emperor saw as strengthening his own position, Magnus was selected, possibly with deliberate irony by Claudius, as one of the messengers despatched to inform the Senate of the conquest of Britain. In spite of his close relationship with the Emperor, Magnus suffered, like so many others, from the malicious gossip poured into the ear of the ageing Claudius by Messalina, and he was executed on trumped-up charges.

The Legionary Commanders

Titus Flavius Vespasianus

The most important figure in the light of subsequent events was undoubtedly Titus Flavius Vespasianus, a future emperor. He came from an obscure family, his grandfather had been one of Pompey's centurions. His father, Flavius Sabinus, was a *publicanus* (tax farmer) in Asia, where although he had a good reputation for honesty, he had made enough money to set up as a money-lender in Helvetia (Switzerland). There were two sons, Sabinus, named after his father and Vespasian, after his mother Vespasia Polla, and it was through the power and influence of her family that they were able to climb the social ladder to the senatorial rung. Vespasian's first military post was as an equestrian tribune in Thrace, and he had to rely on the influence of Narcissus, the powerful Secretary of State to Claudius for a legionary command at the time of the invasion.[54] He also had the backing of L. Vitellius, a boon companion and advisor of Claudius, so trusted that he was left in charge of the Imperial government while the Emperor was away in Britain. Even so, Vespasian's background and plain 'homely' appearance would have remained an obstacle to further advancement, but for his opportunity for victory and glory in Britain. Nor did his close ties with Claudius bring him much favour with Nero, especially after he had noticeably dozed off during one of that Emperor's song recitals. He may have been saved on that occasion by the very factors which had retarded his career, since Nero could hardly have considered him a serious political threat. When he was 56, he was suddenly remembered for his military abilities and brought out of retirement to deal with the serious revolt in Judaea. This appointment, and his subsequent success was the power-base which led him to the purple. His ten year reign was characterized by its sober and stabilizing effect on the Empire.

Flavius Sabinus
Vespasian's brother, Flavius Sabinus, was also in Britain with the invasion forces, but a sentence in Dio (lx 20 3) has been taken to mean that he came as a staff officer to his brother, which for his seniority seems an anomaly. Dio's text is difficult and corrupt, and it has been shown by one scholar that with a minor emendation, it could mean that Sabinus was a legionary commander.[55] Evidence, however, is lacking as to which of the other legions he was *legatus*. Sabinus did not survive to see his brother reach the throne, for he was brutally murdered in Rome in 69 by the Vitellian mob,[56] while Vespasian's younger son, Domitian, then 18 (who became emperor in 81) was more fortunate, escaping in the disguise of a devotee of Isis.

C. Hosidius Geta
It has been assumed by some historians that the praenomen of this man was Gnaeus,[57] which would identify him with the general who completed the conquest of Mauritania in 44, succeeding Suetonius Paullinus there in 42.[58] It is difficult to see how a man so actively engaged in the mountains and deserts of north Africa[59] could have

been in Britain in 43. Also his appearance in the front line at the Medway battle after crossing the river, is hardly consistent with a top-ranking staff officer, who would have been helping to direct the main battle from a rearward headquarters. This Hosidius Geta was clearly a legionary commander[60] acting in concert with the two Flavii. The family of the Hosidii came from Histonium, a town on the Adriatic coast of Southern Italy, and a fragmentary inscription found there refers to someone who took part in the British expedition, but expansion and interpretation is difficult, and the general opinion of scholars is that Caius was the brother of Gnaeus of Mauritanian fame.

A British personality

Tiberius Claudius Cogidubnus

The British leaders who were to be involved in the struggle with Rome have been considered above, but there is a new figure appearing on the scene who also played an important role, although we are not sure precisely what it was. He is the man who became Tiberius Claudius Cogidubnus, client king of the Regni, a full Roman citizen, adopting the name of his patron, the Emperor. This much is clear from an inscription found in 1723 at his capital at Chichester (*RIB* 91). Excavations at Fishbourne at the head of the Bosham Harbour have revealed a sequence of buildings, first a Roman naval base, followed by a substantial and lavishly decorated house which was demolished to make way for a very large palace, the only example in Britain. This has been linked with Cogidubnus, although the dating of the palace would have placed it late in his life.[61] What concerns us here is that Cogidubnus was remarkably well rewarded by Claudius and the question remains as to how he earned such Imperial favour. As we have seen above, in 43 Rome had few allies in Britain, but some of the tribes were very worried by the expansionist ideas of Caratacus. Careful diplomatic pressure by Rome could have been applied to the waverers to win them over. This could have been the task accomplished by Cogidubnus, especially if he had been a Briton of royal blood. One effect of this could have been the surrender of the Dobunni to Plautius soon after his landing. Starting from this assumption, a most ingenious hypothesis has been worked out by Professor C F C Hawkes, and that brilliant scholar C E Stevens. They linked Cogidubnus with Sentius Saturninus to explain the placing of his name so oddly with Plautius by Eutropius. Sentius, they argued, was given power to sign treaties on behalf of Rome, and he travelled round the outlying tribes with Cogidubnus in this dangerous and secret mission. Claudius may not have worried too much if Sentius failed and even lost his life, since he considered him a dangerous man. This cloak and dagger stuff may be attractive to some readers, but is far too speculative to be regarded as remotely possible. More relevant, perhaps, was the vital Bosham

Harbour, the key to the coastal assault, soon to be launched by Vespasian, the rapid and undisputed possession of this alone was of sufficient importance to justify Claudius. The creation of the client kingdom may, however, be more probably associated with a later event as will be considered in the subsequent volume.

5 The Invasion and Advance to Camulodunum

The only account we have of the actual invasion is in Dio (1x 19 – 20; Appendix 1), but it is difficult to make it into a coherent narrative without stretching the meaning and using a good deal of imagination, all of which would not be necessary had we had the lost books of Tacitus. Dio starts with the reason for the campaign, it was all due to persuasion by the exiled King Verica (who is almost certainly the Berikos in the text of Dio) on Claudius and this could have been the of-official political pretext given to justify the event. The army was re-luctant to embark for fear of the Channel crossing. The terror of the superstitious troops brought face to face with the ocean is understand-able, and also they knew that three or four years earlier, the invasion planned by Gaius, (the mad Caligula) had been abandoned. This very strange story told by Suetonius[1] must be accepted as a serious possi-bility because a lighthouse was built at Boulogne, an important step in setting up a permanent communication link across the Channel. Plau-tius was forced to accept a delay until 'late in the season', which sug-gests some months, and we learn also that the landing was unopposed because the Britons had tired of waiting and returned home. A delay is also noted by Suetonius (*Galba* 7) where he specifically stated that the expedition was delayed on account of a minor illness of Galba, but as argued above, this is more likely to refer to the departure of Claudius himself from Rome, when Galba was one of his *comites*. Perhaps the cautious Plautius wanted the British levies to disperse and used the sol-diers' reluctance to embark as an excuse. It seems strange that he was unable to exert his authority as supreme commander, and had to send to Rome for help and advice. Eventually, this came in the form of Nar-cissus, the powerful Secretary of State, and one of Claudius' closest advisors. This wily Greek succeeded in cajoling the troops aboard, his appearance prompting the jibe recorded by Dio, referring to the freedman's former slave status, which dissolved the soldiers into gales of hysterical laughter.[2] One can only guess at the coarse ribaldry used by Narcissus to achieve this end, and to which the stiff Plautius was un-likely to descend.

The next statement by Dio is also difficult to interpret, for he says that the invasion forces sailed in three divisions, so as not to be preven-ted from landing as could happen to a single force. This could mean either that there were three landing places, or there were three groups of ships following each other, so that the second and third only came in after the first task force had secured the landfall. In the subsequent narrative, there are no indications of a divided army, and at the great Medway battle, there were at least three legions engaged, and it is reasonable to assume that the fourth would have been kept in reserve, so there was probably only one landing point.

Fortunately, archaeology comes to our aid over this difficulty, since Richbourgh has produced evidence of a campaign camp which could be associated with the initial landing. There is the possibility that a force could have disembarked in Bosham Harbour, under the friendly eye of Cogidubnus, but apart from protecting this valuable British ally and securing this coast, there seems no other part such a force could have played in the subsequent campaign.[3]

The archaeological evidence for the invasion

The topography of the tip of north-east Kent has changed considerably over the centuries. Caesar was forced to make a beach landing which proved disastrous on both occasions and had there been any kind of haven on this stretch of coast, he would surely have used it. But during the 97 years between the invasions, a dramatic change had taken place with the creation of the Wansum Strait, separating Thanet from the mainland of Kent and forming the small harbour at Richborough. This was probably brought about by a great storm in which a force of water suddenly breached the sand-bar and scoured out the channel.

Between the invasions, as seen above, considerable trade had developed with Gaul and the Rhineland, and although much of this would have come across the North Sea from the latter, some traders would have used the shorter route and made use of the new Strait, which took small ships directly into the Thames Estuary, possibly only at high tide, thus avoiding the dangerous waters of North Foreland. Roman military intelligence would have this information and with such a safe harbour now open to him, Plautius' main primary objective would have been its seizure.

The site remained an important one until the Strait began to silt up, although Richborough was still a port of entry when Count Theodosius embarked there in AD 368 to deal with the effects of the great Barbarian Conspiracy, and the Wansum Strait was still open to small ships until the end of the fifteenth century.[4] Richborough itself is a small sandy hill rising some 60 feet above sea level. Finds indicate a pre-Roman occupation of the late Iron Age and it seems a reasonable assumption that it would have been held by the British in strength when they waited in vain for the invasion fleet to appear. It has been, through subsequent ages, a site made notable by the presence of the massive masonry of a Saxon Shore Fort.

Richborough was a place eminently suitable for excavation in the days when antiquarians dug sites because they were there. Selected by the Society of Antiquaries of London, it was excavated from 1922 to 1938, fortunately under the direction of J P Bushe-Fox, whose techniques were far in advance of his time. This has enabled further study to be done on the records and revised interpretations made of structures and features. Quite unlike the earlier excavators of Silchester, who were content to explore only the uppermost Roman structures, Bushe-Fox saw the need for a total examination of the site. Thus, it is not surprising that he found, buried below everything else, two long ditches of typical military V-shaped profile with an 11 foot opening guarded by a timber gate and having no relationship to later features.[5] They cross the site almost in a north–south direction and have been traced for a distance of 705 yards without finding an end. The northern extremity has been cut off by the Richborough Stream, while at the south there is the beginning of a curve also cut by erosion. It is difficult to reconstruct the site as it was in AD 43 but it could have provided a camp of at least ten acres and possibly more. This would have been quite inadequate for the whole of the Plautian force, and these ditches and gate probably represent the camp of the first task force of several thousand legionaries sent in to secure the harbour and dig in in advance of the main body, possibly the first of Dio's three divisions. Bushe-Fox examined these ditches with care and recognized their purpose and that they were only in use for a short time.[6] Also there are no remains of an extensive occupation with buildings inside. The large flat plateau to the west offers ample space for the whole army which would have required a camp of about 150 acres but no attempt has been made to trace ditches of this site. An alternative possibility is that the smaller site was to protect the ships in the anchorage if the haven was on this site.

To return to the narrative of Dio. Having embarked, the winds blew the ships back, but a flash of light, probably a meteor, shot across the sky towards their goal. This was regarded as a favourable omen. The Romans, like the Etruscans, from whom they derived this lore were great omen watchers, especially signs from the sky, since they were interpreted as sent by their principal god, Jupiter, the head of the Pantheon. Flights of birds were closely observed, and there was a special place in Rome where this was done, but celestial indications were even more significant since they came from the heavens. Lightning was Jupiter's thunderbolt and unusual lights and shooting stars were all invested with special meaning. At such a fearful moment when the soldiers had committed themselves to the god of the ocean it was specially heartening to receive a direct message from this superior deity. This would have done much more for the morale of the army than any pep-talk by their leader.

1 Tombstone of
M. Favonius Facilis
(*RIB* 200)

2 Celtic Arms and equipment – detail of the Triumphal Arch at Orange

3 *Right* A Triumphal Arch commemorating Claudius' victory over the Britons – 'DE BRITANN [IS]' – and showing the emperor mounted between piles of trophies. From an auruns of Claudius

4 A Roman catapult bolt lodged in the backbone of a Durotrigian warrior. Part of a skeleton found in the war cemetery at Maiden Castle

5 A carro-ballista, a spring gun mounted on a cart from Trajans column

6 and **7** Skulls of warriors, showing the fatal sword cuts – from the war cemetery at Maiden Castle

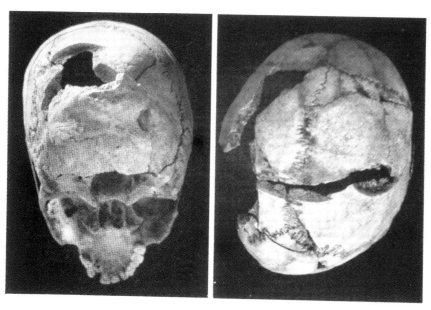

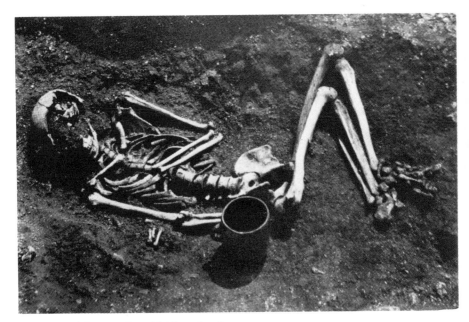

8 A Durotrigian warrior with his tankard

9 *Opposite above* A legionary helmet dredged up from the Thames

10 *Opposite below* A large gilded horse-pendant, with a stylized bird-mount, found at Cirencester

11 A decorated cheek-piece of a cavalry parade helmet, found at Crococalana (Brough in Nottinghamshire)

12 An iron ring, with intaglio of eagle and standards, found at the fort at Great Casterton, Rutland

13 Crop marks of the Roman forts at Great Casterton, Rutland

TI·CLAV
AVG
PONTIFIC
COS·V·IM
SENATVSPO
REGES·BRI
VLLAIACTV
GENTESQVE
PRIMVSINDIC

14 *Left* Roman soldiers building a rampart with spoil from the ditch between turf revetments at front and back – from Trajan's Column

15 *Above* The extant part of the inscription from the Arch of Claudius (see p 170)

16 The Roman army building camps with turf
ramparts, timber towers, gates and
a bridge: from Trajan's Column

17 The fort at Ixworth in East Anglia: aerial photograph by Professor J K St Joseph. The triple ditches are shown as differences in crop growth, and there are indications of internal timber buildings

18 Coins of British rulers showing at the top British copies of the Macedonian stater and lower the improved die-cutting under Roman influence when the British kings added their names and the places of minting

19 The tombstone of Longinus from Colchester

20 One of the ditches of the fort at Wiveliscombe, Somerset (with a six-foot ranging pole for scale)

21 Kirmington

22 Crop marks of two superimposed forts at Baylham House, Suffolk (Photograph: Ordance Survey)

The landing at Richborough was not opposed and the Britons seemed at first reluctant to fight, but the suggestion that Plautius began to search Kent for the missing enemy does not ring true. It is far more likely that reconnaissance parties failed to make contact and finding the way clear, a general advance was ordered. It must have taken some time for Caratacus and his brother to reassemble their levies and allies when the news of the landing reached them and their only strength at first would have been their own warriors and followers. A sound tactician like Caratacus would have fixed a rendezvous for his troops to gather and this seems almost certainly to have been the River Medway, the first place where any kind of defensive stand could have been made. But it was necessary to delay the Romans as much as possible to allow time for their allies to travel from distant parts of Britain. That is why there is the mention of the defeats first of Caratacus and then Togodumnus, since they could not possibly have hoped to hold up the large Roman army for very long, but by harrying tactics, might hope to slow down the advance to the Medway.

The next incident is an embassy from a section of the 'Bodunni' offering their submission to Rome. The statement appearing at this stage of the operations has created in the past much confusion and speculation. The identification of this tribe as the Dobunni was made as long ago as Camden (1551–1623) but was rejected by many scholars because they could not visualize the Roman army in Gloucester so soon after a Channel crossing. But a further comment by Dio resolves this paradox, for he says that this part of the tribe had been subject to the Catuvellauni[7]. It was established above that, on the evidence of coins, the Dobunni had two rulers which implies two sections of this tribe, also that it seems possible that the northern half had an alliance with Cunobeline. This may have helped to bring them in contact with Rome, although the imported pottery found at their capital, Bagendon, dated to AD 15–35[8], may not have come through Camulodunum, but via one of the south-coast points of entry. This section of the Dobunni, already in contact with Roman trade correctly supposed that the wily Cunobeline was an ally of Rome. The sudden change at his death and the mounting hostility towards Rome, must have caused much heart-searching among the tribal leaders. It is evident that they decided the best hopes for their future lay with Rome, but under the terms of any alliance he made, Caratacus would have ordered them to provide levies to meet him on the Medway, rather than risk being involved in such a confrontation, the tribe decided to seek out the Roman commander and sue for peace. This seems to fit very logically into the known framework and Plautius must have regarded this as a useful omen that under pressure the British tribes would fragment and allow him to pursue the old well-tried policy of divide and rule.

The confusion over the 'Bodunni' was compounded by the next phrase of Dio, that Plautius, leaving a garrison there, advanced further and came to a river. This had been thought to mean that a post was established in Dobunnic territory, but as Professor Hawkes has argued the word used by Dio could equally well have meant 'and then' rather than 'at that place' which makes better sense of this passage. The site of this fort is not known but its position may be determined by a consideration of the tactics of the British leaders. Their first harrying efforts were probably at the crossing of the Stour, where wooded terrain would have been much more to their advantage than the open downlands to the west. On this argument, a fort may be found at Canterbury where there is now evidence of a military timber building[9] and of a large Gallo-Belgic *oppidum*[10] and this would have been useful to Plautius in the unlikely event of a retreat. The only known early military site in Kent, apart from Richborough, is at Reculver. This is a small defended area of about an acre, and was probably a signal station, or even a lighthouse at the north entrance to the Wansum Strait, and this, at least, indicates the importance the army attached to this route for military traffic. It has not been precisely dated but coins of Tiberius and Nero in mint condition have been found[11] suggesting that it was maintained at least up to *c*. AD 65.

The Roman army presumably advanced in a broad column along the North Downs – the ancient prehistoric trackway, later to become known as the Pilgrims Way,[12] which traverses the higher ground to the south towards the Wye crossing of the Stour. This old trackway crossed the Medway by a ford somewhere between Snodland and Halling some four miles above Rochester, in a stretch which was probably marshy and unsuitable for a large force. When Plautius reached the chalk ridge overlooking the valley, he was able to study the terrain. From this high vantage point, he could even look across the Estuary to the flat marshes of Essex, but his immediate concern was the large force of Britons strung rather casually on the opposite bank. He also saw to his right the river broadening to a width of some 500 yards, and he probably guessed that the depth would vary, as it does today, between 5 and 20 feet. As he looked straight across the river he saw that it was half this width while to his left it begins to wind and is narrower still up to the fording points of the old trackway. A factor he may not have understood was the effect of the tides which alter the width of the river in its lower reaches. Plautius and his legionary commanders now had to devise a plan of attack, which would avoid an opposed crossing over such an obstacle. The British leaders must have also been wondering how the Romans would face this difficulty, since Dio adds the interesting point that the Britons could not imagine how the Romans would cross without a bridge which, if true, shows a serious ignorance of Roman tactics and training.[13] In his examples of such a contingency, Frontinus emphasizes[14] the need for deception in the timing and the actual point of crossing, and in most of his examples, after the enemy had been persuaded that a crossing is imminent at a certain point, a strong detachment is sent to another place to make a swift unopposed crossing in a typical out-flanking manoeuvre. Plautius had in his army eight Batavian cohorts specially trained to cross large rivers in full battle gear.[15] The Roman commander was a cautious man and he and his legionary commanders would have been well aware of the possibilities open to them and the resources they could deploy.

The account by Dio is very short, but contains two significant pieces of information, firstly, that the battle lasted two days – most unusual in ancient warfare – and, secondly, there were two distinct attacks, the second taking the Britons completely by surprise. It is thus possible to reconstruct the outline of this great battle using these salient facts and the knowledge of Roman tactics[16]. The first step was for the Romans to hold the Britons in their position on the opposite bank and so activities were mounted with men moving about purposefully to convince the enemy that full-scale preparations were being made for an immediate assault. While the Britons watched all this with fascinated anticipation, the Batavians were quietly entering the water and swimming across virtually unnoticed. Their instructions were explicit, to go not for the warriors, but the chariot horses. Plautius would have noted that while the dense mass of Britons were pressed on the bank, their chariots[17] would have been parked to one side or at the rear, but obviously in reach of a swift unexpected attack. Whilst the noise and bustle of the Roman army held the attention of the Britons, these specially trained cohorts could easily have swum across at a point downstream where the river was wider and, therefore, any attack from this direction would be wholly unexpected. The Batavians fell upon the horses slashing them with their swords to wound and ham-string them, and then withdrawing rapidly as the infuriated Britons were thrown into instant confusion when they realized what had happened. This savage unexpected attack on their precious horses would have so enraged the Britons that all other thoughts were driven from their heads. This is the kind of effect Plautius wanted, so attention could be drawn away from the direction of the main attack.

This out-flanking movement must have been out of sight and therefore probably some distance upstream, perhaps near the ancient crossing, the legionaries carefully threading their way across the marshes and regrouping on firmer ground. The spearhead, consisting of two legions under the Flavian brothers,[18] made the crossing successfully and established a bridgehead. The Britons realizing too late they had been out-manoeuvred threw themselves against it but Vespasian and his brother held firm, their task was to hold their position until more troops came across to build up their strength for a break-out. But this did not happen until the next day; so, under the cover of darkness, another legion under Hosidius Geta moved into the bridgehead, and probably at dawn the Romans were ready. According to standard practice, the legionaries held their ground until the Britons attacked and then the legionaries vigorously thrust their wedge-shaped columns into the closely packed ranks carving out their deep channels of carnage. It was a grim and, at first, an indecisive struggle, but Geta's legion broke through and was able to turn and begin an encircling movement, the commander narrowly escaping capture in the process. Presumably at a critical stage Geta was in the middle of this desperate struggle, a splendid example to his men and reviving their flagging energies. So it was he who received special mention from Dio, and gained his *ornamenta triumphalia*[19]. Apart from *Legio II Aug.* it is not possible to say which of the other three legions took part, but Plautius most certainly would have kept one in reserve.

It was one of the greatest and most significant battles fought on British soil signalling not merely a great victory for Rome, but the conquest of lowland Britain. Plautius must have realized that the Province was now virtually his, and all that remained were mopping-up operations and a great deal of talking and argument with the tribal leaders to bring them over to Rome. If the Roman commanders had any intimation of the great struggle ahead with the fierce battles and savage fighting over the next 200 years, they would have been more sober in their jubilation. But there was no time for this since many Britons including Caratacus and his brother had extricated themselves and were disappearing towards the Thames. Plautius had to press home his great advantage and cut down these retreating groups before they could join together and fight again.

Before we take up the chase, it is worth observing that no archaeological trace has ever been found of this momentous event. There is a myth in the minds of many people that battles leave behind masses of skeletons, a debris of armaments and weapons.[20] This remarkable notion is a complete illusion, since all the valuable equipment would have been carefully collected after the fighting, and the bodies removed for proper burial. One could expect ditches of Roman camps, but they have yet to be found.[21] The only possible piece of evidence is a hoard of 34 gold coins found at Bredgar in 1958[22]. The latest of these are four coins – issues of Claudius minted in 41 and 42. The site of this find is on the Downs but almost 11 miles, a day's march, due east of the Medway, so it could hardly have been buried immediately before the battle, but must have been at a stopping point in the advance. An officer may have buried his savings before being despatched to deal with a minor incident and never returned to collect it[23]. One would expect a fort to have been established at Rochester to guard the pontoon bridge that the Roman engineers would immediately have placed across the Medway for the main land supply route from the Richborough base.

The advance to the Thames

After the battle, writes Dio, the Britons fell back to the Thames to a point where it discharged into the ocean and where it forms a lake at flood tide. They crossed with ease since they knew where to find the firm ground and crossing points, the Romans following were not so successful. This difficult passage requires a greater knowledge of the topography of the river and its estuary in the mid-first century than it is possible to reconstruct. There has been a slow, but steady, land subsidence of the eastern coast and this combined with the climatic deterioration in the late Roman period has caused the Thames to rise about 15 feet[24] with the loss of much low-lying land and a continual building of river walls and embankments to preserve some lengths of bank.[25] The broad reaches of the river below Tilbury and Gravesend today bearing a heavy load of ocean traffic, did not exist in AD 43, but at low tide the scene must have been a vista of mud flats through which ran several fresh water streams, the channels of which interchanged as the tides and storms scoured and shifted these alluvial deposits. It would have been possible under these conditions for a crossing to be made, providing the precise route was known. There are indications of a crossing point by ferry in the Middle Ages from Higham via Church Street on the Kent side to East Tilbury on the opposite shore.[26]

This crossing point would appear to be ancient from the evidence at Mucking of a multi-period site on the Essex side of this route. It would have offered Caratacus and his horsemen a quick escape from the Medway and avoided their being overtaken by Roman cavalry with fresh horses. It is at this point too that the river turns sharply north and widens into the Lower Hope into the beginning of the estuary. The sharp bend may have been a cause in the formation of the 'lake' on the flood tide, had the tide turned when the Roman cavalry reached the river bank, it would help to explain their difficulties in making the crossing. Dio continues his narrative with the Germans managing to swim across at this point while the others crossed the river by a bridge a short distance upstream. The width of the river would have presented no problem for the Batavians providing they did not have to struggle over the soft mud flats, but the more conventionally trained troops would have needed an easy way across. The existence of a bridge may occasion surprise, firstly that it was there at all and secondly that the Britons had not destroyed it. The Thames was very much narrower then than it is today and it is known that the tide did not reach London Bridge.[27] This is where eventually a Roman bridge was built but it is not likely to have been the site of an earlier crossing, since there are no significant traces of any pre-Roman occupation on either side of the river at this point and the approach to the river on the south side was very difficult (see p 127 below). It must not be forgotten that Caesar had crossed the Thames with difficulty in his second expedition of 54

BC.[28] There was, he reported, only one place where the river was ford-able and the Britons had fortified the north bank with rows of project-ing pointed stakes, some under the water-line. Antiquarians have made several claims for the identification of this crossing, the most popular being Brentford, where timbers have been found in the river. But this seems too far to the west and wooden structures, not uncom-mon in rivers, are usually old fish-weirs or traps. Another and more at-tractive suggestion is a crossing near Westminster. This is based on the later Roman roads including Watling Street, since if the lines on both sides of the river are projected from the sharp angle on the south bank and the junction with an east-west road on the north, they meet where the Tyburn once flowed into the Thames, and there is another road branching from the river bank on the south side towards London Bridge[29].

With the development of trade with Rome in the pre-conquest period it is possible that there was a land route leading to a Thames crossing used by the traders. The construction of a bridge is not a total impossibility as it could have been built with technical help, not an uncommon Roman practice with friendly states.[30] Maybe Dio's text is garbled and it originally meant that an advance party of Roman engin-eers set up a pontoon bridge[31] which could have been easily brought from Richborough upstream. The main difficulty presented to the advancing cavalry would have been the southern shore where South-wark now stands. This was a wide stretch of sand and silt with marsh and mud flats along the river margin, intersected with innumerable streams and rivulets. When eventually a causeway was built across this difficult area by the Roman engineers, layers of heavy timber had to be laid down, held by revetments along the edge as a foundation.[32] Two Roman roads met at the London Bridge crossing but there is evidence of timber buildings sealed below one of them although, as will be seen, there is a growing amount of evidence of the military presence at London, nothing is known of the very earliest activities when Plautius arrived with his forces.

Having doubtless read Caesar, Plautius would have been fully aware of the possible difficulties of a Thames crossing but on this oc-casion the opposition came after the troops had crossed the river. By now Caratacus had been able to rally his forces and make attempt to delay the advance on Camulodunum. The heavy Medway losses must have forced upon him the realization that the British strength and their fighting methods were quite inadequate to face the four legions in another pitched battle, also information had by now reached him about the tribes making, or preparing to make, overtures to Rome. A new strategy was needed and little time left to redispose the men who had survived the battle and were still prepared to fight. He soon found he was the only leader as Togodumnus died about this time, perhaps from wounds received in battle. Caratacus managed to instil some confidence and there was probably a thirst for revenge, if we are to believe Dio who states that the Britons became all the more determined to resist and avenge the death of their King. But this may be Roman propaganda, since Plautius was unable to make the next obvious move – to advance quickly on to Camulodunum and seize the British capital. He was obliged to respect the quite specific instructions he had received from the Emperor, who reserved the right as commander-in-chief of his army to lead it into the enemy capital. To conform with this, Plautius now wrote a despatch, as prearranged, to the effect that the British resistance was now so obstinate that only the presence of the Emperor would secure victory. This pause, forced upon the Governor, must have been very galling and it could have been highly unfortunate for Rome had the Britons received large reinforcements from the north and west. But more significantly, had Plautius ordered a cavalry swoop on Camulodunum, it is possible he could have captured or destroyed Caratacus. By allowing the British prince time to escape with his family and devoted body-guard, Rome had given the Britons a chance to re-group and cause serious trouble all too soon.

What one now has to consider is what happened in the long interval, at least six weeks, before the Emperor's arrival. Caratacus, highly puzzled no doubt at the strange Roman inactivity, had time to make contact with other British leaders. The most powerful, Cartimandua of the Brigantes, had already been won over by Rome, but in the far west there were determined hill folk prepared to fight for their freedom, and above all the Druids had the insight and intelligence to plan ahead. They may have had their line of retreat to their sanctuary in Anglesey prepared well in advance, and they saw in Caratacus their only hope of a leader who could gain the respect and loyalty of the western tribes in the territory we now know as Wales.[33] Caratacus and his followers bade their anguished farewells to their kinsfolk and set out westwards into areas quite unknown to them, but safe under the protection of the Druids. He may even have advised those left behind to make the best of it and offer only token resistance.

What did Plautius do in the pause? Dio tells us that he merely consolidated the gains he had already made, but this only covered Kent, Sussex and the London bridgehead. It was by now late in the season and he could ill-afford to lose time when so much needed to be done. There was one direction of advance he could make without infringing the prerogative of Claudius and that was towards the south-west. Cogidubnus could have told him about the tribes in this area and also the Romans would have encountered their levies at the Medway, merely on the grounds of stamping out resistance, a campaign could have been mounted and, if necessary, disguised as an armed reconnaissance. Speed was essential and the fleet with its transport which had so successfully brought the army across the Channel was available. The fleet may already have established a base in Bosham Harbour as part of an arrangement with Cogidubnus and this was an ideal place from which to launch a coastal assault. The Britons would naturally expect an approach by land and there is evidence that the most hostile tribe, the Durotriges were busy improving their defences.[34] The task force chosen was *Legio II Augusta* under Vespasian. Plautius could not have afforded to commit a large force to this task, as he had to prepare for Claudius with all the 'spit and polish' and 'red carpeting' that would be involved, and there would have been time to recall Vespasian to be presented to Claudius as one of the victorious generals. The evidence for Vespasian's campaign will be considered later since it is part of the general reduction of Britain under Plautius. Our immediate task is to follow the journey of the Emperor with his large retinue and the time he spent in Britain.

Claudius comes to Britain

The despatch of Plautius would have been sent by a fast military courier. If he had gone on a vehicle used by the Imperial post, he might have emulated Caesar who could achieve 100 miles in a day[35], but the normal speed of post averaged five miles an hour. If he had achieved the high rate of 100 miles a day, it would have taken the courier five or six days[36] and so the despatch would have reached Claudius in Rome 10 to 12 days after leaving Londinium. The Imperial party was waiting for the message and all arrangements would have been made for the journey, but as we have already noted, there was a delay due to the illness of Galba. Dio tells us that the Emperor handed over the control of Rome to his fellow consul in office Lucius Vitellius, so that they both retained these positions for six months[37].

Dio gives some details of the progress; included in the party were not only men of the highest social status, but a section of the Praetorian Guard and elephants[38] and the problem of ensuring the proper degree of comfort and even luxury would have been considerable. Special ships and vehicles would have had to be provided and overnight accommodation carefully planned in advance, as well as all the intermediate stops for rest and refreshment. Such a royal progress demanded a small army of servants and artisans and at no small cost to the tribes of Gaul. It is unfortunate that Dio devotes a single sentence to this prodigious effort. Claudius sailed down the Tibur to Ostia, thence by ship along the coast to Massilia and through Gaul, partly by river and partly by land to the Channel port. Suetonius adds the alarming detail that the party was almost shipwrecked twice, first off the Ligurian coast and later near Îles d'Hyères rounding the headland of the Cote d'Azur before making safe harbour at Massilia. The storms were caused by the penetrating cold wind, known in Provence as the mistral, which still makes this normally warm colourful land so unpleasant for the Easter visitor, but much worse for the inhabitants. One wonders which rivers were used in Gaul – the swift Rhône could only be used by slow barges against the current; but if Claudius crossed the watershed he could have followed the regular transport route by land to Boulogne from Cologne. Although this would have been a much longer route it might have been more comfortable for such a large party.

The accounts of the first Roman Emperor to visit Britain are very brief. Suetonius is quite dismissive – 'he fought no battle nor did he suffer any casualties'. Dio adds a little more – 'Claudius joined his legions at the Thames and led them across the river to engage the Britons who had assembled there. Having defeated them he took Camulodunum'. It is interesting to note that Plautius had his main base on the south bank and it was here that Claudius would have reviewed his troops before crossing the Thames. The site for this is still a matter of conjecture. It could be argued that the Westminster cross-ing would have taken Claudius in the wrong direction, unless he turned sharply to the east on the north bank. The London Bridge crossing would have been the more obvious and the army engineers would have had ample time to have built a timber road and bridges across the difficult channels and banks at Southwark. The 1972–73 excavations in Borough High Street revealed two periods of an early road, the first of which included timber bridges across the channels, but without any trace of road metalling[39]. This suggests the possibility of a timber plank road with side revetments along drainage ditches. The timber could have been covered with rushes or sand to make a more suitable surface for horses. Only in the second phase was a more substantial road, with timber foundations and revetments, construc-ted, presumably as a supply route for Richborough. The lighter tim-berwork would have been adequate for the crossing of Claudius at the head of his army. There is a possibility that some significance may have been seen in the Emperor crossing the river into enemy territory at the head of his army. It was necessary for some token resistance to have been arranged, so that Claudius could claim victories for himself. Dio adds that he was hailed *Imperator* several times – 'contrary to tra-dition' and is credited with five salutations on this occasion, and during his reign collected no less than 27! Camulodunum is 50 miles from London and the army could have marched there in two days without undue difficulty, but to give some air of reality to the Emperor's sequence of victories there may have been some delays with 'serious obstacles' and 'tough groups of resistance' to be overcome. Some of it may even have been real but Claudius, intoxicated by the taste of battle, may have been beguiled into regarding it all as reality. The main purpose was to chalk up successes for home consumption and his two sons-in-law, Magnus and Silanus, were immediately despatched to inform the Senate of his splendid achievements which would ensure the award of a triumph and the title Britannicus. The most important single event of the brief 16 day visit was the submission of the British rulers, which must have been staged with due pomp and ceremony at Camulodunum. Although this is not mentioned by Dio or Suetonius, it is implied on the inscription of his two triumphal arches in Rome. Although only the left hand quarter of one (Pl 15) and three other fragments have survived, it is possible to reconstruct the whole[40] with the help of a similar, but not identical text on an arch at Cyzicus (p 170).[41] The dedication claims that he received the submission of 11 British Kings without any losses (*sine ulla iactura*).[42] The British rulers must have been available and had presumably been gathered together by Plautius in anticipation of their acts of submission at the critical moment when Claudius could be appropriately installed at the British capital. Of the 16 days of his state visit, two or three must have been spent at base camp on the Thames, reviewing his army and preparing for the advance which would have occupied three or four days, leaving about 10 days at Camulodunum but of these several would have been taken up with constructing the audience chamber of sufficient size and splendour. There must have been a small army of orderlies and artisans brought over by Plautius for all this organization and work.

But the most important problem remains – how far can we go in naming the British XI? Would the three client rulers Cogidubnus, Prasutagus and Cartimandua, have been included or would they have been received separately and enriched with Imperial gifts and largesse? Cogidubnus was given the territory of the Atrebates as well as the Regni[43], so there could have been a token chief of the former present. Of the other submissions, one can only be sure of the ruler of the northern section of the Dobunni who may have been the Bodvoc [. . . on the coins, but this leaves us seven more. In view of the raising of Verulamium to municipal status, the ruler of this western part of the Catuvellauni could have been one of them. Nothing is known of the attitude of the Coritani, although as suggested above, the coin hoards in Brigantia may indicate the flight of refugees from this tribe.[44] Presumably the march through Kent had shown the kings there the futility of any further protest, they may have had bitter tribal memories of their harsh treatment under Caesar and their denial of trade, and there could have been two or three petty rulers in this territory with a tradition of fractious bickering[45]. There could have been kings from distant parts if the hints in the Eulogies have a basis in reality, and assuming that they would have felt the need for protection from a more powerful neighbour. It is not difficult to suggest a list of the tribal chiefs who made their formal submission to the Emperor, an act which normally took place in the Capitol in Rome and one must assume that Claudius had received formal authority from the Senate to act on its behalf. After all, he had quite a gathering of senators with him at the time, which could have represented a kind of quorum. The pernickety

Claudius would have taken a perverse delight in going out of his way to observe the strict formalities, as his relationship with the Senate was still a little strained.

All these activities were completed in 16 days which says much for the success of the army in the south-west and the elaborate arrangements made prior to the visit. Before he left Britain Claudius proceeded to disarm the natives as required by Roman law and to instruct Plautius to bring the remaining territory under Roman control. Claudius departed with a sense of great achievement. His position as Emperor could no longer be challenged and he had above all established a strong identity with one of his great provincial armies. He was away from Rome for six months, according to Dio[46], and this would have given him ample time to return via the Rhine to review his troops there and receive their acclaim.

The precise extent of this new province was defined by Claudius and his advisors as a matter for careful examination, before this however, we need to pick up the story of Vespasian's achievements in the south-west.

Vespasian in the south-west

As indicated above, the swift drive towards the south-west was probably started in the interval pending the Emperor's arrival. Identification of the legion and its commander chosen for this task comes mainly from Suetonius, who tells us[47] that Vespasian fought 30 battles, overcame two hostile tribes and took 20 *oppida* in addition to the Isle of Wight (*insulam Vectem*) and it is Tacitus who informs us that he commanded *Legio II Augusta*[48]. The inclusion of the Isle of Wight firmly places this campaign in the south-west, but there is a little difficulty in naming the two tribes. The Durotriges seem to be a certainty, but for the other one there are three possibilities, the Dumnonii, the Belgae and the southern half of the Dobunni. The Dumnonii of Devon and Cornwall can be excluded, since they were not invaded at this time and can be presumed friendly; the Belgae appear to occupy an oddly shaped territory in the geography of Roman Britain but we can only suppose that this was due to a reorganization of the tribal boundaries at a much later date. It is better at this point to keep a firm eye on the distribution pattern of the Celtic coins which show clearly that the western part of the territory later ascribed to the Belgae, was occupied by the southern branch of the Dobunni. The area to the east of the Durotriges, on the basis of a rather thin spread of his coins was the Kingdom of Verica of the Atrebates. It would seem from this that two tribes had land taken from them to create the *civitas Belgarum*. A further guide to the territories involved is provided by the evidence of destruction of the hill-forts and battle casualties associated with the presence of the Roman army. The figures given by Dio are obviously rounded ones and the term *oppidum* must mean no more than a hill-fort. Its usage has recently been confined to the Belgic type of defences, rather than the contoured hill-fort of an older tradition.

The archeological evidence

There are over 50 hill-forts in the territory of the Durotriges alone and only very careful excavation is ever likely to tell us which of them fell to the assault of Vespasian's legionaries. Skeletons would first have to be proved to have been battle casualties and then closely dated to this period, and the same is true of any deliberate reduction of the defences, while casual finds of Roman military equipment may only be a primary indicator. Also this is only the first time the Roman army may have been attacking these sites. There are two later occasions, one in 48, considered below, and another in 60–61 in the aftermath of the great Boudican revolt.

Cadbury Castle

Cadbury Castle in Somerset is a good example of this problem. A brilliantly conceived and directed excavation by Professor Leslie Alcock revealed destruction in the final phase of the south-west gate[49] and associated with this were the scattered remains of about 30 men, women and children strewn along a passage,[50] but it is thought that the gruesome dismemberment of some of the bodies was caused by wild animals and all that it suggests is that there were no kins-folk around to give the bodies proper burial. Although there is little evidence of bones broken or fractured by the sword it seems likely that a massacre took place. Pieces of military equipment of the mid-first century AD point to the presence of the Roman army. To test the date, no less than 10 samples of charred wood and carbonized grain were selected from these layers and subjected to radio-carbon dating. As there had been some controversy over the right calibration methods, five different evaluations were made for each sample, providing a fascinating result, well described and tabulated.[51] The variations were extraordinary and two samples fall well outside the acceptable date range, but six could be placed in the 45–61 bracket, and seven would seem to lean towards the later end of this narrow range. This supports a conclusion previously reached[52] that this particular attack fits the events of 60–61 rather better than anything earlier.

Maiden Castle

Greater certainty can be ascribed to two Dorset hill-forts, Maiden Castle and Hod Hill. The former was the scene of a large-scale excavation by Mortimer Wheeler in 1934–7.[53] Interest was directed especially on the gates and their entrances and the carefully planned ditches forced attackers to make an oblique approach, which exposed them to sling stones from the defences on the towering ramparts above. This kind of tactical arrangement intrigued the military mind of Wheeler and it is hardly surprising that he put so much into a detailed study of these vulnerable points. In doing so, he gained a bonus, for by the east gate he found a group of 28 graves. Although the bodies had been hurriedly buried, provision had been made for their journey into the next world, joints of meat and tankards of ale, or maybe even 'scrumpy' that rough cider which makes a visit to Dorset so memorable, even today. Some of the graves were shared in eternal companionship and in all, there were 23 men and 11 women. Several had severe head injuries inflicted with sharp blades and there was some evidence that the bodies had been hacked about after death (Report, pp 351 – 2). This assault took place late in the history of the hill-fort, but the excavator was left in no doubt when he found embedded in a backbone of one of the skeletons, the head of a *ballista* bolt. This is a type of projectile used by legionaries, and was fired from a small catapult mounted on a cart (Pl 4) one being allocated to each century in the legion, each operated by ten men,[54] which gives a total of 60 machines. They could be used in several ways, the legionary advancing towards a hill-fort could be covered by these guns from the flanks, laying down a barrage by firing high into the air, striking down unexpectedly with devastating effect. By attaching tow or straw, which could be set alight, they could be aimed at the native houses and start fires in the middle of the attack. They could also be employed against selected targets like gate-ways or breeches in a wall where the aim could be directed at individual defenders. This find at Maiden Castle clinched the matter and demonstrated that this great hill-fort had fallen to the 2nd legion, and the excavation revealed also that the army had deliberately slighted the defences by pushing the tops of the rampart into the ditches and levering the large stones out of the tall gateways. After this the site was deserted,[55] its inhabitants massacred or enslaved and those left forced to settle down by a nearby fort[56] where the army could keep an eye on them. This was Dorchester (Durnovaria) which became a thriving little town and tribal centre.

Hod Hill

The other hill-fort to produce reliable evidence of assault is Hod Hill at Stourpaine, near Blandford Forum. It was excavated with masterly precision by Sir Ian Richmond[57] from 1951 to 1958.

The fate of this hill-fort and details of the Roman assault have been graphically described by Richmond. He pointed out how the strengthening of the defences was abruptly ended while the work was in progress, and this is dramatically seen in the air photographs at the north-east corner, where the new outer ditch ends suddenly and very untidily with the spoil heap still at its edge. The excavator also found

15 *ballista* bolts and when their find-spots were plotted that a concentration of fire power had been directed on the chieftain's hut, probably, as Richmond suggests, from a siege-tower over-topping the ramparts. This sudden concentrated and violent assault probably led to a rapid surrender, as there is no war cemetery comparable to that at Maiden Castle.[58] After the capture of the hill-fort came the deliberate reduction and reorganization of the defences for the Roman fort, then built into its north-west corner and considered in detail below (p 150).

6 The Shape of the Roman Province

The Britain Caesar knew from his own observations and those of his surveyors was limited to the Thames Estuary, northern Kent and the woods and marshes of the Lea Valley and perhaps some of the land immediately to the west. The advent of the Roman traders and the establishment of their posts led to more extensive and detailed knowledge, and Rome began also to seek alliances with distant tribes. There were fugitive princes like Tincommius of the Atrebates, who could have given Roman officials first-hand accounts of their tribal territories and the lands beyond. The cautious Plautius would have sought out all the available information and must have had a reasonable idea of the geography of southern Britain. He could even have planned the precise extent of the conquest with the chief advisors of the Empire. What emerges from the subsequent military dispositions is the idea of a strictly limited conquest, with the creation of a new province, the western boundary of which was the Humber Estuary, the Trent, the Warwickshire Avon, the lower Severn, the Bristol Channel and the Exe. This line follows the natural divide formed by the limestone escarpment into which the rivers have cut their valleys.[1] It also marks a cultural boundary, seen most dramatically in the distribution of the British coins[2] since, apart from strays accounted for by fugitives and Roman soldiers, they are found only to the south and east of this line and the tribes beyond never produced coins of their own. If this can be used as a measure of social or economic advance it is a significant watershed. Rome did not particularly want peoples within her Empire who would not be converted into respectable citizens.

Within this area was the mineral wealth they expected to find – the silver lead ore of the Mendips and the abundant iron of the Weald of Kent and the limestone belt. It was the lowland zone and most of it was good agricultural land with no difficult mountain areas. But Rome was also firmly aware of the considerable lands beyond in the west and the north, occupied by fierce independent hill-folk, who would not take so readily to the promise of a bright 'civilized' future. Rome was quite accustomed to establish land frontiers against barbarian peoples, and they had adopted, from their earliest expansionist period, a simple, but highly effective political device – the client relationship with a carefully selected local ruler. Rome's own social relationships were

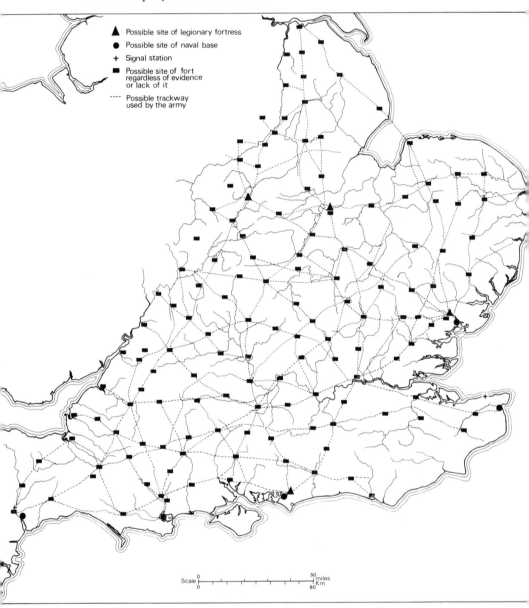

Scale
0 _____ 50 miles
0 _____ 80 Km

Map II Suggested sites of military establishments in the Plautian period. (Not all of their forts would necessarily have been occupied at the same time)

based on the concept of the patron and his clients, which applied in particular to those high in the social order owning land and wealth. It was a natural extension of the hierarchy of the family with the head (the *pater familias*) being obeyed and respected by all the members, and should any of them go astray, become ill or fall on bad times, each could always depend on the 'father' coming to their aid, and at the same time he could count absolutely on their loyalty and obedience. As the great families acquired wealth and land, they naturally extended the system to all their tenants and farm workers and artisans and their families. Thus a small number of men of the senatorial order could command the unquestioned support of a small army of retainers. This helps to explain the background to the late Republic and the bitter social and civil wars, when groups of important men were brought together by political necessity to sustain their power. The greatest of them all in political subtlety and statecraft was Augustus, the first *princeps* (chief among equals) and, of course, the Emperor became the chief patron and his *clientela* was extended to all the inhabitants within the Empire[3]. It seemed obvious and logical to the Roman mind to extend this basic concept to the allies on the frontier, but it was entirely on a personal basis, the Emperor, as the patron, accepted the king or ruler as his client and thus assumed that the subjects of that ruler in turn were held then in the same state of dependence. By this means, Rome secured an outer buffer to her frontiers with little effort and expense. The main object of the treaties would have been to oblige the ruler to protect his territory against any barbarian attack from without, and the Emperor would have agreed to assist his client in the event of a serious invasion or an internal revolt[4].

The client kingdoms in Britain

The northern frontier of Brigantia

The application of this neat arrangement in Britain at least secured the northern frontier. The Pennines and the lands on each side were occupied by a number of small tribes, except those north of the Humber, where the Parisii[5] were numerous and prosperous and, as they were more recent migrants, were socially and culturally more advanced than the dalesmen of the hills. In a diplomatic masterstroke, the Romans managed to bring together this vast loose conglomeration of Brigantian tribes under the client Queen Cartimandua, who must have been acceptable to all these diverse peoples as she was probably a member of one of the leading families. Her position was strengthened politically with a dynastic marriage to Venutius from one of the tribes from the territory to the north. Thus Rome secured in a sense a double security, and Cartimandua was to remain firmly loyal to Rome through the crises of the next 20 years, although most likely under great pressure from her consort and the more independent-minded

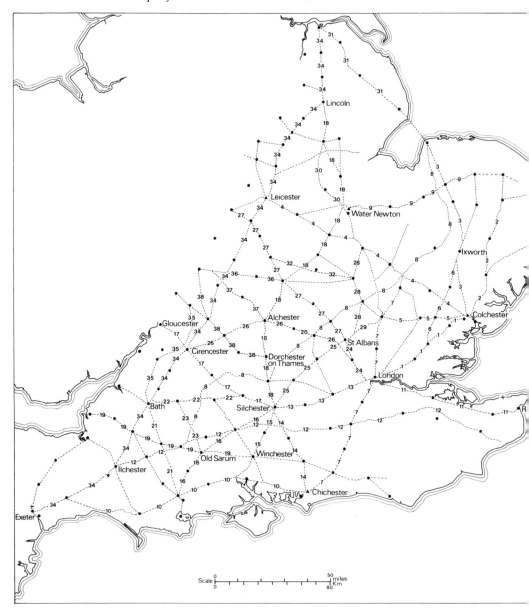

Map III Suggested military routes

sections of her subjects to break the treaty. She was a powerful woman who exercised her feminine wiles to great effect.

The western frontier

It must have been Rome's intention to create client kingdoms on the western frontier along the Severn valley, but all attempts to find amenable rulers failed, since Caratacus had so rapidly and effectively gained control over these areas, and with the Druidic support would have prevented any further defections to Rome. In the extreme southwest, the peninsula of Devon and Cornwall was occupied by the Dumnonii and at this period there may have been a peace treaty which did not extend to a full client relationship. A line roughly from the Exe to the Parrett was the frontier zone and there seemed no advantage to Rome to advance any further. The two other client kingdoms, as already explained, were in an anomalous position relative to the new province, and can only be considered as Claudian rewards for loyal services at the time of the invasion if they had been created by then.

The Plautian defensive strategy (– see also Appendix 2)

It should now be fully appreciated that the suggested network of military sites is an extremely tenuous one with some totally unsupported ideas for the areas which to date have produced no evidence. This exercise is an attempt to understand the military consequences of the campaigns and pacification in the period from AD 43 to 47. No account has been taken of the campaign camps with units in the field, or in winter quarters, nor the adjustments made necessary by the hostility of some of the tribes or sections of them. The initial positions held by some of the units may have been solely determined by the presence of a large concentration of potentially hostile Britons. Only when they had been quietened and tensions eased would it have been possible for the dispositions to be adjusted for a more effective control of communications. It should, therefore, occasion little surprise to find two forts within a short distance of each other, as the sites may have been changed to suit a change in local circumstances within this short period of the first governor. Our present knowledge is quite inadequate to make any more but the most tentative suggestions at this stage. Forts may be known only from aerial photographs, or indicated by finds of equipment; there are very few examples of large-scale excavations like that at Hod Hill (No 64*) which presented such a mass of detail that one can begin to understand the site. It is, however, salutory to discover that when this happens the evidence is far more complicated and very difficult to interpret. Given little pieces of information from here and there and a powerful imagination, one can build patterns of the campaigns which may satisfy their creator, but can be guaranteed

* The numbers following the fort sites are shown on the three maps.

Sites on Map VI

Legionary Fortresses
L 1 Colchester
L 2 Chichester

Naval Bases
S 1 Richborough
S 2 Bosham Harbour
S 4 Fingeringhoe Wick

Signal Station
1 Reculver

Forts
 1 Canterbury
 2 Rochester
 3 London
 4 near Billericay
 5 Chelmsford
 6 Kelvedon
 7 Colchester (Stanway)
 8 Baylham House
 9 Scole
10 Caistor St Edmunds
11 Brampton
12 Ixworth
13 Saham Toney
15 Wixoe

20 Braintree
21 Great Dunmow
22 Braughing
23 Long Melford
24 near Waltham Abbey
25 Great Chesterford
26 Lackford, near Lakenheath
27 near Morley Hall
28 near Billingford
33 Newhaven
34 near Hassocks
35 Hardham
41 near Wye
42 near Maidstone (at the crossing of the Medway)
43 near Sevenoaks
44 near Dorking (at the crossing of Stane Street)
45 near Guildford (at the crossing of the Wey)
52 Staines
54 Iping
85 Brockley Hill
132 Alfoldean
133 North of Ewell

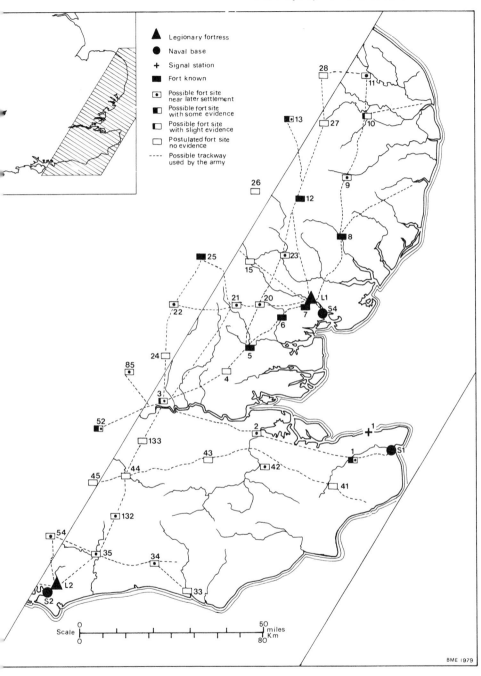

Sites on Map V

Legionary Fortresses
L 2 Chichester
L 3 Longthorpe

Naval Bases
S 2 Bosham Harbour
S 5 Hamworthy

Forts
 3 London
13 Saham Toney
14 On the Wash
16 Cambridge
17 Godmanchester
18 Aldwinkle (at the crossing of the Nene)
20 Braintree
22 Braughing
24 near Waltham Abbey
25 Great Chesterton
27 Lackford, near Lakenheath
28 near Billingford
29 Castle Acre (at the crossing of the Icknield Way)
31 near March
32 Water Newton
36 Bittern (Clausentum)
37 near Ibsley (at the crossing of the Avon)
38 Shapwick
39 Dorchester, Dorset
45 near Guildford (at the crossing of the Wey)
46 near East Anton (Leucomagus)
47 Stockton
50 Silchester
51 near Bagshot

52 Staines
53 Neatham
54 Iping
55 Popham
56 Winchester
57 Old Sarum
58 near Rotherly
59 Lake Farm (Wimbourne)
60 near Boxford
61 Wanborough
64 Hod Hill
65 near Basildon
66 Dorchester-on-Thames
67 Alchester
68 Towcester
69 Irchester
76 near Bourne
81 Mildenhall, Wilts
84 St Albans (Verulamium)
85 Brockley Hill
86 near Latimer
87 near Henley
88 Northchurch
89 near Fleet Marston
90 Dunstable
91 Dropshort
96 Baldock
97 Sandy
100 Burgh-le-Marsh
102 Harrold (at the crossing of the Ouse)
130 near Standlake (at the crossing of the Thames)
135 near Amesbury (at the crossing of the Avon)

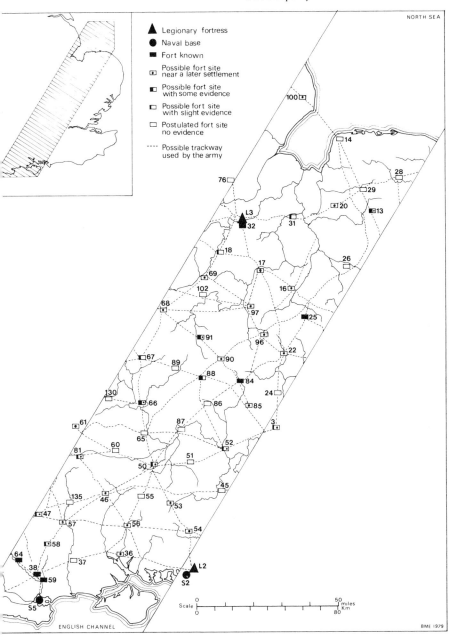

NORTH SEA

Legend:
- ▲ Legionary fortress
- ● Naval base
- ■ Fort known
- ⊡ Possible fort site near a later settlement
- ◧ Possible fort site with some evidence
- ▫ Possible fort site with slight evidence
- ▫ Postulated fort site no evidence
- ---- Possible trackway used by the army

100

14

28

29

76

20

13

L3
32

31

18

26

17

69

16

102

68

97

25

91

96

22

67

89

90

88

84

24

130

66

86

85

61

87

3

65

60

52

81

51

50

45

135

55

46

53

47

57

56

54

58

36

64

37

38

L2

59

S2

S5

Scale
0 — 50 miles
0 — 80 Km

ENGLISH CHANNEL

BME 1979

Sites on Map IV

Legionary fortress
L4 Leicester

Naval Base
S 3 Topsham

Signal Station
2 Stoke Hill, Exeter

Forts
19 Medbourne
39 Dorchester, Dorset
40 Exeter
47 Stockton
48 near Wincanton
49 Ilchester
61 Wanborough
62 Cirencester
63 Gloucester
64 Hod Hill
67 Alchester
68 Towcester
70 Great Casterton
71 Ancaster
72 Lincoln
73 Owmby
74 Hibaldstow
75 Winteringham
76 near Bourne
77 Cold Kitchen Hill
78 North of Shepton Mallet (at the crossing of the Fosse Way)
79 Charterhouse
80 Uphill (Weston-super-Mare)
81 Mildenhall, Wilts
82 Bath
83 Sandy Lane
92 Whilton Lodge
93 Caves Inn
94 High Cross
95 Mancetter

98 Kirmington
99 Burgh-on-Bain
101 Old Sleaford
103 Alcester
104 near Chipping Warden
105 Lower Lea
106 Nettleton
107 White Walls
108 near Bourton-on-the-Water
109 near Halford (at the crossing of the Stour)
110 near Chesterton
111 Willoughby-on-the-Wolds (Vernemetum)
112 Margidunum
113 Thorpe-by-Newark
114 Brough
115 Owston on the Trent
116 Marton
117 near Bilsthorpe
118 Broxstowe
119 near Radcliffe
120 near Bardon
121 near Temple Balsall
122 near Eckington
123 Andoversford
124 Kingscote
125 near Berkeley
126 Sea Mills
127 at the mouth of the Parrett
128 Wiveliscombe
129 near Tiverton
130 near Standlake (at the crossing of the Thames)
131 Asthall
134 Ham Hill
136 near Honiton
137 Rodborough Common

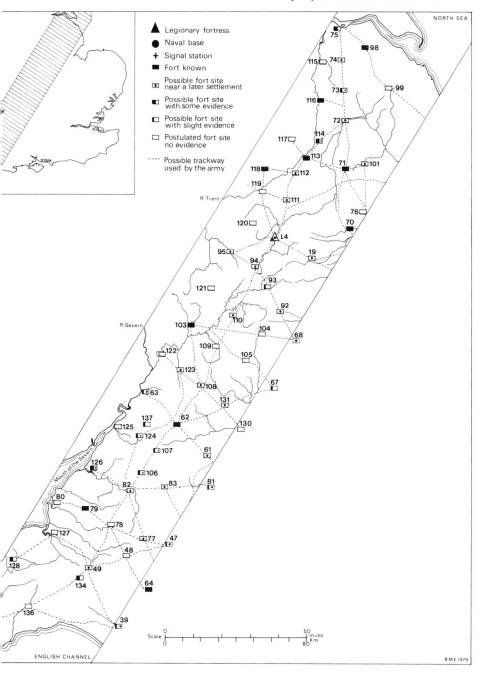

NORTH SEA

▲ Legionary fortress
● Naval base
+ Signal station
■ Fort known
⊡ Possible fort site
  near a later settlement
◼ Possible fort site
  with some evidence
▢ Possible fort site
  with slight evidence
▢ Postulated fort site
  no evidence
--- Possible trackway
  used by the army

R.Trent

R.Severn

Mouth of the Severn

ENGLISH CHANNEL

Scale

0   50 miles
0   80 Km

B M E 1979

to be remote from the actuality. One might, therefore, ask: why bother until sufficient evidence is available for study? The answer to that is that ignorance is no excuse for inertia, and one needs a framework for conjectural thinking. The truth can only be approached by hard work and effort in collecting information and working out possible solutions. This may stimulate others to look for more evidence to add to the body of knowledge and the hypotheses can be continually corrected and adjusted.

The normal Roman practice was to plant a tight net-work of forts, about a day's march apart, over a newly conquered area to control all the key strategic points with the object of preventing hostile elements from gathering together and thus depriving them of mobility. These positions are quite often at river crossings or along the ancient trackways.[6] When there were large concentations of Britons in a settlement, military units would not be far away to maintain a constant watch. Once the sites of some of the forts are known, it is not difficult to predict where others may be found. Apart from the strategic and geographic factors, one looks for a small flat plateau above the flood plain of a river at points where crossings could have been made. There is, however, another important aspect which helps in the identification of sites of forts. When troops had been stationed anywhere for a few years, they attracted local natives and traders from more distant places to settle nearby and supply the basic needs of soldiers, women, drink, food and those extras which give comfort and enjoyment not obtained in a barrack life. These little settlements sprawling along the roads leading to the fort usually survived as permanent towns and settlements on the departure of the troops, to continue to provide the same services for travellers using the roads.

Even the two client kingdoms of Cogidubnus and Prasutagus, were not exempt from military occupation, at least in the Plautian phase. There is evidence of a large military establishment at Chichester, the capital of the Kingdom of Cogidubnus and a hint of troops at Silchester (No 50), and this implies forts of this period must also be expected in Icenian territory. The pro-Roman elements of the western Catuvellauni at Verulamium also were obliged to suffer the presence of a unit guarding the crossing of the Ver (No 84).

Using these criteria, it is possible to reconstruct a network of forts with a fair degree of plausibility (but see Appendix 2); there is, however, a difficulty in not knowing the precise date of the military occupation of these sites. This would not seriously invalidate the proposed scheme except that there were constant adjustments and the more important variant is connected with the events of the later campaigns following the defeat of Boudica and the crushing of the great revolt in AD 60 – 61, which led to the military reorganization of much of the Midlands and East Anglia. It is quite impossible without pottery or coins which can be very narrowly dated to decide whether any particular fort belongs to the Plautian scheme (AD 43 – 48), or that of Suetonius Paullinus (AD 60 – 65).

The Fosse Way frontier

The most important decision Plautius had to make in his arrangements for the fort network was the precise western limit. Having decided which of the tribes were to be included in the province, he would naturally have looked for a great physical barrier, like a river. The rivers of Britain were very small compared with those of the continent but he found in the Jurassic limestone escarpment a suitable geographic feature. The best he could do was to use this high ground for his frontier road (the original meaning of the word *limes*) and site his forward position on the Rivers-Trent, Avon and lower Severn, to guard the main crossing points. This arrangement was to some extent already determined by the landscape and the use made of the escarpment in earlier times of the trackways known collectively as the Jurassic Way[7]. The attribution of the Fosse Frontier to Plautius is clear from a passage of Tacitus, relating to the second governor Ostorius Scapula who, soon after his arrival, 'disarmed all those suspected on the Roman side of the Trent and Severn'[8] which demonstrates that this line was already in existence when he arrived. A more detailed study of this frontier and its forts will be given below (p 159).

The legionary fortresses

Of the four legionary fortresses dating from this period, the sites of only two are known. One is that of *Legio XX* at Camulodunum, discovered in excavations under the western part of the later *colonia*.[9] Its size is 48 acres; although three sides are known, the line of the fourth can be assumed since it was dictated by the presence of a steep slope. The only buildings so far identified are the barrack-blocks in the south-east corner of Lion Walk. Unfortunately, the basic plan remains uncertain, but the probability is that the *via principalis* is on the north–south axis. Indications were found in 1974[10] of possible earlier defences under the northern part of the fortress.

Bearing in mind the evidence from Hod Hill (p 150) and Longthorpe (No L3), one must not expect to find the stylized type of 50-to 60-acre fortress of the Flavian period. At this earlier stage in Britain it was evidently the practice to detail legionary cohorts for out-post duties, even sharing a fort with auxiliaries. There would, however, have been a base for the *legatus legionis* (legionary commander), his HQ staff, workshops, hospital and the cohort in training. There are large forts of 20 to 30 acres which may fall into this category, and Professor Frere has called them 'vexillation' forts,[11] implying occupation by a mixed force of different units. Unfortunately, only one of these has been excavated, that at Longthorpe on the Nene, near Peterborough[12] and had resources allowed, an extensive area could

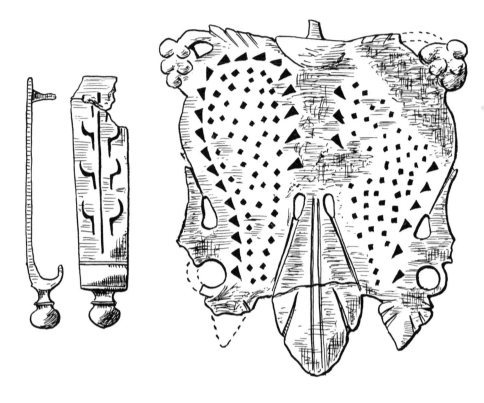

Left An apron-mount with a tinned surface and decorated with niello
Right A pendant with niello inlay from Colchester

have been stripped and a plan obtained which might have been very helpful in giving us a better understanding of these anomalous establishments. The system of trenching, however, to which the excavators were restricted, has only created more problems and left a very tantalizing glimpse of strangely irregular buildings, far removed from the rigid military planning of the later periods. Those buildings for which positive identification is possible are two granaries and the large central structure which should be the *principia*, and there are two others which have the appearance of barrack-blocks.

Legio II Augusta was in the south-west with one of its cohorts at Hod Hill (No 64), but its main base appears to have been at Chichester (No L 2), near the supply base at Fishbourne on Bosham Harbour. The evidence has come from a series of rescue excavations carried out by Alec Down and published by him.[13] Unfortunately, he could only open up small areas at a time, so it has not been possible to plot a coherent plan of the fort. The timber buildings cover an area of *c.* 1100 feet by *c.* 550 feet – an area of about 13 acres (Plan I) and the large quantity of equip-

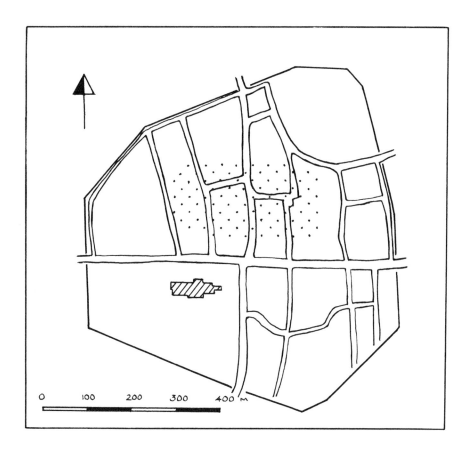

Plan I Chichester – dotted area shows extent of early military timber buildings

ment is all legionary. Items so far recovered include a fine *gladius* blade from Chapel Street in remarkable condition and which seems hardly to have been used, and an officer's decorated belt-mount depicting five dogs chasing a boar.[14]

The fourth legion in Britain was *Legio XIV Gemina*, which at a later stage was to advance along Watling Street to its Wroxeter site. The nodal point of communication in the Plautian scheme was Camulodunum and not London and this raises the possibility of Leicester (No L 4) being its base at this stage.[15] The name Ratae[16] and finds suggest the presence of a large native settlement.[17] Evidence of military activity has been found here, this includes a typical legionary belt-mount decorated with niello.[18] Although the tile stamp LVIII (retro) must be discounted,[19] a ditch of military type has been noted near the river Soar with early pottery in its filling[20] and timber buildings of 'immediately post-conquest date' have been found in Blackfriars Street.[21]

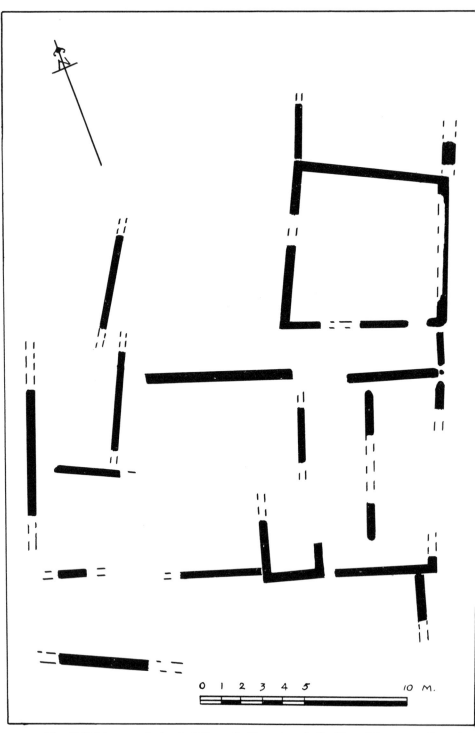

Plan II Chichester – timber buildings of military type in the Chapel Street area (based on a plan kindly supplied by Alec Down)

Another significant find near the Jewry Wall Museum, has been a decorated cheek-piece, normally associated with cavalry. The relief depicts a winged female holding in her left hand a bunch of what may be poppy heads or grapes. There is also the remarkable blue glass medallion[22] found at a depth of 10 feet when putting in a gas main on a housing estate, two miles west of Leicester. It is one of a set of nine military awards (*dona militaria*) and depicts Germanicus with his three children, probably issued in AD 23. This was presumably lost by a veteran or one of his descendants and, although it has a military interest, it may not have any direct connection with a possible unit stationed here. A number of lead seals have been recovered from various parts of the City, including one stamped L(EG)XXV, but others have the names of different units and may not relate to the unit in occupation, but merely indicate that there was a military depôt here receiving or despatching packages.[23]

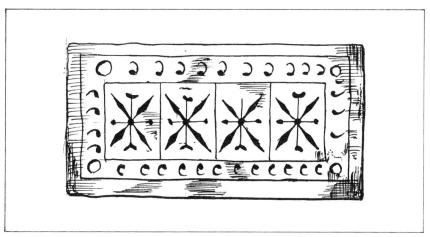

A legionary belt-plate from Leicester

The auxiliary forts – Londinium (No 3)

The evidence for the presence of auxiliary units can be summarized briefly, but first one should deal with Londinium. Before the conquest this had been a place of no particular significance, although there were tracks leading to crossings of the Thames. It was the astute eyes of the Romans who saw the enormous importance of the site as a nodal point in their provincial communication network. Nevertheless it took time for this to become effective because the first obvious centre was the British capital at Camulodunum, and it is possible to trace the first network of routes radiating from it (Map III), but this was soon to be superseded by the more logical choice. As suggested above, the first Plautian base camp must have been on the south bank of the Thames, but as soon as Colchester was in Roman hands a permanent fort would have been erected on the north side to protect the London Bridge crossing. In spite of the large-scale excavations of recent years carried out in advance of development by the Department of Urban Archaeology, the traces are still very slight,[24] and there is no sound evidence, as yet, to suggest a possible site or sites. In the years which followed, several forts could have been erected at different points as the military needs changed. It may be of significance that so many objects of first-century military origin have been found dumped in the Walbrook[25] which suggests that a fort was not too far away, most probably on the east side. What was thought to have been a military type ditch was found by Dr Hugh Chapman in 1971 at Aldgate[26] but this could merely have been a transit camp on the Camulodunum road, starting from the bridgehead on an alignment diagonal to the later city grid, in itself an indication of an earlier origin.

A decorated pendant from the Walbrook

North of the Thames estuary
The route to Camulodunum should be well marked with at least three forts, but only two are so far known. The first should be expected where it meets the north-south route from the Tilbury Thames crossing discussed above (p 101) near Billericay (No 4).[27] The first known fort is at Chelmsford (No 5) which bears the interesting name of *Caes-*

aromagus, which must have an imperial significance. The Celtic suffix *magus* is as difficult to interpret as *venta* – both seem to indicate some kind of meeting place or point of assembly. If, as would seem most probable, it was linked with Claudius, there are two possible suggestions.[28] It could have been where the Emperor gained one of his victories for which he received a salutation, in which case, the meaning could be 'Caesar's field of victory'. The second possibility is that it was specially granted to the Trinovantes when the *colonia* at Camulodunum was founded. The evidence of a military presence came in excavation and observation in 1969–71 with pieces of equipment and Claudian coins and samian associated with timber buildings.[29] The Cables Yard excavation in 1975 produced a demolished turf rampart and a V-ditch.[30] A road was found heading off in a south-easterly direction. This was thought[31] to divide after a short distance, one branch bending to the south of the crossing of the Crouch at Wichford, where excavations in 1971 produced a military type ditch thought to belong to a campaign base.[32] Several military objects were recovered including a scabbard chape and trumpet mouth-piece[33] and they may have come from a fort in the vicinity. Such a fort may have been in contact with the two-acre signal station at Hadleigh[34] to the south-east; there is a similar one at Orsett on the north-south route of the Thames crossing.[35] The other branch of the road from Chelmsford appears to be directed eastwards towards Heybridge on the Black-water Estuary. There is evidence of a considerable settlement and harbour[36] here, which may be linked with the military system.

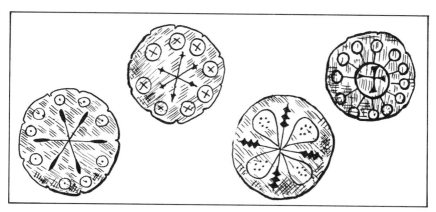

Four studs decorated with niello from London

The third site is at Kelvedon (Canonium) (No 6) where excavations in 1971–3 produced evidence of the south-west corner of a fort on the 22.3metre contour above the flood plain of the River Blackwater.[37] There were kilns, thought to be of this period, on the edge of the ditch, a situation similar to Longthorpe (p 123) above. At Camulodunum there is an auxiliary fort of *ala* size at Stanway,[38] (No 7) clearly sited near Gosbecks the presumed site of the British capital (see p 131 above). It has been furthermore suggested that this was the fort of the Thracian *Ala.* and may be earlier than the legionary base if the XXth was needed by Plautius in his reduction of the rest of the province in the first years of occupation.

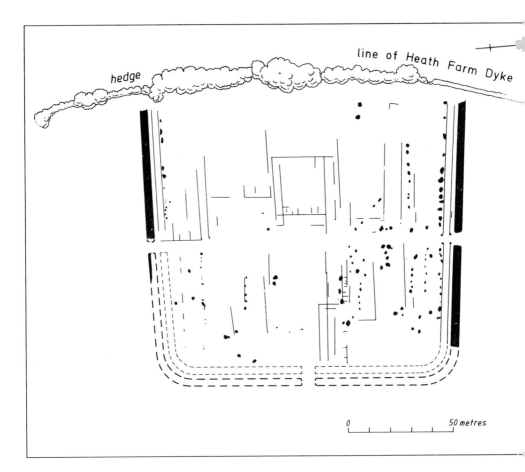

Plan III The auxiliary fort at Stanway

Fingringhoe Wick

Military equipment (p 133) and Claudian coins have been found in gravel workings on the headlands of Fingringhoe Wick[39] (No 54) on the River Colne, which suggests the possible presence there at this time of a naval base supplying *Legio XX* direct from the Rhineland.

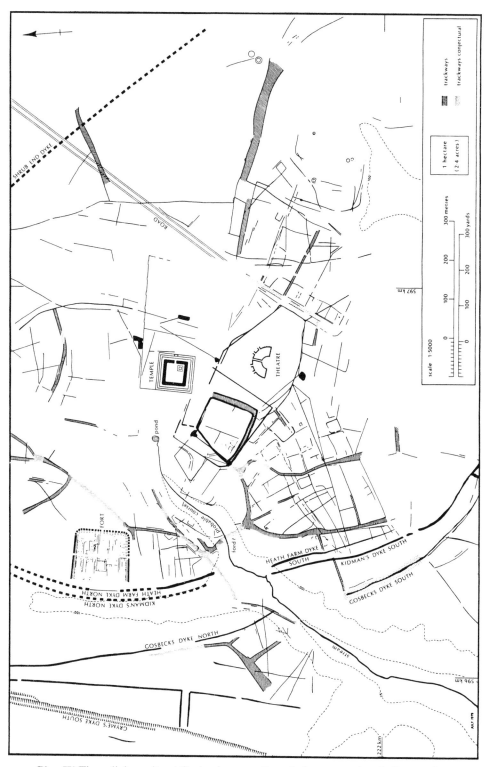

Plan IV The religious site at Gosbecks, near Camulodunum, and early Roman fort, with crop marks from aerial photographs of the British capital

The military dispositions – East Anglia

Since forts have been found at Verulamium and at Chichester, and there is evidence of the possibility of one at Silchester (No 50), it follows that the two client kingdoms were occupied by the army, at least under Plautius. The territories of the Iceni and Trinovantes would also have been under military control after the Boudican revolt and only a close study of the relationships between buildings or defences of different periods, or of critical pieces of pottery, could help to separate the two different phases of occupation. Bearing in mind the factors which determined the siting of forts, i.e. the river crossings and the presence of British communities, the simplest method of studying the possible military network is by the routes the army would wish to control. Excluding the one from London (Route 1) one starts with the four military routes radiating from Camulodunum, some of which later developed into a system of roads:

2 North-north-east passing Baylham House, (No 8, Combretovium), Scole (No 4) and Caistor St Edmund (No 10, Venta Icenorum) and Brampton.

3 North and towards Ixworth (No 12), then swinging slightly to the west towards the Wash, through Saham Toney (No 13) and known as the Peddars Way.

4 North-west towards Leicester (No 4, Ratae) which was probably a nodal point in the Plautian frontier, passing through Cambridge (No 16, Duroliponte) and Godmanchester (No 17, Durovigutum). This main supply route to the frontier zone was later superseded when London became the chief road centre.

5 West, presumably along an earlier trackway, towards the important pro-Roman centre at Braughing (No 22) and connected with Verulamium (No 84).

There is another route from the Thames crossing near Tilbury, and which strikes north towards Great Dunmow (No 21) and beyond to link with the Icknield Way, an early trackway which skirts the Fen margin, passing through the important Lakenheath area, almost to merge into Route 3 above. To these must be added the two routes from London linking with Great Dunmow, and another (Route 7) up the Lea Valley to Braughing (No 22) and Great Chesterford (No 25) and the Icknield Way. There may have been interconnecting routes within this main system. The suggested siting of forts is based on this network, although the evidence at present is slight, it seems to support the validity of the scheme.

Forts on Route 2

The first fort of Camulodunum is at the crossing of the Gipping at Baylham House (No 8), whichhas produced over the years evidence of

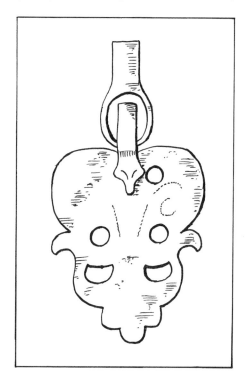

A pendant from Fingeringhoe Wick

a military presence[40] including a saddle-cloth weight, indicating cavalry. The most spectacular find made in 1795 is a bronze statuette of Nero, now in the British Museum, the fine craftsmanship of which is seen in the silver and niello inlay.[41] It must have belonged to an official cult shrine and taken out and deliberately broken and cast away, when Nero received the *damnatio* after his assassination in AD 68. A piece of bronze of this outstanding quality is hardly likely to have belonged to a native temple, but its military association is only a speculation. The site of this fort has been seen over the years in small lengths of ditches,[42] but in 1978, an aerial photograph taken for the Ordnance Survey shows it with remarkable clarity (Pl 22). There are, in fact, two superimposed forts of different periods, the larger had three ditches and is over 11 acres,[43] two opposing corners of the other are visible within the south-western part of the large enclosure, and it is about five and a half acres. It is not possible to assess their relationship, although the later is a normal-sized auxiliary fort.

Sites of three more forts on this route could be expected. The first

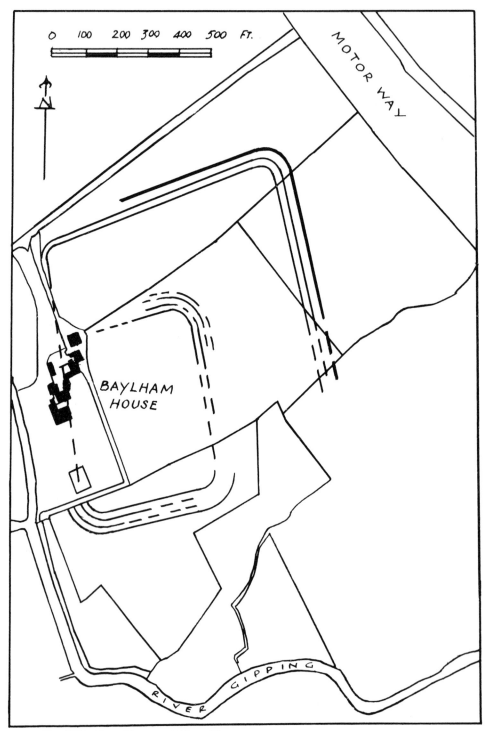

Plan V Baylham House – cf. Plate 22

Part of a fitted saddle-cloth weight from Baylham House, Suffolk (½)

should be at the Waveney crossing near Scole where the latter civil settlement developed on the north side of the river and although excavations here[44] have produced very little pre-Flavian material, there are
several military artefacts including a cuirass hinge, a fragment of a decorated officer's belt-mount and what could be a harness-band
buckle.[45] The fort is probably on the south side of the river where
traces of possible campaign camps have been noted.

The next site was probably near the later cantonal capital at Caistor
St Edmund at the crossing of the Chet, but the only scraps of evidence
to date are pieces of military equipment including a cuirass hinge now
in the Castle Museum, Norwich. To the north, the next site may be at
the Bure crossing and a 25-acre campaign camp has been observed by
Derek Edwards at Horstead-with-Stanninghall[46] so the permanent
fort maybe in this neighbourhood, possibly east of Brampton (No 11)
where the route meets the east-west route aimed for the coast at the
mouth of the Yare.

Forts on Route 3 (Peddars Way)

The first certain fort along this route is at Ixworth (No 12), where it was
first noted by Derrick Riley in 1945[47] and has since been under observation by Professor St Joseph.[48] This is a fine triple-ditched fort of
seven acres, south of the modern village. The next site is 20 miles away
to the north-north-west at Saham Toney (No 13) and there is probably
an intermediate fort about half way. The site near Saham Toney has

long been known as an important British settlement,[49] it lies on the Peddars Way and is on a small flat plateau, about 250 by 200 yards, overlooking a stream on the north side of which appears to be a large native settlement with continuing occupation into Roman times. A local resident, Robin Brown, has been watching these sites for some years, especially after ploughing, and picked up a number of objects from the surface.[50] Many of these have cavalry associations, but there are also pieces of legionary equipment. A military establishment was probably sited here near a large native community rather than in a position of strategic advantage.

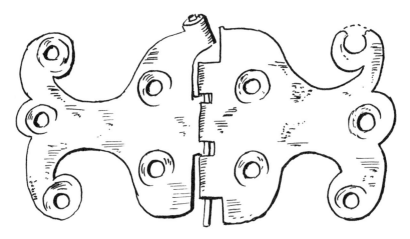

A pair of cuirass hinges from Caistor St Edmunds

The route continues in a straight line towards the Wash presumably to connect with an ancient ferry-point[51] and a fort (No 30) may be expected at its junction with the important east-west route at the crossing of the Nar.

Forts on Route 4
This was an important military route linking the Plautian rear-base and *Legio XX* with the frontier at Leicester (No L4), yet it was not a Roman road to survive for its full length and 25 miles of it near Colchester have vanished, but should be recoverable with careful fieldwork. The only known fort on its whole length is at Godmanchester (No 17, Durovigutum) where Michael Green's excavations over many years have brought to light much evidence of this site on the crossing of the Ouse, at the junction of another important route from London which meets the Fens on its way to Lincoln and the Humber. Traces of the defences and internal buildings of an early fort have been found to the south of the civil settlement.[52] The sites of two other forts can be extrapolated at the crossing of the Stour near Wixoe (No 15) and at Cambridge (No 16, Duroliponte) on the Cam, where, in spite of much

excavation, nothing of military significance has been noted. The fort may, like so many others, be on the south side of the river.

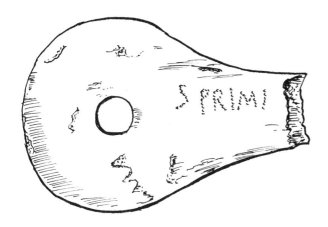

A pendant from the Lakenheath area

The stretch between Godmanchester and Leicester probably has at least two forts on it. The first of which is likely at the junction with the route along the Nene Valley from Towcester. In his work on a Roman bridge over an earlier course of the Nene at Aldwincle (No 18) by Dennis Jackson in 1967–71 found a concentration of prehistoric occupation and a baldric link of a Roman military type[53] lost by a soldier passing along this way. The other fort could be at the crossing of the Welland, or just beyond it at Medbourne (No 19), the site of a Roman settlement.

Forts on Route 5
This route due west of Camulodunum connected with the key nodal point in an early system at Braughing (No 22), where a fort must be expected. There ought also to have been one near Great Dunmow[54] (No 21) at the crossing of the Chelmer where there is a larger civil settlement and possibly another near Braintree (No 20) by the later civil settlement[55] at the Blackwater crossing.

The other routes of East Anglia help to complete the military network. One of these (Route 5) is parallel to Route 2, stemming from Chelmsford (No 5), proceeding north-north-west crossing the Stour at Long Melford[56] (No 23) a known civil settlement, joining Route 2 at Ixworth (No 12) and appears to continue towards the Brampton area in the Bure Valley, and a fort site may be extrapolated in the Crownthorpe-Morley area (No 27). Yet another important route, already mentioned is that starting from London, proceeding up the Lea Valley to Braughing (No 22), then on to Great Chesterford (No 25), where an early fort is known at the crossing of the Cam.[57] Excavations and aerial photographs have helped to piece together a reasonably convincing plan of a large fort of 35 to 37 acres lying below the northern half of the later Roman walled town[58]. The dating evidence suggests a Neronian rather than a Claudian occupation,[59] and it could be considered an excellent position for a rearward base in the aftermath of AD 60. This does not, of course, rule out the presence of a Plautian fort, but not necessarily on or near the same site and possibly on the Braughing road south of the river. This route then crosses the Granta to join the famous early trackway, the Icknield Way, which passes through the main concentration of Icenian sites in the Little Ouse Valley. The obvious wealth of this area, especially round Lakenheath[60] suggests that the Icenian capital may have been here. An area with such a comparative native density of occupation would have demanded a military presence (No 26), but no evidence has so far been produced[61]. North of this, the trackway merges with Route 2 towards the mouth of the Wash.

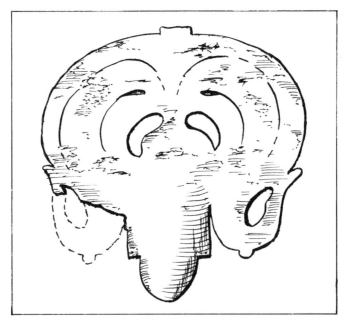

Part of a saucepan handle with a punched inscription: 'of the century of Primus' from Saham Toney

The only other Route (9) to be considered is another early trackway running almost east-west from the Fens across Norfolk through Brampton to the coast. To the west it picks its way across the Fen causeway making for the rich Fengate area in the Nene Valley, where it peters out, but from its general direction it may have been an ancient salt way from the important brine springs at Droitwich. At least three forts could be expected west of Brampton (No 11), the first at the crossing of the Wensum near Billingford, the second either at the crossing of Route 3 or of the Icknield Way at Castle Acre (No 29) and the third perhaps near Fincham. Another may be found west of March (No 31) where Timothy Potter has drawn my attention to a native site of the mid-first century and a kink in the road at a place called Stonea Camp[62].

This brief review of a possible military network of routes and forts deals almost exclusively with the interior, but it seems likely that the coastal areas would also be controlled, especially the main estuaries such as the Crouch, Orwell, Deben, Alde, Waverley and Yare. It would also have been necessary to restrict free movement of the Britons at the ferry-point at the ends of the Icknield Way and Peddars Way across the mouth of the Wash.

The military dispositions south of the Thames

The arrangement of forts in Kent has already been considered in the section on the advance to the Thames, but apart from forts at Canterbury (No 1) and Rochester (No 2) to protect the main supply route from Richborough to London, it is possible that it was necessary to watch the tribal movements to the south, and forts may have been placed along the North Downs trackway, on the Stour near Wye (No 41); perhaps near Maidstone (No 42) on the Medway and at the Darenth crossing (No 43) and that of the Mole, where this route crosses Stane Street near Dorking (No 44). The friendly areas of the Regini and Atrebates would have had their quota of troops and a route network can be suggested, but unlike East Anglia, there was the important sea route which enabled Vespasian to carry out his rapid advance and conquest.

There is also the continuation of Route 7 from London which was to become known as Stane Street.[63] In its length of 62 miles one might expect at least four fort sites at intervals of about 15 miles. The first out of London would have been buried under the suburbia, north of Ewell (No 133), and the second may have been at the junction of the Pilgrims Way (Route 12) and the crossing of the River Mole north of Dorking, where there could have been a small civil settlement (No 44). The third site is most probably at Alfoldean (No 132), at the crossing of the River Avon; a square defined enclosure of 2.5 acres bisected by the river and Stane Street, was investigated by S E Winbolt in the Twenties.[64] His conclusion, as with Hardham, the next site to the south was that it was a small posting station with a defended *mansio*; but it seems more likely to have been a small *burgus* like those along Watling Street.[65] Nothing very early has been found here, so if there is a fort here it may be on the north side of the river. A similar site at Hardham (No 35), the fourth possibility, is a definite rectangle of just over four acres. The pottery from this includes some Claudian pieces[66] and this to date is the only scrap of evidence from all four sites of the remote possibility of an early military presence.

The naval and supply bases along the south coast Route 10

The harbours which were the keys to this were established in Bosham, the Solent, Poole Bay and the Exe Estuary, all linked together with a coastal land route: Chichester (No L 2), Bittern (No 36), Lake Farm (No 54), Dorchester (No 34), Topsham (No S 3). Another possibility exists at the mouth of the Ouse where Newhaven Harbour now stands (No 33). Rescue excavations in the town centre in 1973 revealed a first-century ditch and a timber granary.[67]

Fishbourne (No S 2)

Apart from Newhaven, the most easterly of these bases was discovered in Bosham Harbour by Professor Barry Cunliffe.[68] It was an unexpected discovery below the great palace which has been associated with Cogidubnus, the British prince and an ally of Rome. Although only a small area of this primary occupation could be studied, enough was found to identify two timber buildings of a military type of construction. The foundations of Building 1, *c* 22 feet by 100 feet, consisted of at least six close-set rows of construction trenches, with posts at intervals, typical of a raised granary and similar to those at Richborough and elsewhere. Building 2, *c* 97 feet by 52 feet, had been built on six rows of posts (78 in all) spaced at 8 foot intervals and appears to be another raised granary or store building. The buildings are flanked by drainage gullies or eaves drips and gravelled ways, all set out in a precise military pattern. It is clearly part of a store-base and Professor Cunliffe estimated that the total area of this site could have been over 50 acres. The pottery was abundant and all pre-Flavian, with a few pieces of military equipment including the legionary helmet dredged out of the harbour[69], which shows that this was an army supply base in the Plautian phase, probably receiving cargoes directly from Gaul for the troops engaged in the conquest and occupation of southern Britain.

Bittern on the Solent (No 36)

The next site proceeding in a westerly direction along the coast is the important sea-entry into Britain provided by the Solent. Unfortunately, very little is known about the site on the River Itchen – now buried under a housing estate on the outskirts of Southampton. The excavations, started in 1938, were stopped by the war[70] but when further development was proposed, a rescue excavation was organized from 1951 on the western part of the site, the only area by that time free of building except the ruins of the Manor House, which in the

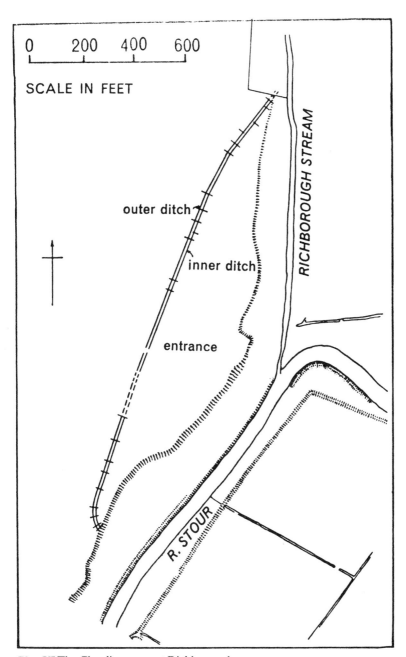

Plan VI The Claudian camp at Richborough

Middle Ages belonged to the See of Winchester. No early structural features were recognized but the amount of Claudian/Neronian samian[71] and Claudian coins, some of which were in fresh condition, seem to point to an early occupation. The only published equipment has been two prick-spurs of a military type[72]. The Roman name of the place was Clausentum, and its possible derivation from that of the Emperor Claudius has created speculation, but with no satisfactory conclusion.[73]

Hamworthy in Poole Bay (No S 5)

Another fine enclosed harbour existed in Poole Bay and early Roman pottery and a large hand-mill of Niedermendig lava[74] has been found at Hamworthy.[75] This site, with such interesting potential has been destroyed by gravel pits and the building of factories. Whatever existed here at this period will now never be known, but it must have been closely connected with the military establishment at Lake Farm (No 59), west of Wimborne Minster. It was discovered and investigated by a local archaeologist, Norman Field,[76] and further work was carried out on the site of a disused railway line in 1972–73.[77] Although this was on a very small scale it clearly demonstrated that it was a complicated site with possible associations with a works depôt.[78] Only a large-scale excavation will uncover the problems of what is obviously a military site which probably remained in use in the course of the later campaigns.

Topsham on the Exe Estuary (No S 3)

This was the most westerly of these coastal bases, but whether it was established as early as this or belongs to the next military phase is not clear, since very little is yet known about this site except that it has produced some early pottery[79] but this has no proven military connection.

The land routes

The most important nodal point of the routes south of the Thames was the capital of the Atrebates, Silchester (No 50, Calleva), where no less than six of them met.
They were:

13 From London where it linked with Camulodunum
14 South-east to Chichester (No L 2, Noviomagus) and the Bosham Harbour store-base (No S 2)
15 South to Winchester (No 56, Venta Belgarum) and the Solent
16 South-west towards Old Sarum (No 57, Sorviodunum) and to Shapwick (No 38) near Badbury where it joins the coastal route, No 15
17 North-west to Cirencester (No 62, Corinium) and the crossing of the lower Severn to Gloucester (No 63, Glevum)

18 North to the Thames crossing at Dorchester-on-Thames (No 66) into the South Midlands.

Route 13
The most important military site on this route was probably the crossing of the Thames at Staines (No 52, Pontes), indicating the presence of a bridge, and it is hardly surprising that military material has turned up in excavations with ditches and timber buildings.[80] Among the artefacts found was part of a helmet cheek-piece made of iron covered by a thin embossed bronze sheet, with the typical Roman cable-moulded border round a bust, but not enough of this survives for identification. It belonged to a well known type of cavalry helmet like the ones described from Leicester (see p 127 above), Brough on the Fosse and the Kingsholm site at Gloucester, and this indicates the presence of a cavalry unit base possibly at this time, and may account for the harness-mount found further along the road at Egham.[81] It is 25 miles from Pontes to Silchester (No 50) and a fort is possible at about the mid-point in the Bagshot area (No 51).

Route 14
The south-east route to Chichester may be a continuation of an ancient trackway to the north linking with the Jurassic Way. It passes through two almost equally spaced settlements (No 53) on the Wey and Iping (No 54). The former has produced a first-century ditch 6.5 feet by 6.5 feet, about the right dimensions for a fort with no military associations.[82] Chichester the terminal point, and a probable legionary site, has been considered above (p 125).

Route 15
This route runs south-west to Winchester (No 56) and presumably on to Bittern (No 36). There are no certain sites or forts, but Winchester (Venta) occupies such a key position at the Itchen crossing that it seems a highly likely possibility. The city has been subject to the most extensive series of excavations of any Roman town in Britain with the possible exception of London. They were part of a well-planned and executed scheme directed by Martin Biddle, but although they have been of enormous importance for Roman, post-Roman and medieval studies,[83] no trace has been found of any military activity.

There is a faint but tantalizing suggestion from the earlier excavations in St George Street, almost in the centre of the city.[84] When the contractor's trench went deeper than those of the excavator, it was observed that where the natural gravel had been levelled there were traces of rectangular timber buildings above which was a spread of destruction material,[85] which the excavator thought to be the result of a fire (Report p. 23). This in itself would not be significant, but for the collection of pottery from these levels (Report Fig. 13 Nos. 1 – 21).

This contains some small fine colour-coated bowls decorated with scale pattern and dot-covered roundels imported from Central Gaul and extensively used by the army at this period. Furthermore, the effect of burning could have been caused by the demolition when the fort was given up by the army. In the area immediately to the east there is on the Kingdon's workshop site further levelling to an astounding depth of six feet (Report p 23) which is explained as necessary to compensate for the natural slope of 1 in 20. This certainly looks like Roman engineering but the dating evidence although somewhat scanty, includes nothing later than the Claudian period. It was however, unusual to level military sites at this period since, in the palisade type of construction, the floors of buildings were laid horizontally and upright foundation posts cut to the appropriate lengths to provide for this on sloping or uneven ground. This large-scale levelling work at Winchester would fit more readily into the construction of the town, which presumably belongs to the late first-century and all the artefacts are residual, as so often is the case in massive earth-moving operations. Otherwise one can only assume that the site of any fort must lie outside excavated areas, even beyond the Roman and medieval city. The important factors would have been the ancient crossing points of the river and the presence of any British settlements.

Winchester is at the point where an important ancient trackway over the chalk uplands crosses the river, and there is an Iron Age hill-fort of modest size on St Catherine's Hill to the south. The problem of a pre-Roman settlement under Winchester itself has been a vexing one. There is a defended enclosure known as Orams Arbor, extending beyond the north-west limit of the Roman town and excavations in the Castle area have shown these defences to extend below the town, Martin Biddle has estimated its possible area as 46 acres (including the defences). Among the buildings found in the enclosure is a circular one with a four-post structure in an off-central position, which has been identified as an Iron Age shrine.[86] The pottery found in the early levels is entirely of local native types, including the so-called 'saucepan' pots, peculiar to the area east of Southampton Water.[87] A strong case has been made for the establishment of a native community here before the invasion, as it seems from evidence elsewhere that the pottery was in use in the century before the conquest.[88] Another possibility is that a fort may have been sited at a crossing to the north of the city in the Hyde area, the direction along which the route from the south appears to be aiming. Early Roman burials have been found here, but the area has been built over and also the ground has been drastically altered in levelling for the North Walls Recreation Ground, so there is little hope of further investigation.

One might also expect a fort between Winchester and Silchester and the junction with the ancient east-west trackway near Basingstoke is a possibility.

Route 16

This route is a continuation of Route 13 from London, joining the coastal route at Badbury (Vindocladia); a fort was discovered in 1975 from the air by John Boyden at Shapwick (No 38). As Norman Field has pointed out[89] it is clearly in a relationship to the Iron Age hill-forts at Badbury and Spettisbury, since there is a hint of the army in action at the latter. The new fort appears to be triple-ditched and is about six acres in size within its defences. Surface pottery indicates a mid-first-century-occupation, although only a detailed investigation will pin it down to a definite phase, but its obvious link with the Hod Hill route and the nodal forts makes it a strong candidate for the Plautian phase.

The other sites where forts may be expected between Shapwick and Silchester are at the crossing of the Avon tributaries near Old Sarum (No 57) at the crossing point by the river and it is significant that early samian has been recovered from Stratford-sub-Castle.[90] There is another possibility at the point where the ancient east-west trackway crosses the route at the settlement of Leucomagus (No 46) near East Anton, although there are no indications at present of a military presence.

Halfway between Old Sarum (No 57) and Shapwick (No 38) the route passes over Cranborne Chase, where the clusters of native settlements at Woodcuts and Rotherly were subject to the meticulous investigations of the great Pitt-Rivers[91]. This was an area which may have needed watching but the only evidence of military presence are the two ballista-bolts from Rotherly (No 58)[92] one of which was found in the filling of the ditch of the Main Circle. Following Richmond's suggestion of the distribution of similar missiles at Hod Hill, one might speculate that this was a target[93].

Route 17

This route is aimed towards the north-west at the lower Severn crossing at Gloucester (No 63) where there must have been an auxiliary fort in the pre-legionary Plautian phase. The evidence for this rests solely on the tombstone of Rufus Sita (P1; *RIB* 121) found in 1824 at Wotton, where there must have been a military cemetery on this route. It gives us the name of the unit (*Coh VI Thracum*) and presumably the fort is below the fortress of *Legio XX* at Kingsholme. The other fort which there is some certainty is at Cirencester (No 62, *Corinium Dobunnorum*) at the crossing of the Fosse Way. There are two tombstones of differerent units, Dannicus was a trooper of the *Ala Indiana* (P1 *RIB* 108) and Sextus Valerius Genialis, a trooper of the *Ala Thracum* (p1 *RIB* 109). It seems unlikely that these two crack units would have brigaded together and it could represent a change in establishment. There have been extensive excavations in the Roman city over recent years and pieces of cavalry equipment have been found.[94] Evidence of the site of a fort came in 1961 with the discovery of a stretch of its northern defences below the later basilica of this forum, but its size and shape have yet to be determined.[95] The position is complicated by the discovery of two other possible military sites one in the southern part of the town at Watermoor and the second in Chester Street. As the construction dates and sizes of the forts are not known, it is impossible to assess their relationships to each other or which belonged to the Plautian phase.[96]

Between Cirencester and Silchester, a fort could have been established at Wanborough (No 61), an extensive later settlement[97] which dates back to the mid-first century, and it has been suggested that the road itself was built in the mid 40s.[98] Another may have been the junction of the road from Bath, about four miles north-west of Newbury (No 60).

Route 18

This route, possibly part of an ancient trackway, runs almost due north to the important Thames crossing at Dorchester (No 66) and then to Alchester (No 67): The former is 20 miles from Silchester and there may have been a fort at the mid-way point where the Icknield Way crosses near Basildon (No 65). At Dorchester-on-Thames, there was a native settlement and a hint of a fort from a crop-mark south of the small town,[99] but this has not yet been tested. Alchester was another small Roman town at an important road junction and two items of cavalry equipment suggest the possibility of the presence of a fort.[100] The route joins Watling Street at Towcester (No 68, Lactodurum) a site which will be considered below (p 156) and continues north to meet the Jurassic Way.

The nodal point of this key route pattern is Silchester (No 50, Calleva) the capital of the Atrebates. The Roman town was subject to a complete stripping at the end of the last century by the Society of Antiquaries. The excavators totally ignored the lessons of the great pioneer work of Pitt-Rivers, and it is interesting to note that he resigned from the Excavation Committee, as soon as he realized the methods being adopted. It is ironic that the town plan so produced became a model example of the garden city, so attractive to the planners of the twenties and it has been accepted as the plan of a typical Roman town. Yet the failure of the excavators to observe any timber buildings completely invalidates it, since there were probably more of this construction that there were with stone foundations. The large-scale work produced a very large collection of objects which have pride of place in the Reading Museum. Among them is a small number of interesting military items, including parts of a cuirass from pit XXIII in the northern part of the town. They have been listed and some illustrated by Mr George Boon[101] and include four cuirass

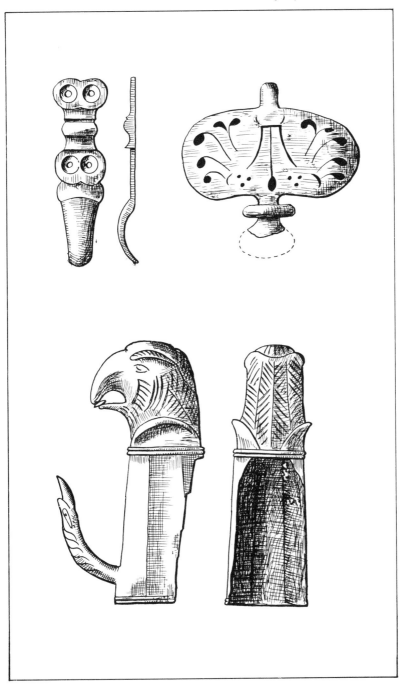

Top left Part of a baldric-clip from Gloucester (½)
Top right A harness pendant decorated with niello
Bottom An eagle-head rein-loop terminal from a cart   from Cirencester (½)

hinges, seven rosette studs, with scraps of iron, all from a *lorica segmentata*. In the general collection are two cuirass hooks, an apron mount, two nielloed belt-plates, several typical military buckles, a bronze toggle, and two possible cavalry items, i.e. a harness-clip and a heavy circular mount. This leaves little doubt about the presence of legionaries. The pit was probably the work of a demolition party when the fort was dismantled. The nineteenth-century excavation was restricted to the upper levels of the town and the remains of a fort would be several feet below the successive layers of civil buildings and deposits, so it is not surprising that any traces of military defences were never encountered. The street grid has been shown by Mr Boon to be Flavian in origin,[102] and the earlier town may have been on a different alignment, the relationship of this and the native *oppidum* to the fort will only be known when further large-scale excavations are carried out, this time in totality, until then speculation is useless.

Cross routes

The great eastway trackway (Route 12) across the Chalk uplands extends as far as Exeter (No 40) on the Exe, and probably beyond, but this is the limit of the Plautian frontier and there would in all probability have been an auxiliary fort here in this phase, although it has so far escaped observation. One would anticipate a fort also near Ilchester (No 49, Lindinis), where the road crosses the Fosse Way, unless Ham Hill (No 134) had been preferred (see p 159 below), one would expect at least three forts between Ilchester and the Leucomagus junction. Travelling from east to west, the first suitable point would be the Avon crossing, just north of Amesbury (No 135), the next is at the River Wylye crossing immediately to the west of which the important Winchester–Charterhouse route crosses obliquely. Pieces of cavalry equipment[103] have been found near here in the Iron-Age hill-fort at Bilbury Rings[104] but whether they are the residue of some captured loot, or are indications of the presence of a unit is difficult to judge, without any other evidence. Another possible site for a fort is at Stockton (No 47), at the crossing of Route 19. There was a very large native settlement here and this in itself could have required the presence of a unit. An apron-mount, early brooches and pottery of types often associated with military occupation have been found here.[105]

The trackway crosses two of the routes from Silchester on which forts have already been postulated, but further east, a useful control point could have been the crossing of the Wey near Guildford (No 45) where a castle reminds us of its significance as a defence position in the Middle Ages.

The next great cross-route (Route 19) to be considered is the one through Winchester (No 56) and Old Sarum (No 57), which may have extended eastwards along the South Downs to Iping (No 54) and Hardham (No 35). It continued westwards along the higher ground to the important silver deposits of the Mendips at Charterhouse. The first fort west of Old Sarum would have been that already suggested, at the Wylye crossing (No 47). Between this point and the Fosse Way a fort may have been sited half-way but the only evidence so far is a pelta-mount from Cold Kitchen Hill (No 77) and this is also the junction with Route 21[106]. Nothing is known of a fort at the Fosse crossing, although it would have been well placed half-way between Bath and Ilchester north of Shepton Mallet (No 78). The next to the west is at Charterhouse (No 79), where a fort is known,[107] presumably with troops to guard the valuable silver mines. A lead pig found in 1883 at Saint Valery-sur-Somme[108] bears a cast inscription of the name Nero followed by L 11, which must indicate that during the reign of this emperor, *Legio II Aug* was involved in silver production. There are, however, two earlier pigs, one found *c.* 1540, now alas lost, and another with a cold-struck stamp, both of which can be dated to AD 49.[109] The Route continued no doubt down to the mouth of the River Axe, where there is a small Roman settlement[110] at Uphill (No 80) south of Weston-Super-Mare.

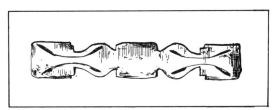

An apron-mount from Bilbury Camp, Wyle, Wilts (½)

One must add to the network some link routes. There is one (Route 20) from Winchester (No 56) to Wanborough (No 61), passing through Leucomagus (No 46) and Mildenhall (No 81, Cunetio), a small walled Roman town in Wiltshire, which has produced early coins and brooches, as well as imported pottery.[111] A well found below the footings of the west wall of the town produced a military apron mount with some Claudian pottery,[112] and an aerial photograph published by Professor St Joseph in 1953 shows a pair of ditches with a well-turned corner below the western part of the town.[113] and which have been assumed to have been civil since they appear to enclose an area of almost 15 acres. A section cut across these ditches has produced evidence of late pottery in the fill of one of them which seems to rule out an early origin.[114] One cannot discuss Mildenhall without including the remarkable deposit at Oare, about four miles to the south-west. This was described as a 'late Celtic rubbish heap' by the Cunningtons who investigated it in 1907 – 8.[115] It is a mixture of black earth and pottery, and has been re-studied by Vivien Swan,[116] who identifies it as a waste dump of a pottery works of the mid-first century, and clearly the vessels made here have little resemblance to the normal native late Iron Age types. The conclusion reached by Mrs Swan is that potters came here from the south-east to supply a new market, which she is probably correct in assuming would have been the Roman army, settling in and demanding the table and kitchen wares to which they were accustomed (see p 22 above). The factory established at Oare not only supplied Mildenhall, but its wares were found in military deposits at Cirencester (No 62), Rodborough Common in Gloucestershire (see p 22–23 above) and Nettleton Shrub (No 106, see p 116 above) At Huist Hill, near Oare, was found a very finely moulded penannular brooch with ribbed terminals of a type used by the army.[117]

Another link (Route 21) runs from Shapwick (No 38) in a northerly direction up the Stour Valley to Hod Hill (No 64), the most famous of all the Claudian forts, excavated in such superb fashion by Sir Ian Richmond. Norman Field has since found a metalled road at the foot of the hill[118]. Ploughing in the nineteenth century turned up a great collection of objects, many of which were collected by a local ironmonger named Durden, and it is said that he spent so much time and money on this hobby that he went bankrupt! This great collection was bought by the British Museum in 1862[119] and has always been considered indisputable evidence for the presence of the army. It is, however, surprising to find tucked away into a corner of the hill-fort an intriguing and unusual situation. It was a desire to find out more about the relationship of this fort to the hill-fort that prompted the Trustees of the British Museum to invite Sir Ian Richmond to carry out an excavation for them.[120] The plan he produced of the fort is a very odd one and tested Richmond's splendid deductive gifts. Serious abnormalities had been created by the presence of two different units, a cohort of legionaries and half an *ala* of cavalry[121]. It is a mixture which was potentially unwise, since the *ala* commander would have been an equestrian of higher social status than the centurion in charge of the legionaries, but the latter would normally have had much greater military experience. The difference is reflected in the sizes and internal arrangements of their living quarters, *praetoriae* 1 and 2. The equestrian officer was allocated 6565 square feet and the centurion only 4900 square feet,[122] the former also had a fine dining room with a row of columns to support clerestory lighting.

The dating evidence consists of 60 coins ending with Claudius[123] and the samian which has been studied by Dr Grace Simpson (Report pp 103–111). The 35 Claudian pieces impressed Dr Simpson by their striking differences in fabric and surface gloss from the later Neronian wares, and, although it is impossible to be so precise with the coarse wares, these too have a distinctly Claudian appearance (Report p 112).

This evidence suggests that the fort was abandoned by *c.* 50 and so belongs only to the Plautian phase.

This route if continued would have linked at a point (NGR 7429) about four miles east of Wincanton (No 48) with the great early east-west Downland trackway (Route 12) heading for Exeter (No 40) and mentioned above (p 139). Extended northwards beyond this it would have joined the Fosse Way at its crossing point with Route 19 near Shepton Mallet (No 78).

Another useful cross-route (22) would have run east-west from Mildenhall (No 81) to Bath (No 82) and beyond to the mouth of the Avon at Sea Mills (No 126). It starts from a point on Route 17, where a fort site has been postulated near Newbury (No 60). Almost halfway between Mildenhall and Bath is a Roman settlement at Sandy Lane (No 83, Verlucio)[124]and where one would be tempted to look for a military site. A fine martingale with a projecting horse's head which could be military has been found at Easton Grey.[125] The western terminal would have been a small but useful harbour for the fleet and also a ferry-point for crossing the Bristol Channel. Enough evidence has come from Sea Mills (No 126 Abona) to mark this as an early fort site[126]and possibly a naval base which was probably occupied at this period and in subsequent phases.

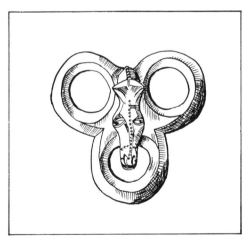

A martingale with a projecting horse's head
from Easton Grey, near White Walls, Wilts (½)

The hostile territory of north Wiltshire with its hill-forts would also have been tightly held in a military net-work. A cross-route (No 23) bisecting this large area would have connected Old Sarum (No 57) and

Sandy Lane (No 83). There are two stray military objects which seem to be unconnected with any suggested route. One comes from Casterly Camp at Upavon, which was excavated by the Cunningtons in the early part of the century.[127] This produced a large quantity of material which included some early, probably pre-conquest, imported Roman pottery and a circular harness mount.[128] The other object, a belt-mount, decorated with niello was found at Manton Down.[129] Another possible site is at Westbury Ironworks, where early pottery and brooches have been found.[130]

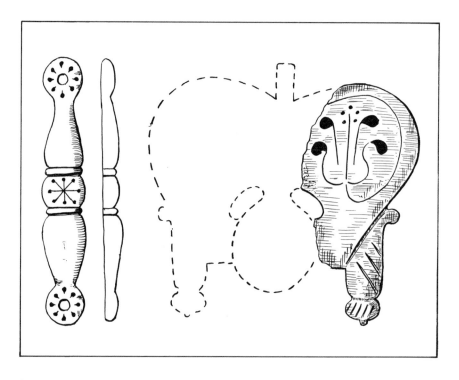

Left A belt-mount from Manton Down, near Casterley Camp, Wilts (½)
Right Part of a large harness pendant decorated with niello from Sea Mills (½)

The routes north of the Thames and the South Midlands

A nodal point for the early route system appears to have been Verulamium (no 84), an important pre-conquest centre which was to become the capital city of the Catuvellauni. In the rescue excavation directed by Professor Frere in 1956 along Bluehouse Hill, a section was cut through the north-east defences of the Roman city. Buried below the later rampart was an early one of turf, the front of which was revetted in timber. Below it was nothing but a humus layer from which were recovered fragments of coin moulds from a Celtic mint. On the tail of the bank were fragments of a building burnt in the great conflagration of the Boudican sack in AD 60. The published section[131] is ideal for teaching stratigraphy, structual relationships and historical implications. Unfortunately, nothing more is known of these defences, or the size of the fort, but military objects have turned up in earlier excavations[132] while others are published in Professor Frere's report, although not always identified as such.[133] They appear to indicate both legionary and cavalry items of equipment.

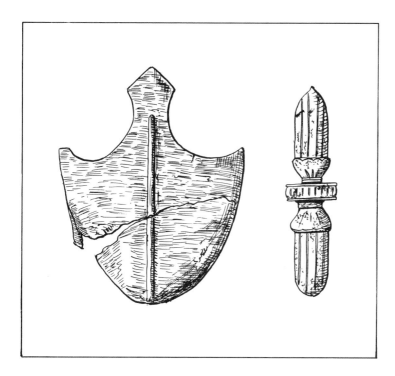

A bronze dagger chape from Verulamium (½)
An acorn mount from Cow Roast, Northchurch (½)

A bronze dagger chape from Verulamium
An acorn mount from Cow Roast, Northchurch

The routes from Verulamium can be listed as follows:

24 South to join the London–Silchester road
25 South-west to Silchester (No 50)
26 Westerly to Alchester (No 67) and Cirencester (No 62)
27 North-west (Watling Street) to Mancetter (No 95)
28 North-west to Baldock (No 96) then north to Lincoln (No 72)
29 East to Braughing (No 22)

Route 24

This route clearly begins as an off-shoot from the main route to the west, and a fort might be expected half-way to Verulamium at Brockley Hill (No 85, Sulloniacis) where a large pottery factory later became established.

Route 25

This route extended Nos 5 and 29 from Camulodunum and Braughing (No 22) and linked the two tribal centres passing through the Chilterns and crossing the Thames, presumably near Reading. There are at present no indications of any forts along this, but in the length of 40 miles, two might be expected possibly one near Latimer (No 86) and the other near Henley (No 87).

Route 26

This was the main westerly link with the Fosse frontier joining it at Cirencester (No 62). There are indications in the Tring Gap of a fort at the oddly named place Cow Roast (No 88), a mile north-west of Northchurch, with pieces of military equipment found in excavations there.[134] In 1811, a fine bronze legionary helmet, now in the British Museum, was found during the construction of the canal[135] at Dodswell, half-a-mile away, it is of a Claudian type like the one from Bosham Harbour. A site for a fort might be considered more likely a little further to the north-west at the junction of the route with the Icknield Way. The siting at the Cow Roast was probably due to a native concentration there, and for which there is some evidence from the excavations. There may have been an Iron Age fort at the significantly named Aldbury, which overlooks this narrow valley. The Cow Roast, includes imitation coins of Claudius, early brooches, a skillet handle, an unusual belt-mount of opposed acorns (p 153) and a hinge from a *lorica segmentata*. The evidence from Alchester (No 67) has already been noted (p 146) and a half-way point between here and Corinium would indicate a fort at the crossing of the Windrush near Asthall (No 131), where there is a small settlement.[136] From here there may have been a link-route to Dorchester (No 66) with a mid-point fort at the Thames crossing near Standlake (No 130).

Route 27

This follows the road later to become known as Watling Street, the important trunk road from London to the north-west and Ireland. At this early period it was a link route with the frontier, although its significance was soon to be realized when London became the main nodal point of the Roman road system. There were almost certainly forts along it, firstly at the edge of the Chilterns where it crosses the Icknield Way, near Dunstable (No 90) the small Roman settlement of Durocobrivis.[137] In spite of considerable excavation and constant watching by an amateur local society, no trace of a fort has come to light, and it may, like so many more, be some distance from the civil site. This certainly applies to the next place at the crossing of the Oussel near Bletchley which developed on the west bank. The small settlement of Magiovinium has long been recognized at Dropshort Farm (No 91) and the outlines of two forts of different periods have shown up as crop-marks in a field to the south-west of Watling Street, and a trench cut for a water main revealed a ditch system and Neronian pottery was recovered from one of them.[138]

Route 28

This route strikes north-east to Baldock (No 96), where it joins an important route (5) from Camulodunum, which swung north from Braughing to skirt the Fens margin. Baldock was a place of some wealth and importance in the late Iron Age, as rescue excavations by Dr Ian Stead and chance finds have clearly shown[139] and the site of a fort should be in this vicinity. The route continues north to Sandy (No 97), skirting the river Ivel. As at Baldock, intensive market gardening has been responsible for the discovery of large collections of material over the years.[140] There is a considerable pre-conquest settlement on the high ground to the north and east but this had spread into the valley by the time of the conquest.[141] A fort may have been placed on the east-west trackway which may originally have started from Camulodunum[142] and this presumably would have extended from Sandy to Irchester (No 69). No specific military associations are known at Sandy, although there is an amusing reference to a 'Roman sword' being found in such a remarkable state of preservation that the landowner, Captain Peel, had it copied for his service in India.[143]

The route continued to Godmanchester (No 17) but soon after this divides, one branch aimed at Leicester (No L 4) is a continuation of the main communication link (Route 4) with Camulodunum, and has been considered above. The other branch ending at the Humber, crosses the Nene Valley by Water Newton (Durobrivae) and there are two military sites. On the north bank of the river stands the legionary base at Longthorpe (No L 3) (see p 123 above), but on the south side of the Nene is the unmistakeable outline of an auxiliary fort (No 32). This has been known from air photographs published as long ago as 1930 by O G S Crawford,[144] but it has not yet been excavated, it could either have preceded or succeeded Longthorpe and a special case could be made for either, so it is better to wait for some evidence.[145]

The next site along this route should be at the crossing of the River Tove at Towcester (No 68), where the Roman town of Lactodurum developed. A very long route traceable from Chichester (No L2), crosses Watling Street at this point and continues in a north-east direction towards the Fens along the Nene Valley. No military finds have been made at Towcester, but it is possible that a fort would have been built on the high ground to the south overlooking the valley and is now either buried under a housing estate or all traces have been removed by the construction of the race course.[146] Proceeding along the Watling Street route one reaches Whilton Lodge (No 92), the Roman walled settlement of Bannaventa. When part of this was excavated to build a marina connected with the Grand Union Canal, nothing early was found[147] but a fort could have been established on the south side of the settlement where a unit could have kept an eye on the large hill fort on Borough Hill near Daventry.[148]

The next probable site is near the Roman settlement of Tripontium at Caves Inn (No 93), north of Rugby, but the only piece of evidence is a fine bronze saucepan of typical campaign issue, almost identical with others from Gloucester and Broxstowe. It was found in gravel workings about a mile to the south[149] of the later civil settlement, but the landscape has now been so changed that it is impossible to know if this single find is indicative of a fort here. The next two sites at High Cross (No 94) and Mancetter (No 95) are considered in the section on the frontier (p 165).

Beyond the Nene, the route divides, one branch striking due north skirts the Fens through Bourne to Sleaford, while the other Route (30) loops round to the west where there was a fort at the crossing of the Wash at Great Casterton (No 70). This was found in 1951 by Professor St Joseph during a year of exceptional drought, unfortunately, it came just too late, as houses were already being built over part of it. Two seasons of excavations were possible as an extension of a summer training school by the extramural department of the University of Nottingham under the direction of Dr Philip Corder. There were in fact two forts, the later (5.16 acres) being a reduction of the earlier (6 acres) which was a double-ditch enclosure. The ditches joined at the gates like Hod Hill.[150] Both forts are large and probably held mixed units; unfortunately, very little equipment was found, so it is impossible to suggest the types of unit, except that a length of *pilum* head may indicate legionary presence, as may also an iron ring with a superb engraved intaglio. This shows an eagle standing on a round pedestal between two centurial standards (Pl 12) and which could have been the ring of a legionary centurion. There was enough Claudian samian to make it fairly certain that the first fort belongs to the Plautian phase. A construction trench of the second phase, however, produced a coin of AD 60 – 68 which fixes this change of garrison probably to the movement of *Legio IX* to Lincoln, but that will be considered in due course.

The next fort along the route is at Ancaster (No 71), where the river Slea cuts through the Jurassic ridge. Excavations have produced details of the defences[151] and a possible gate.[152] The size of the fort is not yet known although the east – west width has been suggested as 420 feet.[153] The route proceeds from Ancaster in a direct northerly line, as if it is deliberately aimed at the Humber crossing, and the way the Fosse joins it south of Lincoln suggests that this is the earlier alignment of the two.

The area of Lincolnshire to the east of this route and north of the undrained Fens must have had some military control, and fortunately an indication of this comes with the discovery of a fort at Kirmington (No 98) from the air by Derrick Riley (Pl 21).[154] Observations over several years have helped to build up a plan of a large 8.5-acre double-ditched fort with a later civil settlement sprawling over it. A military post here would have guarded a gap through the Wolds which has since attracted a railway line and main road. It is also on the line of a Wolds trackway which presumably made its way towards the north edge of The Wash, where a ferry point must have existed connecting across with the north end of the Icknield Way on the Norfolk coast. The fort on the Lincolnshire side may have been at Burgh-le-Marsh (No 100), where a concentration of finds suggests a late settlement. A half-way point on the Wolds route could have been on the Bain Gap at Burgh-on-Bain, (No 99), another suggestive place-name. The only other possibility in this large area is the native site at Old Sleaford (No 101). This large and important site was excavated by Mrs MU Jones in 1960–61[155] and one of the most significant finds was the four thousand odd fragments of clay coin moulds, one of the largest finds from any Celtic site clearing indicating the presence of an important mint. Not enough coins of the Coritani have been found to indicate a definite division of the tribe with centres at Old Sleaford and Leicester.[156] As in other cases one element may have been more pro-Roman than the other, which could account for Leicester prospering as the tribal capital, while Old Sleaford became a minor settlement. A unit in this vicinity may have been needed under Plautius, although it is only eight miles from Ancaster (No 71).[157]

Midland cross-routes

This still leaves a very large area north-west of Watling Street between Towcester (No 68) and Dunstable (No 40). There is in the northern section of this area a suggestion of a route from Sandy (No 97) to Whilton Lodge (No 92), passing by the settlement at Duston, near Northampton, where sand extraction has turned up a large amount of pottery[158] including early sherds now in the Northampton Museum. A mid-point position on such a route would be at Harrold (No 102) on the Ouse, where Tony Brown has investigated an important pottery factory[159] providing kitchen wares in the mid-first century in a sophisticated type of kiln which may, as at Rushden, reflect a sudden introduction of new techniques, perhaps in the wake of the army and even supplying local units.

The area south of the junction of the Fosse Way and Watling Street at High Cross (No 94) is at present a large blank triangle. One cross route is the old salt-way from Droitwich, which crosses the Avon at Tiddington, a short distance upstream from the later crossing at Stratford-on-Avon, one branch would have been south-east to Alchester (No 67) to join the route to the south-west. There is a possibility that another branch made a more easterly turn towards Towcester (No 68) and stretched even beyond towards the Essex coastal inlets. Although this is highly speculative, it may help to indicate possible military sites, such as one at the crossing of the upper reaches of the Cherwell (No 104). Similarly, on the southern branch of the Avon, one might find a fort near Lower Lea (No 105) where there is a large Roman settlement.

Perhaps the most important cross-route is a major route which, through adopting the system of nodal points, has so far escaped attention. This starts from Bosham Harbour on the south coast and proceeds north through Silchester (No 50, Route 14), Dorchester-on-Thames (No 66) and Alchester (No 67) to Towcester (No 68, Route 18). There is then an unfortunate gap in the map of Roman Britain, but there must have been a route and, later a road, along the Nene Valley[160] to Durobrivae and thence to skirt the Fens margin. The only fort not already accounted for on this long route (No 18) must be near the small walled town at Irchester (No 69) on the Nene, but the excavations there in 1962–63 failed to produce any sign of a military presence,[161] and the only evidence for this still remains part of a belt-buckle in the Northampton Museum. The excavation showed a large spread of early material below and beyond the south defences of the town, and this has been claimed as a pre-conquest occupation, but just how much of the pottery can be placed in this early context is doubtful. Jeremy Knight has suggested that the early site was possibly the civil occupation attached to a fort (Report p 113), which he concludes is likely to be found on the river edge under the northern part of the town. Aerial photographs of the town show a very strange street pattern[162] but there is no trace of a road to a gate on the river side of the defences, and this seems to indicate that the bridge position had been established in the military period, and that it was to one side, probably the east, of the town. Providing, of course, that there was a north-south route, for which there is at present little evidence.

What may be a find of some significance is the quite extraordinary pottery from a site near Rushden, but actually in the parish of Irchester (Nat Grid SP943660). This was the result of a rescue excavation in advance of levelling for playing fields and was directed by Peter Woods.[163] He found pottery kilns of sophisticated types of the Claudian-Neronian period, some of the pottery from which includes vessels of a most unusual shape decorated in red and yellow slip with incised patterns of squares and 'ladders'.[164] Nothing like this is known in Britain and the only possible explanation seems to be that potters from a distant part of the Empire followed troops to Britain to make pottery familiar to them.

The Fosse Way Frontier (Route 34)

Perhaps the most important element in the Plautian scheme was the frontier itself and the communication link in the rear. The basic concept and date has been considered above (p 123) and the sites along its abnormally long stretch must now be considered. The names attached to the Roman roads are, of course, post-Roman and have no relationship to the original stretches or functions. This frontier route, known as the Fosse Way, began in the south-west at Exeter (No 40, Isca) at the head of the Exe Estuary. This inlet supplied a valuable harbour for the Fleet and its base was presumably at Topsham (No S 3, see p 142 above) and it is probable that there was an auxiliary fort at Exeter itself, which remains to be found below the later legionary base.

There would in all probability have been a fort at the crossing of the River Otter north-east of Honiton (No 136), where the route was joined by the coastal link-route (No 10) considered above (p 140) and where a spur with steep slopes on the west side of the river is guarded by the massive Iron Age defences of Dumpdon Camp.[165] Another link route may have branched away to the south towards Axmouth and Seaton on the coast, where some first-century material has been found at the Honeyditches villa by Henrietta Miles, but there are no obvious military connections.[166]

The next site along the route is Ham Hill (No 134), which dominates the landscape. There is an extensive 200-acre Iron Age hill fort on the top, one of the largest in Britain, unfortunately, the hill consists of a very fine building stone which has been quarried since the early Middle Ages, if not before, and since this is such a long established practice, it cannot be legally stopped without very large compensation.[167] The quarrying has uncovered large areas of the hill top and one can see in the vertical sides of the cuttings the outlines of pits and structual features, and the work over the years has produced a great deal of material, most of which is in the County Museum of Taunton.[168] Some of this has come from the quarry workers, but most from the excavations of H St George Gray,[169] the great Somerset antiquary who had been Pitt-Rivers' assistant. The large number of finds include military equipment, which is outstanding in its quality and almost certainly legionary, although the large fragment of scale-cuirass could have been from an auxiliary and there are some cavalry pieces. The quality of finds and the dominant position of the site gives a clear indication of the probable presence of a fort inside the Iron Age fort, as at Hod Hill (No 64), although there is as yet no structual evidence noted.[170]

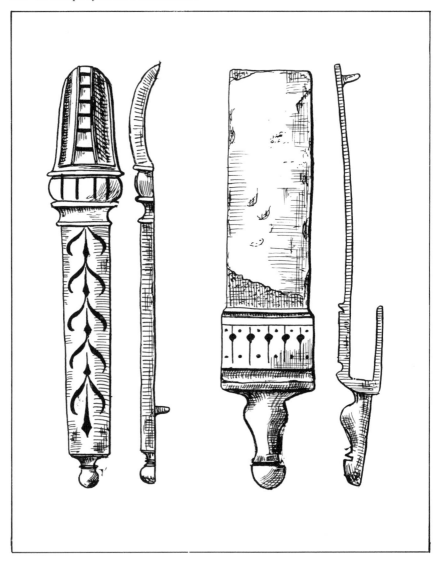

Left Part of a baldric clip with niello decoration
Right An apron-mount with tinned surface and niello inlay from Ham Hill

Five miles along the route is Ilchester (No 49, Lindinis) on the River Parrett at the junction of the east-west trackways and also the route from Dorchester (No 39) to the south-east. A military presence could be expected here, but it is too near to Ham Hill (No 134) for two forts to have been occupied at the same time, so one could have replaced the other in the next phase when legionaries were needed for new forward positions under Scapula. Large scale rescue excavations under John Casey have been carried out recently, but although there is an undoubted first-century occupation, no trace of military presence has been detected.[171]

The route changes its alignment at Ilchester, now pointing in a north-easterly direction towards Lincoln (No 72), and it is interesting to note that it does not deviate in the whole of this long length more than five miles from a straight line. The next fort site might be expected north of Shepton Mallett (No 78) at the crossing with the east-west link route from Winchester (No 56) to Charterhouse (No 74) and the mouth of the Axe. The next key site is at Bath (No 82, Aquae Sulis), where the fine hot springs provided a focus for one of the largest temple-spas of the Roman world. If there is a fort site here it will be found beyond the marshy ground round the famous spring, possibly on the east side of the river in the vicinity of Henrietta Park and Sydney Gardens. A fort here would have guarded the river crossing of an early trackway (Route 35) from the hills to the west. The area is dominated by the large Iron Age single ditch fortress on Bathampton Down, and a fort here would have been more secure and also occupied a commanding position, but little is known of this native site. As noted above (p 87) the military tombstone of L. Vitellius Tancinus, a trooper of the *Ala Vettones* (*RIB* 159) should now be considered no earlier than Vespasian and so he must have died while seeking a cure. Proceeding along the route, the small settlement at Camerton has been extensively excavated without producing any military evidence; further on, evidence[172] for a fort at Nettleton Shrub (No 106) has been accepted by the Ordnance Survey.[173] In the excavations of this fascinating religious site, items of military equipment and early pottery types[174] used by the army elsewhere have been found, although the site of the actual fort has not yet been securely established. Further along at a convenient distance is a small settlement – White Walls (No 107), where early pottery of distinctive types has been identified by Mrs Swan and a fine martingale has turned up nearby at Easton Grey; this gives hope of the eventual discovery of military presence. The next proven fort site is at Cirencester (No 62), considered above (p 145), at an important junction of six routes which form a fascinating pattern round the city. The Fosse Way, for example, makes a sharp angle to join the road from Alchester (No 67), and if projected, seems to be aimed at the north gate of the Roman city. One of the roads is the White Way, an earlier trackway from the north, and along which may have travelled the salt traders from the brine springs at modern Droitwich. This passes by the great Iron Age *oppidum* at Bagendon, where small scale excavations by Mrs Clifford have produced interesting early material (see p 60 above). It is difficult to project the original military routes until more is known of the sites, sizes and chronological order of the forts (see above p 115).

Continuing along the route, the first possible fort site beyond Cirencester is at the crossing of the Windrush near Bourton-on-the-Water

(No 108), where there was a branch route north towards Alcester (No 103) in South Warwickshire, and also the large and important 56-acre Iron Age stronghold at Salmonsbury. The work of many years by Helen O'Neil has shown how rich this area was in pre-Roman occupation, and a fort on the level ground at the foot of the Cotswold escarpment is a distinct possibility, although no trace has so far been observed. Another suggestion is the small settlement at Dorn, eight miles away, but there is no evidence here either and perhaps a better site would have been the crossing of the Stour at Halford[175] (No 109). The level of evidence does not improve as one proceeds further along the route – the next possible site, for example, is Chesterton (No 110), a walled settlement on the Fosse, but in spite of excavation, not a shred of evidence has appeared, and it is now more likely that the military site may be some distance away.[176]

A site where considerable military activity could well be expected is High Cross (No 94, Venonae) at the important junction with Watling Street, but in spite of constant vigilance from the air and some rescue excavations, nothing has been detected, except for a possible signal station less than an acre in size which was originally noticed by Professor St Joseph to the west of the road-crossing and investigated by Miss Elizabeth Blank.[177] Proceeding further one arrives at Leicester (No L4), considered above (p 125) as the possible base of *Legio XIV* in the Plautian scheme. The next possibility is at Willoughby (No 111, Vernemetum)[178] but there is no evidence to report. About 25 miles from Leicester lies Margidunum No 112, a place of great interest to the student of the development of Romano-British studies. It is here that Dr Felix Oswald, a learned and indefatigable local archeologist, excavated almost single-handed over 20 years what he claimed to be a Claudian fort.[179] It always was an anomalous site and it is now seen as a later defended civil settlement, but there is no doubt about its early origin, and the great quantities of iron slag in the first century layers has suggested that it could have been a military works depôt during this period.[180] It seems unlikely, however, that such an establishment would have been in a forward position and it seems more possible that there was a fort here under Plautius and the iron works belonged to a later military phase.

Eight miles further along the Fosse is Thorpe-by-Newark (No 113), (Ad Pontem) at a crossing of the Trent[181] The aerial photographs published by Professor St Joseph[182] clearly show the several phases of defences, both military and civil. Of the attempts to interpret them by excavations,[183] the most recent has been that of John Wacher, who established at least two military periods,[184] but this needs to be confirmed by better dating evidence and some identifiable military objects. Only seven miles along the route is Brough (No 114 Crococalana), another small settlement at which a military site has been postulated, on the strength of a cheek-piece of a cavalry parade

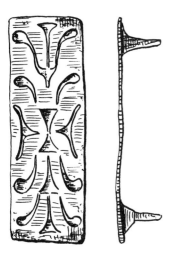

A belt-mount with emplacements
for niello inlay from Margidunum, Notts

helmet,[185] (pl 11) now in Newark Museum. This depicts Epona, the
Celtic goddess of horses[186] in relief. Although aerial photographs by
Professor St Joseph[187] show a mass of pits and ditches, there is no hint
of any crop-marks of a military character. If there had been a military
cavalry unit there, it seems unlikely on the basis of distance that it was
at the time when Thorpe was also occupied, and it is possible that there
was a shift in the dispositions of units in the subsequent changes in the
frontier.

Lincoln (No 72), the next site, occupies a key position on the
Witham Gap with considerable military significance which is reflected
in its history. It became the fortress of *Legio IX*, but not until AD 65 or
66 when Nero withdrew *Legio XIV* from Britain and this does not
belong to our present study.[188] In the period AD 43 – 65, it is almost
certain that a military presence would have been established here
although there are few indications; however, the odd changes in the
line of the Fosse Way may be one of them. As it approaches Lincoln it
makes a sudden change of direction and if its alignment is continued it
is seen to be directed at the South Common where it could have joined
the route from the south which was probably established first. This
raises the possibility of an early fort in this area.[189] Excavations in 1972
on the south of the river on the site of Holmes Grainhouse have produced early material with a native type hut below timber buildings of a
military type[190] and similar buildings were also encountered between
Saltergate and Silver Street in the south-east corner of the lower
colonia.[191] But these discoveries have been on such a small scale that it
is not possible to decide whether there are early forts here, or, as

should seem more probable by the river, a store-base by the quay-side.

At Lincoln the Fosse Way route turns almost directly north along the edge of the escarpment to the crossing of the Humber, and at Old Winteringham (No 75) a first-century fort has been postulated on the site of a villa.[192] This is based on the presence of buildings of a military type of construction, two early roads, coins and pottery. There were five coins of Claudius and one of Tiberius (Report p 39) and 13 pieces of pre-Flavian samian (Report pp 102 – 103) and the other fine wares are also early (Report pp 127 – 135) but the group is very similar to that from North Ferriby on the other side of the Humber, and this raises the possibility of this early material having been the result of pre-conquest trade.[193] A few military objects would make a fort here virtually certain, but the excavations could only produce two lengths of bronze scabbard binding (Report Fig 114 Nos 132 and 133) and a fragment of a possible axe-head sheath (*ibid* No 141).[194] There is no doubt that a Claudian fort ought to have been hereabouts.

There are probably two intermediate sites between the Humber and Lincoln, one at Hibaldstow (No 74) and the other at Owmby (No 73). Extensive rescue excavations[195] at the former have not produced any indication, but there is from Owmby in the Scunthorpe Museum, a cuirass-hinge and a military type buckle.[196]

The outposts beyond the Fosse Way

The limits of the actual frontier are difficult to define and would not necessarily have been fixed lines like the international frontiers of today, but areas under patrol and surveillance. It is most likely, however, that rivers played a significant role, especially the Trent and the Severn, but this would have left a stretch of some 70 miles in the centre where the small streams like the Avon, Alne and Soar could not have provided any effective protection from sudden attack. Efforts would have been made to establish and maintain friendly relations with the peoples in these areas so that advance warning of any assault could be given. The units in these vulnerable areas would have been mounted and the more expendable *cohortes equitatae* would have been chosen rather than the *alae*. The only one to have been identified is the sixth cohort of Thracians at Gloucester (No 63, *RIB* 121). A list of possible out-post forts is given in a north to south order and the first two are on the east bank of the Trent.

1 If there is a fort at Hibaldstow (No 74), another should be found due west on the Trent where the little River Eau joins it, or by the old ferry point at Owston (No 115).

2 There is firmer evidence for the next site at Littleborough (Segolocum), where there is a posting station on the west bank connected to Lincoln by Tilbridge Lane. An earthwork on the east bank

was seen by Stukeley[197] but all traces of it have long since vanished. It may, however, be the crop-mark recorded by Professor St Joseph in 1976, half a mile west of Marton (No 116)[198] where a fort has been placed by the OS. To the south of this, the Trent runs close to the Fosse Way.

3 Outposts beyond the river can be anticipated. One has been found at Broxstowe(No 118) on the north-western outskirts of Nottingham. Unfortunately, this site disappeared below a housing estate before its significance was realized and it has only been identified by the finds in the Castle Museum in Nottingham and Margidunum Collection in the University.[199]

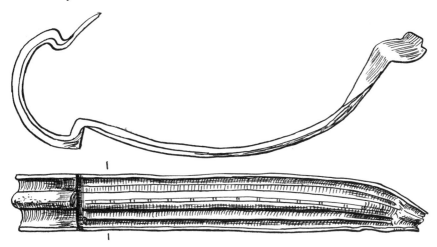

A scabbard-mount from Broxstowe, Notts

4 A post half-way between Broxstowe and Littleborough would be in the Bilsthorpe-Eakring area (No 117). A scatter of late Roman finds to the west suggests that a route was eventually established to Temple-borough, probably with branches to Chesterfield and Doncaster.

5 Moving south-west again, a site suggests itself on the road linking Littlechester (Derventio) with Vernemetum (No 111) on the Fosse at the crossing of the Soar between Ratcliffe and Thrumpton (No 119).

6 The alignment of the modern road B 567 may reflect an early link with Leicester through Charnwood Forest to a possible fort site near Whitwick and Swannington (No 120). This is a mid-point position between the Soar crossing and the next known fort.

7 Mancetter (No 95 Manduessedum) on Watling Street is a site which was to have considerable military significance in the next phase as the probable legionary base of *Legio XIV*. It is a very complicated site,[200] and it may be a long time before a fort of the Plautian phase can be identified. The distance from here to the next known out-post fort at Alcester (No 103), Warwickshire, is almost 30 miles, and continuing with the same line of reasoning, a mid-point site may be found at the crossing of the Blythe in the vicinity of Temple Balsall (No 121).[201] The presence of an early fort has been suggested at The Lunt, famous for its Neronian military establishment, but the only evidence of earlier occupation is in the form of a remarkable decorated samian jug (Déchelette form 62) dated to AD 30 – 45[202] and now in the Ashmolean Museum, Oxford. It was found in fragments in gravel workings by a local antiquary, J H Edwards,[203] but among the many finds he re- covered, some of which are in the Coventry City Museum, there is nothing to suggest a military presence. Such a fine piece of treasured tableware could be expected to have a long life, and in itself cannot suggest an early fort in this intermediate position on the frontier.

8 An aerial photograph by Arnold Baker has given us a fort at Alcester (No 103), some distance south of the later Roman town on the hill overlooking the River Alne, a typical strong defence position to be expected for an out-post fort facing potentially dangerous terrain. The date has yet to be established by excavation. Looking to the south-west, the next known site is at Gloucester (No 63, Glevum)

9 A mid-point position on the Avon would be Eckington (No 122), where a unit could have kept an eye on the concentration of settle- ments on and around Bredon Hill.[204] It is very easy to pin-point fort sites on a map from the comfort of an arm-chair, and although the Roman commander did not have this great benefit, he could hardly have failed to notice the very large area inside the quadrilateral Eckington-Burton-Cirencester (Glevum). He may have felt the need for a post somewhere in the middle of this to watch the White Way (Route 35), an early trackway. A suitable point is perhaps near Whit- tington, at the site known as Andoversford (No 123), where a large Roman settlement was to develop.[205] This area includes the remark- able Belgic-type *oppidum* at Bagendon which must have featured in the early conquest as it was the capital of the northern Dobunni. Small scale excavations by Elsie Clifford in 1954 – 56 produced a wealth of in- teresting material which has led to much speculation over its date.[206] The latest opinions favour an immediate pre-occupation date i.e. AD 20–40 for trading contacts with the Roman world, but the view expressed by Geoff Dannell, that this ended abruptly with the conquest[207] has been challenged by Vivien Swan.[208] She considers the imported non-samian wares indicate some occupation after the conquest, which could even have military associations if the identi- fication of the Savernake ware from Oare is upheld by petrological examination. The same thinking could apply to the area south-west of Gloucester-Cirencester, bounded by the Severn and the Fosse, and one then has the choice of two possible sites, one at Rodborough

Common (No 137), Gloucestershire and the other at Kingscote (No 124) on the southern part of the White Way, as it traverses the high ground towards the Avon crossing at Bath (No 82). The Rodborough Common site has been suggested as a fort by Vivien Swan[209] on the strength of pottery found in the excavation of 1954–56.[210] This is Claudian and includes Savernake ware from the Oare factory, but Mrs Swan also points out the discovery of a V-shaped ditch and possible military equipment in the published report. The plan of the ditch certainly shows a right-angle turn (Report Fig 1) and a section of the typical V-profile with a flat bottom (Report Fig 2 Section 1955), but there is nothing specifically military in the published finds. With the Kingscote site, one is on firmer ground. Although this prolific site has been known for a long time it was not closely studied until visited by the Royal Commission staff in 1971, for the Gloucestershire-Cotswold Inventory[211] and a brief account was also published[212] which includes early brooches and items of military equipment (Report Nos 16, 18 and possibly 19). A programme of excavations has since then been initiated by a local amateur group,[213] but not on or near the site of the fort. There is no evidence to help to phase these two sites in a chronological sequence, if indeed Rodborough Common is a military site.

The frontier posts on the Bristol Channel at Sea Mills (No 126) and at the mouths of the Axe and Parrett, have already been mentioned above. This leaves for consideration the larger area north of Exeter and south-west of the Parrett. Probably the Dumnonii were friendly, and no rigid line was fixed in this difficult country, regular patrols by cavalry may have been considered adequate. Only one fort site has been postulated, that at Wiveliscombe (No 128), but the small scale excavation in 1956 produced no positive evidence[214] although the defences were built to a military pattern (Pl 20) and a unit here would have had command over the little valleys emerging from the Brendon Hills. Assuming this probability, the spacing could indicate another fort on the east bank of the River Exe at Tiverton, (No 129)[215] where the Iron Age fort of Cranmore Castle protects the crossing. There is also in this zone one of the few known signal stations, that at Stoke Hill, north of Exeter. Although at one time thought to belong to a much later period[216] its plan slightly suggests a first-century context, as has been more recently appreciated.[217] It is a site which could send signals both up the Exe and Culm valleys, and could have formed part of the essential communication network.

10 The site for the fort of *Coh VI Thracum* has yet to be found at Gloucester (No 63), but it may be expected below the later legionary base of *Legio XX* on the Kingsholm site. The limit of the frontier to the south must be the edge of the Bristol Channel and the half-way point between Gloucester and Sea Mills (No 126) would be in the vicinity of Berkeley Castle (No 125).

7 The Claudian Celebrations and Departure of Plautius

The person to gain the greatest satisfaction from the British conquest was the Emperor Claudius. He had seized on the venture as a means of escaping from the hostility of the Senate and of swinging popular sentiment towards him, but, above all, to gain acceptance of the provincial armies as a victorious commander-in-chief. It also brought him for the first time in close personal touch with the provincials of the north-west with whom he developed a sympathy, especially towards the Gauls. Claudius, now established as an acceptable Emperor, a full member of a ruling dynasty with the loyalty of his army, felt he had every reason for a celebration to place a seal on his achievements. The events and monuments had to be carefully planned and one can glimpse the hand of Claudius himself with his leanings towards tradition and archaic antiquarianism. There were the formal honours voted by the Senate, with its underlying irony which Claudius would have relished; the triumph celebrated in 44 with officially and unofficially inspired poems of commemoration, the special issue of coins and the two triumphal arches[1]. A fiction was carefully maintained that the Emperor could not award himself special honours and privileges, since this was the perogative of the Senate. It must be assumed that this was all worked out with care and due attention to tradition well in advance, before, in fact, the Emperor set out on his journey. A special session of the Senate was called immediately after receiving the despatch from Cn Pompeius Magnus and L Julius Silanus[2]. Suitable speeches were made and Claudius was voted a triumph and the building of two triumphal arches, the sites specifically mentioned – one in Rome and the other on the Channel coast. Both Claudius and his son were given the title Britannicus, since it had become an established custom of the Senate to grant honorific titles of the names of conquered territories. What may be seen as a departure from tradition was a seat in the Senate for the Emperor's wife, Messalina, but this followed the precedent set by Livia, the wife of Augustus[3]. Also Messalina had been allowed the use of the *carpentum*[4] at state ceremonies, a right reserved for the Vestal Virgins and the consuls. These honours for the Imperial consort are an early indication of the development of the concept of royalty in the reigning dynasty, a step deliberately avoided by Augustus.

The triumph was carefully planned and executed on a grand scale. It gave Claudius an opportunity for establishing himself in popular favour with the people of Rome. Provincial governors were given the rare privilege of leaving their posts to journey to Rome to take part. Claudius believed that he had completed the task begun by his distinguished uncle, Julius Caesar and that this had created a special bond between them. The Emperor would have enjoyed the research into the archives this entailed, and he must have studied all the official acts of Caesar to discover which he could pointedly emulate. One which offered the correct touch of traditional *pietas* in the full public view was his ascent of the steps of the *podium* of the great state temple on the Capitol, which he painfully achieved on his knees with the help of his sons-in-law.

Processions were always difficult to organize, since it was of the greatest importance to ensure that everyone was placed in the order demanded by precedent and protocol. These details were carefully copied from the records of the great triple triumph of Augustus celebrated in 29 BC although there had been the later triumphs of Tiberius in AD 12 and Germanicus in AD 17. Behind the royal couple came the commanders on whom the *triumphalia ornamenta* had been conferred but whether they included Flavius Vespasian is in doubt.[5] M. Crassus Frugi had been awarded this honour before and so was allowed to ride a horse to distinguish him from the others. The ceremonies were not confined to Rome as there is an interesting reference in Pliny[6] to Claudius sailing from Ravenna in a ship that was more like a palace when celebrating his triumph over Britain.

Cities of municipal status were expected to donate gold wreaths of victory to the Emperor, a practice soon to be regarded as a heavy tax, rather than an honour and obligation joyously accepted. This practice was also spread to guilds and similar incorporated bodies, and, by chance, the text of a letter has survived in which Claudius acknowledged such a gift of a gold crown sent by the Guild of Travelling Athletes[7]. Donald Dudley made a special comment on the poems written for the occasion[8]. It is, as to be expected, a very mixed collection, but it tells us something of the concepts of Britain in the minds of the residents of Rome. Its very remoteness on the edge of the world and detached from the mainland by the great ocean with its mighty waves and tides creating an awesome vision in those with only experience of the Mediterranean. Add to this the speed of the conquest in the tradition of Caesar, giving Claudius an unexpected lustre as head of the victorious army. But the main theme is the conquest of the ocean which brought this strange remote country into the orbit of Rome – 'what were separate worlds are now one'[9].

The commemorative coins were minted in 46, 49, 50 and 51, all of them showing a triumphal arch inscribed DE BRITANN (*RIC* 8–17) (Pl 3) and there are others with victories (*RIC* 49–51) and the eastern mint at Cappadocia produced a *denarius* showing Claudius riding in a triumphal quadriga with the legend DE BRITANNIS (*RIC* 52). In another issue the Emperor is closely identified with his troops with the legend PRAETOR RECEPT (*RIC* 38–44). The permanent memorials were the two triumphal arches, that in Rome was not dedicated until 52, presumably because it took time to design and build. The site of the arch needed careful consideration. It obviously had to be on the main road, leading to the city centre in the Forum and Capitol to the north-west. This was the Via Lata which left the walled city by the Porta Flaminia. It was the road which passed the Ara Pacis and the mausoleum of Augustus, establishing a link with the first Emperor. The monument has not survived and it is only known by some of its fragments and its appearance on the coins where it is shown surmounted by a figure on a horse between two trophies, and it is possible that Claudius used as his model the arch of Drusus the younger, erected in AD 23.

The restoration of the dedicatory inscription on the Arch of Claudius

About a third of the dedicatory inscription survives and can be seen built into a wall in the courtyard of the Conservatori Museum in the Capitol. The text can be restored with some confidence from the inscription of an arch set up by the local community at Cyzicus.[10] After reciting the titles of the Emperor, it states that he received the submission of 11 kings of the Britons, the words *in deditionem acceperit* are those used in any formal act of submission, when voluntary or by defeat. The phrase *sine ulla iactura*, as noted above, is somewhat archaic and may have been deliberately selected by Claudius in the sense used by Caesar not in describing losses in battle, as most translations imply, but without any loss of honour by Rome, especially in the fulfilment of her treaty obligations. This refers back to the official reason for the invasion – as a response to the call of an ally for assistance, although Verica himself was conveniently forgotten. The final line echoes the constant theme of the poems, the victory over the ocean. Claudius was the first to bring the barbarians beyond the ocean under the people of Rome. This achievement was evidently regarded by Claudius as the culmination of the campaigns of the Julio – Claudian House on the north-western frontier[11].

Plautius departs

Plautius had good reason to view his achievements with some satisfaction. The invasion had gone very smoothly, his victory at the Medway battle was notable and effectively placed most of the province in his hands. The only serious opposition came from the south-west but Vespasian had overwhelmed the hostile tribes with speed and boldness. But it must have been the sheer professionalism of the directed skill of the second legion in storming the hill-forts, considered as their impregnable bulwarks, which left the Britons stunned. They had no answer to this since the open downlands denied them the possibility of guerilla tactics. But Plautius knew perfectly well that his rapid conquest needed time for consolidation to enable the Britons to assimilate Roman ideas especially in economic development. There was still a great swell of bitter resentment against the loss of freedom and the tribal way of life. The kings and chiefs had to be won over by diplomacy and substantial gifts or loans to enable them to establish markets and the flow of trade. This would take at least a generation and meantime, the army had to maintain a close and watchful hold. The retiring governor's main concern must have been his western frontier. Rome's allies, the northern Dobunni would have given full reports of the activities of Caratacus whose influence on the western border tribes was thwarting Roman diplomacy. It must have been evident to Plautius that very soon serious trouble could be expected, but he may not have known that it would happen immediately he sailed away. As he was by nature a careful and cautious man it is possible that Claudius may have dismissed the fears he must have expressed in his report. The Emperor was still in a state of euphoria and went out of his way to greet Plautius when he arrived in Rome. Contrary to normal practice, Claudius came out of the city to meet him and allowed him precedence in the ascent to the Capitol. With a typical sense of history, the Emperor awarded him an *ovatio*[12] the first time this had been given to a senator for 66 years and the last, since thereafter, it was strictly reserved for close members of the Imperial family. Claudius clearly wished to keep Britain before the public eye and these ceremonies would have reflected on him and his unusual gestures rather than on Plautius, who thereafter lapsed into dignified retirement, sullied only by the unfortunate behaviour of members of his family.

The attitudes of the Britons to the Roman occupation would have varied considerably. There were those like Cogidubnus and Prasutagus, who were well pleased with the new wealth and position they now enjoyed. The western section of the Catuvellauni were one of the first to react to urban ideas, and as Professor Frere has demonstrated,[13] was soon building a city with some pretension of civil planning, although to a critical eye the reconstruction drawing may give an appearance of an American mid-western street of the cowboy era. But we do not as yet know about the public buildings of Verulamium in their early period. There is certainly solid achievement at Chichester (Noviomagus) for the new foundation was to have in the life-time of Cogidubnus a guild of ship-wrights, wealthy enough to erect a temple to Neptune and Minerva (*RIB* 91). This would surely indicate a very early development of a typical Roman institution, although the guild may have been given a good start through naval contracts with the unit in the Bosham Harbour base at Fishbourne. Evidence from Silchester can only come from an excavation of the earliest levels of Calleva, which has not yet been possible, although the street grid, as we know it, seems to be later (see p 148 above). However, George Boon has pointed out the extent of trade at the conquest period from the finds of pottery.[14] It is far too early in the investigation of the south-eastern towns to be able to make an assessment of the rapidity of urban development in the forties and early fifties, but the first indications we have point to an advance which must have given the Roman government and the traders some satisfaction. However, elsewhere in the Province there was quite a different story. Beyond the area of post-Caesarian trading contact, the tribes were not yet aware of the need to adjust to capitalism and produce a surplus for the market. Also they were remote from contact except for the more adventurous Gallic traders and these carpet-baggers had not left a very favourable impression with their sharp practices. A great deal of resentment and open hostility must have existed and this Rome had to overcome before any serious advance could be made toward urbanization. Evidence to date seems to indicate the beginnings of the main towns to have been not until the end of the first century, but this may have been due not so much to British resistance but to the army, holding their forts and fortresses long after the units had moved out of them.

In view of the subsequent and immediate events, it is unwise to speculate further, but as will be seen Britain was far from conquered and Rome may not have realized the immense effort they still had to put into the Britannia before it became a viable province of Rome. The conquest must, therefore, be considered as merely the first step towards this achievement. The second governor, Ostorius Scapula was impatiently waiting in Gaul for Plautius to cross the Channel so he could reach his new command. Whatever may have been in his thoughts, high-minded or ambitious, they were quickly dispelled on reaching his headquarters at Camulodunum with the devastating news from the west.

References

Abbreviations

AE – Anneé Épigraphique
BAR – British Archaeol Reports (122 Banbury Road Oxford)
Brit – Britannia (published by the Soc for the Promotion of Roman Stud)
Britannia – S S Frere 3rd ed 1978
CIL – Corpus Inscriptionum Latinarum
Déchelette – form numbers for samian vessels (see B R Hartley Chapter 13 in *The Archaeology of Roman Britain* by R G Collingwood and Ian Richmond 2nd ed 1969)
Epig Stud – Epigraphische Studien
ILS – H Dessau *Inscriptiones Latinae Selectae*
JRS – Journal of Roman Studies
Mack – *The Coinage of Ancient Britain* Spink 1953
RIB – R G Collingwood and R P Wright *The Roman Inscriptions of Britain* i 1965
RIC – Roman Imperial Coinage Spink
VCH – Victoria County History

1 The Sources of Evidence

1 *Brit* 8 (1977) 185–188
2 *Romano-British Imitations of Bronze Coins of Claudius I* Numismatic Notes and Monographs No 65 published by the American Numismatic Society 1935; see also Michael Hammerson in *Southwark Excavations 1972–74* ii 1978, 587–593
3 Any effect on this trade by the anti-Roman activities of Caratacus was probably too brief to have been of any significance
4 *Hengistbury Head* Elek 1978
5 There was a flourishing factory at Arretine (Arezzo) in Tuscany producing fine red-slip wares with moulded reliefs in Augustan and Tiberian times, but it declined as potters in south and central Gaul took advantage of the expanding markets of the north-western provinces. They produced varieties of wares in the Arretine tradition but in quite different fabrics up to early Flavian times. (For the first steps towards a scientific study of this problem see D F Williams and G B Dannell 'Petrological analysis of Arretine and early Samian: a

preliminary report' in *Early Fine Wares in Roman Britain* ed P Arthur and G Marsh BAR 1978, 5–14; see also Kevin Greene *The Pre-Flavian Fine Wares* Report on the excavations at Usk 1965–76, 1979, 9 –11. It is unfortunate that this was not published until after this book had been completed. This will now be the starting point for all future work on the imported wares of this period and it is interesting to note how closely the distribution maps follow the army across Britain

6 I am most indebted to him for allowing me to see a copy of his paper which he will be publishing shortly

7 In any case, it is hardly possible that the troops would have appreciated any difference in the stocks of varying dates

8 At Cirencester and Wroxeter; publications forthcoming

9 *Brit* 6 (1975) 37–61

10 This is a Gallo-Belgic ware in an orange or light-red colour-coat, most of the vessels were platters and shallow dishes

11 C M Wells *The German Policy of Augustus* 1972, 163–211; S von Schnurbein 'Haltern' in *Der Niedergermanische Limes* 1974 ed J E Bogaers and C B Rueger

12 *Brit* 6 (1975) 58–59; I am most grateful to Valerie Rigby for her helpful comments on this point

13 In the only example at present known at Longthorpe, near Peterborough, natives appear to be working on the perimeter of the site (J B Wild 'Eine Militärische Töpferei beim Legionlager in Longthorpe, Peterborough' *Studien zu den militärgrenzen Roms* ii 1977, 75–80; by the end of the first century there were properly established works depôts like that of *Legio XX* at Holt, (W F Grimes 'Holt, Denbighshire: The Works Depôt of the Twentieth Legion at Castle Lyons' *Y Cymmrodor* 41 (1930)

14 The kilns at Longthorpe are a surface or bonfire type and do not require any elaborate structure, and potters using them could have moved from fort to fort, as needed

15 A very interesting type of painted ware has been found near Rushden, Northants, for which no parallels have yet been found (see below p 157)

16 One must exclude containers such as the salt-pots made in the Malverns for the Droitwich salt extractors

17 A useful introduction is *British Prehistory* ed by Colin Renfrew Duckworth paperback 1974

18 eg. Barry Cunliffe *Iron Age Communities in Britain* Routledge 1974 and D W Harding *The Iron Age in Lowland Britain* Routledge 1974; both of which are considered in *The Iron Age in Britain – a review* ed J Collis University of Sheffield 1977

19 Summarized by E von Sacken *Das Grabfolk von Hallstatt* 1868

20 *The Personality of Britain* Fig 5

21 This problem was recognized in 1931 by Professor Hawkes, but renaming them Iron Age A and B only helped to perpetuate the problem. A useful statement of the present thinking is given by John Collis see fn 18 above, 1–7

22 *British Barrows* 1877; *Archaeologia* 52 (1890) 1–72

23 *Forty years Researches in British and Saxon Burial Mounds of East Yorkshire* 1905

24 *The La Tène Cultures of Eastern Yorkshire 1965*; *The Arras Culture* Yorks Philosop Soc 1979

25 *Gallic Wars* vi 3; but there is no known connection between the Parisi and the Arras Culture and this tribe presumably came to Britain much later

26 See J D G Clark 'The Invasion hypothesis in British Archaeology' *Antiquity* 40 (1966) 172–189; John Collis see fn 18 above 1–7; and a careful analysis of the problem by Professor D W Harding see fn 18 above 5–17

27 Cyril Fox *The Archaeology of the Cambridge Region* 1923, 81 and Pls XV and XVIII

2 The Celts and Julius Caesar

1 That solitary traveller, St Jerome, noted in the fourth century AD that the Galatians spoke a language which he considered very similar to that of the Treveri on the Moselle (T E G Powell *The Celts* 1958 p 23; see also P Stähelin *Geschichte der Kleinasiatischen Galater* 1907

2 *Archaeol J* (1902) 211; R F Jessup *The Archaeology of Kent* 1930 144–146

3 Caesar stated that the Trinovantes were the strongest of the tribes in these parts which implies that the other allies were probably smaller in numbers

3 The Tribes of South-East Britain and their Rulers

1 *OS Map of Southern Britain in the Iron Age* 1962 Map 8

2 J G Milne 'The Philippus coin at Rome' *JRS* 30 (1940) 11–15

3 'The Origins of Coinage in Britain: A reappraisal' *Problems of the Iron Age in Southern Britain* ed S S Frere Institute of Archaeology London Occasional Paper No 11

4 Simone Scheers 'Coinage and currency of the Belgic tribes during the Gallic War' *British Numismatic J* 41 (1977) 1–6

5 Warwick Rodwell 'Coinage, Oppida and the rise of Belgic power in South-Eastern Britain' in *Oppida in Barbarian Europe* eds B Cunliffe and T Rowley *BAR* 1976 Figs 1 and 2

6 'The Origin and Development of Celtic Gold Coinage in Britain' *Actes du Colloque International D'Archéologie* 1978, 313–324

7 The use of local minted coins to pay levies was the practice in Gaul under Caesar and probably later. This study has been developed from Dr Scheers *Les Monnaies de la Gauls inspirée de celles de la République romaine* 1969 by Dr Edith Wightman 'Soldier and Civilian in early Roman Gaul' *Akten des XI Internationalen Limeskongresses* 1978, 78–86

8 It must be assumed that these small groups had been absorbed by the Catuvellauni by the time Addedomaros was their ruler

9 His investigations there were not conclusive: *Verulamium, A Belgic and two Roman Cities* 1936, 20–22

10 Except Gallo-Belgic 'E', the uniface stater of the Ambiani and which usually show no signs of wear and which Dr Scheers considers is post-58

11 See fn 4 above para 45, 109

12 This was the subject of a very thoughtful paper by Derek Allen 'Wealth, money and coinage in a Celtic society' in *To Illustrate the Monuments* ed by J V S Megaw 1976, 200–208

13 *Early Land Allotment* eds H C Bowen and P J Fowler *BAR* 1978, 89–98

14 D F Allen 'British Potin Coins: A Review' *The Iron Age and its Hill-Forts* eds M Jesson and D Hill 1971, 127–154

15 See fn 5 above Figs 22–27

16 One from Canterbury seems to read SE [. . . .

17 It so happens that the name of the large Roman settlement here has not survived. One of his series had the letters VIR on the reverse (Mack 190) which also appears on one of DIAS (Mack 188). This would make a more acceptable place-name, possibly cognate with the Latin *viridis*, or it could be a slip for VER

18 'Roman Amphorae in Pre-Roman Britain' in Jesson and Hill 1971 see fn 14 above 161–188

19 Knowledge of the contents occasionally comes from painted or inked lettering on the surface, known as *depinti*

20 *CIL* xv i

21 See fn 5 above Fig 18, 1976

22 Barry Cunliffe *Hengistbury Head* Elek 1978; at least 12 Dressel 1 A *amphorae* have been found here, making this the main port for this trade on the south coast; see also John Collis 'Market and Money' in M Jesson and D Hill 1971 see fn 14 above 97–103

23 'The Rhine and the Problems of Gaulish Ware in Roman Britain' *Roman Shipping and Trade, Britain and the Rhine Province* eds J du Plat Taylor and H Cleere CBA Research Report No 24, 1978, 48–51

24 'A La Tène III Burial at Welwyn Garden City' *Archaeologia* 101 (1967) 1–62

25 *Archaeologia* 63 (1912) Pl II

26 *CIL* iii 768–799; Lewis and Reinhold *Roman Civilisation* ii *The Empire* 1955 9–19; E G Hardy *The Monumentum Ancyranum* 1923

27 *Iron Age Communities in Britain* 1974, 89

28 These people used to be called the Regnenses, i.e. the people of the Kingdom (of Cogidubnus), but Professor Kenneth Jackson has shown this to be an improbable assumption (*JRS* 38 (1948) 58; *Brit* 1 (1970) 78–79). He offers an ingenious alternative, the Regini, which means 'The Proud Ones' with similar examples in Gaul. Professor Rivet, arguing that this may have been the original Celtic name of the tribe, thinks it was later latinized into Regni (*Brit* 1 (1970) 50). To avoid confusion of these two different names of the same tribe, this latter suggestion is adopted here, but these people would probably have been known to Commius as the Regini

29 A detailed study has been made by Richard Bradley and published in B Cunliffe's *Excavations at Fishbourne, 1961–1969*, 17–36; see also B Cunliffe's *The Regni* 1977

30 *Brit* 7 (1976) 97–98

31 Information kindly given by Grahame Soffe and *Chichester Excavations* 2, 1977, 55 and 3, 1978, 331 No 10

32 See fn 1 above Map 6

33 *Bagendon, a Belgic Oppidum* 1961

34 'The samian from Bagendon' in *Roman Pottery Studies in Britain and Beyond* eds J Dore and K Greene *BAR* 1977, 229–234

35 *Iron Age and Romano-British Monuments in the Gloucestershire Cotswolds* RCHM (England) 1976, 7 and 92

36 See fn 1 above Map 6

37 *Current Research in Romano-British Coarse Pottery* CBA Research Report No 10 ed A Detsicas 1973, 63–103

38 There is fortunately an excellent study of the gold issues of Cunobeline by Derek Allen in *Brit* 6 (1974) 1–19 which establishes the chronology of his prolific series

39 Marcus Lollius suffered a defeat by a group of German tribes and had lost the eagle of the Vth Legion

40 Tiberius had retired to Rhodes, having become disenchanted by the attitude of Augustus, who regarded him merely as a work-horse and refused him a proper place in the ruling hierarchy

41 Harold von Petrikovits 'Arminius' *Bonner Jahrbuch* 166 (1966) 175–193

42 Derek Allen *Brit* 7 (1976) 96–100

43 Suetonius *Gaius* 46, 47

44 The Celtic ending –ON is used here, as elsewhere, for the period of British control

45 See fn 5 above 339–349

46 *Camulodunum* 1947, 51

47 I am most grateful to Philip Crummy and Nicholas Smith for allowing me to use the report prepared on behalf of the Colchester Archaeological Trust to support the acceptance of a preservation scheme. An earlier plan was published by the Trust in an archaeological survey *Not only a matter of time* 1975, 13

48 *Archaeologia* 76 (1927) 241–254

49 It could be suggested that these fragments represent deliberate breakage at the time of burial, a common practice of this period, but it applies only to personal objects which needed to be 'killed' to join their owners, and in such a case, all the broken fragments could be present

50 See fn 5 above 358

51 *Bronze Boar Figurines in Iron Age and Roman Britain BAR* No 39, 1977, 10

52 See fn 28 above. The Finds 1971, 24

53 *A Guide to Greek and Roman Life* 3rd ed 1929 Fig 10

54 It was common Roman practice for kings on the frontier to send their children to Rome for this purpose, it not only moulded them into Roman ways, but they could also be treated as hostages, should the occasion arise

55 S S Frere *Britannia* 1974, 64

56 *Archaeologia* 52 (1890) 317–388

57 *Excavations of the Late Celtic Urn Field at Swarling* Soc of Antiq Research Report No V 1925

58 *Proc Prehist Soc* 31 (1965) 241–367; see also the conclusions reached by P Harbison and Lloyd Laing *Some Iron Age Mediterranean Imports in England* BAR 1974, 27–29

59 This vessel has pie-crust frilling round the rim and often at the carination, and the common occurrence of burning on the inside indicates a possible ritual use

60 See fn 4 above, 237

61 *Supplementary Gazetteer of Find-Spots of Celtic Coins in Britain, 1977* Occ Pap No 11a of the Inst of Archaeol London 1978, 82–83

62 P H Robinson *Brit Numismatic J* 45 (175) 6. I am grateful for information to Roger Goodburn who also tells me that one of the more recent finds may be a forgery. The one from Calleva, listed by Derek Allen as a coin of Epaticcus, is a silver-plated copy, but the name of the ruler is missing, however, it is identical with the coins of Caratacus; Mack 265; G Boon *Silchester* 1974, 42, where attention is drawn to the presence here of clay coin moulds very similar to ones from Camulodunon; *Bull Board of Celtic Stud* 25 ii (1973) 243–245; 26 (1974) 94–95

63 The word used by Dio (lx 19, 1) indicates an internal political upheaval so Caratacus may initially have been acting through supporters of Epaticcus (see p 72 above) since Caratacus had a family link with him and this shows in his coins

4 The Opposing Forces

1 Professor A L F Rivet has contributed a very scholarly note on this subject; *Antiquity* 53 (1979) 130–132

2 *L'Arc d'Orange* XVᵉ Supplément à *Gallia* 1962

3 i.e. FE[CIT, RE[FECIT and AVOT; this last, a Celtic word with the same meaning

4 *Gallia Supplement XV* 93

5 Accepted opinion has it that this shield was a votive offering made to a Roman order

6 'The Witham Shield' *Prehistoric and Roman Studies* ed G de G Sieveking 1971, 61–69

7 *Annals* xii 35

8 *Gallic War* i 48

9 *Nigro plumbo ad fistulas lammisque utimus, laboriosius in Hispania eruto, totasque per Gallias: sed in Britannia summo terrae corio adeo large, ut lex ultro dictatur, ne plus certo modo fiat Nat Hist* XXXIV 49

10 Although he specially states that iron occurred only in small quantities in the maritime districts (v 12), but this description of Britain was probably taken from an earlier writer, probably, Posidonius and inserted by Hirtius when he edited the *Gallic War*

11 This figure, may of course, be a deliberate underestimate for the greater glory of his subsequent victory. Caesar certainly took pains to make the enemy believe that his force was much smaller by building his camps with maximum compression (v 49)

12 These are the titles in AD 43 after the victory over Boudica in AD 60 *Legio XIV* became *Gemina Martia Victrix* and *Legio XX – Valeria Victrix*. The positive evidence for the participation of these four legions in the invasion is incomplete. The one about which there is certainty is *11 Aug* from the ancient authorities (*Hist* iii 4) which also informs us that Vespasian was its commander. The presence of the future emperor in Britain, in such a post, is confirmed by Suetonius (*Vesp* 4). There is also epigraphic evidence for this legion (*ILS* 2696). The inclusion of *XX Val* is implied by its early appearance at Colchester, and a further inscription at Ephesus, recording a *praefectus fabrum* who was decorated in the war (*AE* (1924) 78). For *IX Hisp*, Dr Lawrence Keppie has drawn attention to an epigraphic fragment, recording someone accompanying Claudius to Britain, and who had *hospitium cum leg V* . . . and this could only be the VIII th (*CIL* V 7165; *Brit* 2 (1971) 155). The earliest evidence of *XIV Gem* is on the Wroxeter tombstones (*RIB* 292, 294 and probably 296), which, as will be seen below, are not likely to be earlier than c. 56, and the presence of this legion in the defeat of Boudica in 60 or 61

13 Dio lv 31 informs us that when Augustus became suspicious at the delay of Tiberius in reducing the revolt, he raised an army of free born citizens and freedmen for Germanicus to take to Pannonia to bring the war to an end

14 A suggestion I owe to Professor A Birley

15 Mark Hassall, 'Britain and the Rhine Province: epigraphic evidence for Roman trade, *Roman Shipping and trade in Britain and the Rhine provinces* ed J du Plat Taylor and H Cleere CBA Research Report No 24, 1978, 41–48

16 A Mocsy *Pannonia and Upper Moesia* 1974, 43

17 LVIII retrograde; *VCH Leics* i 179–180; *Archaeol J* 75 (1918) 25–27

18 *CIL* v 7003

19 'Legio VIII Augustus and the Claudian invasion' *Brit* 2 (1971) 149–155

20 *CIL* xi 6163

21 *ILS* 974

22 *CIL* xiii 5093, i.e. an ex-guardsman probably serving as a centurion in one of the British legions

23 The plates were copies of originals fixed to the Temple of Minerva in Rome. These certificates list the units in a province from which troops were being discharged at that time, and were legal proof of this grant of citizenship and sometimes of *conubium*, i.e. the legitimization of any union and offspring. *Diplomata* found up to 1964 are in *CIL* xvi, and those discovered subsequently listed by Margaret M Roxan; *Roman Military Diplomas* 1954–1977, Occasional Publication No. 2, Inst of Archaeol London 1978

24 *Brit* i (1970), 'Batavians and the Roman conquest of Britain' 131–136

25 *Annals* iv 46

26 Auxiliary units do not appear to have received these awards until Vespasian, according to P A Holder, to whom I am indebted for his opinion. 46-year-old Vitellius Tancinus from Caurium in Lusitania must, therefore, have died at Bath when seeking a cure

27 I am most indebted to Professor A Birley for his kind help with information and advice in this section

28 Plautius was governor of Pannonia in 42 when C Arruntius Camillus Scribonianus was governor of neighbouring Dalmatia. This distinguished patrician, revolted against Claudius, but was soon deserted by his two legions, who found that divine intervention rooted their standards to the ground and prevented their withdrawal to hail the ursurper (Suetonius *Claud* 13). The rapidity with which this serious rebellion was put down, may have been due to prompt intervention by Plautius, even earning him the British command

29 According to Suetonius, she was divorced for scandalous misconduct and on a suspicion of murder (*Claud* 26), but this seems to have made no difference to the status of the Plautian family. The young Drusus was choked to death by a pear he tossed in the air and caught in his mouth. There was some doubt as to the father of Claudia, since Claudius disowned her (*ibid* 27)

30 These difficult relationships are best seen in Table I in the *Cambridge Ancient History* X 1966

31 *Annals* xiii 32

32 The worship of Cybele and Attis received Imperial acceptance in imperial circles under Claudius, (*Lydus* a Byzantine monk who collected pieces of ancient references to religious practices; *de mensibus* IV 54)

33 *idque illi imperitante Claudio inpune, mox ad gloriam vertit*; 'earning her no punishment under Claudius, later it brought her glory'. She was not, however, mourning the loss of Plautius, but her dear friend Julia, the grand-daughter of Tiberius, and who had married Nero Caesar, son of Germanicus and fallen under the tyranny of Sejanus. Julia fell foul of the capricious Messalina (Dio lx 18)

34 His name is perpetuated by the Lateran Palace in Rome on the site of his mansion, and which was donated by Constantius to the Papacy.

35 As he had great physical strength, his part in the plot was to pin Nero to the ground while the other conspirators dispatched him; *Annals* xv 53 and 60

36 lx 23; this statement of Dio was not correct since earlier examples are known

37 Dio lx 18

38 Seneca *Apocolocyntosis* 13

39 They acted as a police force, night watch and fire brigade

40 Dio may have made a slip here and the actual honour given was the award of the *consularia insignia* as was the case of another procurator (*Annals* xii 21)

41 The responsibilities of procurators were extended under Claudius to include the collection of the *annona* (*Pap Brit School of Rome* (1939) ll). It is, therefore, possible that Laco could have been collecting supplies for the invasion (I owe this suggestion to A Barrett)

42 There is a detailed description of the trial in the *Annals* xi 1–3. Unfortunately, part of this book is missing, but the first sentence indicates that Messalina coveted the famous Gardens of Lucullus which were owned by Asiaticus. After the trial held privately in a room of the Palace, Claudius, in view of his considerable service to the State, allowed Asiaticus to take his own life. He did this with typical Roman composure, even organizing his funeral pyre which had been built in his Gardens, but on inspection, thought it was too near some of the trees, and ordered it to be moved before he retired to his bath and opened his veins

43 According to Dio (lx 27) he refused to have intercourse with her, but he was held in high enough esteem to have a public funeral with eulogies

44 *fratrumque non incestum, sed incustoditum amorem ad infamiam traxit* (*Annals* xii 4)

45 This extraordinary relationship, basically incestuous, was manipulated by Vitellius who forced a decision through the Senate legalizing unions between uncles and their brothers' daughters (*ibid*

xii 7)

46 Domaszeski thought that this inscription referred to the son of Gallus (*Rom Mitt* (1841) 163 ff) and a Flavian date for this kind of command seems more likely; see Geza Alfoldy 'Die Hilfstruppen der römischen provinz Germania Inferior' *Epigrapische Studien* 6 (1968) 131–135

47 *Galba* 7, *non adeo*

48 Suetonius alleged that, during the field manoeuvres in Germany carried out by Caligula, Galba ran by the side of the Emperor's chariot for 20 miles, directing his army at the same time (*Galba* 6)

49 Studied in detail by Sir Ronald Syme *J Roman Stud* 50 (1960) 12–20

50 *Apolcolocyntosis* 11

51 *ILS* 954. This fragment only preserved the first name – M of the province, but this seems a reasonable assumption

52 Suet *Claud* 17

53 He was ordered to drop the *cognomen*, although only a boy at the time (Dio lx 5), but Claudius allowed him to continue to use it

54 Suet *Vesp* 4

55 G Vrind *De Cassii Dionis vocabulis quae ad ius publicum pertinent*, 1923, 90. It still, however, presents a difficulty in explaining how Sabinus received this command so late in his career and when presumably he was already senior to his brother

56 This was Aulus, brother of Lucius who befriended the Flavians

57 Both surviving manuscripts of Dio read 'Caius'; Gnaeus was suggested by Reimar

58 The problem was seen by Sir Ronald Syme *American J of Philology* 77 (1956) 270; D E Eichholz *Brit* 3 (1972) 151

59 Dio lx 9

60 *Revue épigraphique* VIII 2 (1913) 2490; *Prosopographia Imperii Romani* 2 H 217

61 This problem will be considered in greater detail in the later period under Ostorius Scapula

5 The Invasion and Advance to Camulodunum

1 *Gaius* 46 and 47; The troops are said to have collected sea shells and offered them as trophies of war, but it could be a garbled version of a practice landing

2 They all began to shout *Io Saturnalia*, the cry at that festival when slaves put on their masters' clothes, and roles were reversed, like our own 'Merry Christmas' in the military mess. Antony Barrett has suggested to me that the presence of Narcissus may have been necessary if the troops were offered extra pay, this could explain their jubilant exclamation since Saturnalia was the time for receiving gifts

3 I did at one time have the speculative idea that such a force could press rapidly along the Stane Street route to seize any crossing point on the Thames, but this presupposes a greater knowledge of the terrain than Plautius may have had, and a daring tactic which not even Caesar could have conceived

4 J A Steers *The Coastline of England and Wales* 1946, 334–337. For a brief account of the physical geography of Richborough, see Sonia Chadwick Hawkes in *Richborough* V 1968, 224–231 and 'The development of Richborough' by Barry Cunliffe *ibid* 231–251

5 *Richborough* V 232–234 and Fig 26

6 The timber gateway might suggest its use continuing at least for a season. If stores were stocked here, a controlled entrance would have been desirable

7 A detailed study of Dio's statement and its implications was made by Professor C F C Hawkes in his contribution to *Bagendon a Belgic Oppidum Excavations 1954–1956* by Elsie M Clifford 1961, 56–67

8 G B Dannell 'The Samian from Bagendon' *Roman Pottery Studies in Britain* eds J Dore and Kevin Greene 1977, 231

9 In the Marlowe Street area, so Tim Tatton-Brown kindly informs me

10 S S Frere *Britannia* 1974, 64

11 Brian Philp *The Roman Fort at Reculver* p 3, a booklet published by the Kent Archaeological Rescue Unit

12 The medieval route across the Medway by the Roman/medieval bridge at Rochester and so turned along the north bank of the river through Cuxton (see map at the end of R F Jessup's *Kent*, in the County Archaeologies 1930)

13 It has been interpreted by some as indicating that an existing bridge had been destroyed. This is not impossible if Rochester had been the site of an important native community of which the discovery of Celtic coin moulds there may be an indication; S S Frere *Britannia* 1974, 64

14 *Stratagems* I iv 8–10

15 For examples see Tacitus *Hist* ii 17; iv 12, *Annals* ii 8; there is a detailed study of their role in Britain by Mark Hassall in *Brit* I (1970) 131–136

16 One of the first attempts to make a sensible pattern of these events was A R Burn, in his short paper 'The Battle of the Medway, AD 43' in *History* 39 No 133 (1953) 105–115

17 Whether these belonged to the Catavellauni or their allies is a matter of debate

18 Assuming that Sabinus was one of the legionary commanders

19 Claudius displayed oustanding generosity in these awards, and it is probable that all the legionary commanders had the same, as was certainly the case with Vespasian (Suet *Vesp* 4)

20 Provincial museums often have such collections which on investigation are usually found to have been misdated to make this association. There is a fine leather boot in the Grosvenor Museum, Chester, said to have come from the site of the Battle of Rowton Moor of the seventeenth-century civil war. This was accepted until a knowledgeable person identified it as a gunner's boot of the time of the Crimean War!

21 A possibility is a ditch traced for 230 feet below the villa at Eccles which lies on the east side of the river about a mile south of the ancient crossing; *Archaeol Cantiana* 81 (1966). It has a V-profile with a square channel at the bottom and its filling produced a few bronzes similar to ones from Richborough, but the pottery is Claudio-Neronian which indicates occupation certainly into the early 60s. (I am grateful to Alec Detsicas for this information)

22 *Numismatic Chronicle* 6th ser 19 (1959) 17

23 He could have banked it with his unit *deposita* under the charge of his *aquilifer*, then at least his dependants would have had a share

24 A B Woodward 'The geology of the London district' in the *Memoirs of the Geological Survey* ed C E N Bromehead, 2nd edition 1922 and A V Akeroyd 'Archaeological and Historical Evidence of subsidence in Southern Britain', *Trans Royal Phil Soc Lond* 272 (1972) 151–169

25 The dramatic effects of this on the Port of London has been revealed in recent excavations on the water-front; such as T Tatton-Brown, 'Excavations at the Customs House Site, City of London' *Trans London and Middlesex Archaeol Soc* 25 (1974) 117–219; 26 (1975) 103–170, Brian Hobley and John Schofield 'Excavations in the City of London 1974–1975' *Antiq J* 57 (1977) 31–66 and summarised by Brian Hobley in *Ill London News* Oct 1977 *Archaeology* 2932, 75–79

26 Patrick Thornhill 'A lower Thames ford and the campaigns of 54 BC and AD 43. *Archaeol Cantiana* 92 (1976) 119–128. There was a small twelfth-century priory on the Kent side which took the tolls and in 1293 the prioress found herself liable for the maintenance of a causeway and bridge to the ferry point. On the Essex side the road appears to belong to a north-south route which passes through Billericay and Chelmsford, dividing at Little Waltham. Two bronze skillets, if they are of this period, said to have been found near Cliffe and now in the Rochester Museum, may have come from a fort overlooking this crucial crossing point; *Archaeol Cantiana* 70 (1956) 273–277 for early pottery

27 Where extensive excavations have been undertaken by Mrs M U Jones in recent years; *Antiq J* 48 (1968) 210–230; 54 (1974) 183–199

28 *Gallic War* v 18

29 If the Edgware Road alignment is extended it meets the river at Millbank near the Tate Gallery by the Vauxhall Bridge on the south side the line is continued with Camberwell New Road

30 Domitian sent artisans to Dacia to assist with construction work (Dio lxvii 4) but Dio's source is so hostile to the Emperor that it makes little sense of a treaty devised to give Rome time to stabilize this frontier problem

31 This was normal military equipment (Vegetius i 10; I A Richmond 'Trajan's army on Trajan's column' (*Papers of the Brit School at Rome* 13 (1935) 7, 28–29

32 Ralph Merrifield and Harvey Sheldon 'Roman London Bridge, a view from both banks' *The London Archaeologist* 2 No 8; I am most grateful to Brian Hobley and Harvey Sheldon for discoveries and information on the problems of London

33 This name was very much later given by the Saxons who called the Britons the *Walas* or foreigners

34 At Hod Hill and Maiden Castle

35 Suet *Iul* 57

36 Pliny the Elder *Nat Hist* 19 1

37 This does not accord with Suetonius who stated that Claudius had only one six-month consulship—AD 51. Presumably the intention in 43 was to ensure that the Emperor and Vitellius held their joint offices until Claudius returned to Rome the following year

38 Dio lx 21 2; these large creatures used entirely for impressive ceremonial purposes would hardly have come with the Emperor from Rome and they must have been waiting for him at the port of embarkation

39 *Southwark Excavations 1972–74* 1978 59–65 and Fig 15

40 *CIL* vi 920. It can be seen on a wall in the courtyard of the Conservatori Museum in the Capitol in Rome

41 *CIL* iii, 7061 = *ILS* 217

42 This word was often used in the sacrifice of one's honour and could, on the inscription, indicate merely that the obligations of Rome had been satisfied without any stain on her honour rather than simply 'battle casualties' or it could alternatively mean that the act of submission of so many rulers in itself saved Rome having to fight for their territories and so avoid serious losses

43 Although it is not certain whether this happened at this time or later

44 They could have fled north after AD 60

45 There is even to-day a feeling between the peoples on either side of the Medway, distinguished by the names 'The Men of Kent' and 'The Kentish Men'

46 When Gaius Crispus for the second time and Titus Statilius were consuls i.e. in AD 44 (lx 23 1)

47 *Vesp* 4

48 *Hist* iii 44

49 *Antiq J* 51 (1971) 1–7

50 L Alcock *By South Cadbury is that Camelot* 1972 105–106; one of the oddities found among the native weapons was the presence of over a hundred brooches. The Roman military equipment is illustrated on

Pls 70–72

51 J A Campbell, M S Baxter and Leslie Alcock 'Radiocarbon dates from the Cadbury Massacre' *Antiquity* 53 (1979) 31–38

52 *Conquest* 1953 79 and accepted by Dr W Manning. 'The Conquest of the West Country', in *The Roman West Country: Classical Culture and Celtic Society* eds K Brannigan and P J Fowler 1976

53 *Maiden Castle Dorset* 1943 Research Report of the Society of Antiquities No 12

54 According to Vegetius (ii 25); as shown on a scene on Trajan's Column (Pl 5); Cichorius, Taf 46 164. It is evident from finds of pieces of these machines that there were variations of different size; D Baatz 'Recent Finds of Ancient Artillery' *Brit* 9 (1978) 1–18

55 Apart from the old Celtic shrines which continued to be venerated throughout the following centuries and turned into small Romano-Celtic temples with votive objects associated with Minerva and the Celtic triple-horned bull

56 No traces of this fort have yet been found, but it must be under the later town. Scrap pieces of military equipment have turned up from time to time; *Archaeol J* 115 (1960) 79 and Nos 86–88

57 *Hod Hill* ii 1968

58 Only one burial has been recorded, but as a casual find in 1953, and its association with this event cannot be proven (Report p 31)

6 The Shape of the Province

1 One can only appreciate this geographic pattern in relationship to the main watersheds before the glacial period; see G Dury *The Face of the Earth* 1959 Pelican 171–172 and Figs 85 and 100

2 Discussed above p 111; see also OS *Map of Southern Britain in the Iron Age* 1962

3 A concept later to be put into the title *pater patriae* (father of his people), and later still, in stronger form – *dominus noster* (our lord and master)

4 It is interesting to note that the same concept is today applied by the great powers, but on a global basis to protect not frontiers, but trade routes and oil and mineral resources

5 H Ramm *The Parisii* 1978; I Stead *The Arras Culture* 1979

6 These trackways had been in existence for centuries, if not millenia, and they had grown in importance with the development of trade (B Cunliffe *Hengistbury Head* 1978, 64). They kept to the higher and firmer ground and so are known in places as ridge-ways and had a special significance for the Roman army as they were defended by the tribes by blocking them at strategic places by hill-forts. In considering the operations of the army and its network of forts, the word 'route' has been deliberately chosen since it is considered unlikely that metalled roads would have been laid at such an early stage of the conquest. The army engineers cleared ways through woodlands, provided firm ways across marshes and soft areas with log foundations and when necessary built timber bridges, all to provide the army with rapid means of movement and communication by horse and pack-mule. Only when heavy transport waggons were introduced would drainage and a good firm surface be required, but the amount of labour to do this would have to be very great and the army could ill-afford to divert soldiers to this task in terrain most of which was still potentially, if not directly, hostile

7 W F Grimes 'The Jurassic Way across England' in *Aspects of Archaeology in Britain and Beyond* ed W F Grimes 1951, 144–171

8 *Annals* xii 31 *detrahere arma suspectis cunctaque cis Trisantonam et Sabrinam fluvios cohibere parat* according to the famous Bradley emendation (*Academy* April 28th and May 19th 1883)

9 *Brit* 8 (1977) 65–76

10 By Miss R Dunnett *Trans Essex Archaeol Soc* 3rd ser 3 (1971) 38–41

11 *Brit* 5 (1974) 6 and Fig 3

12 *ibid* 1–129

13 *Chichester Excavations* 1, 1971; 2, 1974; 3, 1978

14 *ibid* 3 Fig 10.30 No 13

15 An idea suggested by Alan McWhirr (*Leics Archaeol and Hist Soc* 45 for 1969–70, 5

16 A Celtic word for fortification. Pre-conquest imports imply trade with Rome (*Brit* 9 (1978) 435). I am grateful to Jean Mellor for help and information about Leicester

17 There is high ground of a suitable size and shape for an *oppidum* to the south-west of the Roman town

18 *Archaeol J* 115 (1960) 84 and Fig 5 No 134; there is also an unusual type of harness-pendant of gilded bronze (*Brit* 4 (1973) Fig 18 No 3)

19 No military tile stamps can be dated before the end of the first century in Britain, and in any case, it is unlikely that *Legio VIII* served in Britain (*Brit* 2 (1971) 149–155)

20 E Blank *Ratae Coritanorum* (Ginn Hist Patch Series) 1971, 9–12

21 *Brit* 9 (1978), 435

22 *Antiq J* 52 (1972) 350–353

23 The other units are *Coh I Aquitanorum* (*ibid* No 36, 386); *Ala Vocontiorum* (*Brit* 9 (1976) No 46, 479) and *Legio VI* (*ibid* No 47), but if this reading is correct the depôt continued in use into the early second century.

24 Summarized by Peter Marsden in *Collectanea Londiniensa* 1978, 89–92

25 *Archaeol J* 115 (1960) 84–86; most of them are in the Museum of London and include legionary equipment and pieces of leather

26 *Trans London and Middlesex Archaeol Soc* 23 (1973) 60–62

27 It may be significant the road to Braintree and Ixworth would join the London–Camulodunum road if projected at this point, and not at Chelmsford.

28 A third suggestion has been made by J G F Hind that it was here that Claudius received the British chiefs (*Greece and Rome* 21 (1974) 68–70), but this would surely have been at the British capital?

29 P J Drury Trans Essex Archaeol Soc (1972) 4–5; *Brit* 7 (1970) 342

30 *ibid* p 343

31 As shown in the small inset map in the preliminary report (Fig 1)

32 *Brit* 3 (1972) 335; it has a typical shovel-slot at the bottom

33 Information kindly supplied by Dr Warwick Rodwell

34 Discovered by Professor St Joseph (*JRS* 43 (1953) 97 and Pl XVI No 2)

35 Found by Dr Rodwell (*Trans Essex Archaeol Soc* 9, 3rd ser (1977) 338; although their signal station bears a superficial resemblance to those on the north coast of Devon of a Neronian date, they could belong to a much later relay system connecting the Saxon Shore forts with London

36 *VCH Roman Essex* 1963, 17. Dr Rodwell has noted a similar rectangular enclosure on the other side of the river at Maldon (*Roman Essex* pub by the *Essex Archaeol Soc* 1972, 6) Military presence here may have been needed for the lucrative saltings

37 *Brit* 3 (1973) 305; 5 (1974) 442 and Fig 15. Assuming the correct placing of the gate of this plan, the width of the fort would have been *c*. 300 m

38 A bronze barnacle-type pendant, often associated with cavalry, was found nearby on the Gosbecks temple site in 1967 (*Brit* 2 (1971) 45 and Fig 6 No 1)

39 This material is now in the Colchester and Essex Museum (*VCH Roman Essex* 1963, 3)

40 Summarized in *Boudica* 1978, 106–107

41 *Roman Crafts* 1976 Pl 11

42 Credit for this initial discovery must go to R Farrands who has persistently flown over this site for several years; *Proc Suffolk Inst Archaeol* 27 (1958) 179; 27 (1961) 91; *Brit* 5 (1973) 439

43 *Brit* 9 (1978) 448

44 *East Anglian Archaeol* No 5 (1977) 97–224

45 *ibid* Fig 57 Nos 26, 25 and 24 respectively; No 25 is of the type noted from Dorchester, Dorset, p 146 and No 26 can be paralleled from the military sites of Aislingen (*Limesforschungen* No 1 (1959) Taf 23 No 11 and *Saalburg* (1897) Fig 78 No 11)

46 *East Anglian Archaeol* No 5 (1975) 261 Fig 71 and Pl XXVIII

47 *J Roman Stud* 35 (1945) 82

48 *J Roman Stud* 43 (1953) 82; 59 (1969) 127–128 and Pl II 2

49 R Rainbird Clark *East Anglia* 1960, 112 and 117. It has been known also for a hoard of bronzes found here (*VCH Norfolk* I 1900,

273)

50 I am most grateful to Robin Brown for showing me the site and the material he has collected and meticulously recorded. Although there are no surface indications to show a fort was there, the finds and the suitability of the site itself are sufficient to make this a very possible one

51 There is a route across the Wolds at Lincolnshire aimed at a ferry-point on the north side of the Wash

52 Summary in *Small Towns of Roman Britain* eds W Rodwell and T Rowley *BAR* 1975, 185 and Figs 1 and 2. The only equipment noted is a *dolabra*, an axe-pick used by legionaries.

53 *Northants Archaeol* 12 (1977) 52 and Fig 13; *ibid* 13 (1978) 169

54 *VCH Essex* iii 1963, 125–126; *Brit* 2 (1971) 272; 3 (1972) 333; 4 (1973) 304

55 *Brit* 6 (1975) 262–263

56 *Proc Suffolk Inst Archaeol* 28.3 (1961) 272–289

57 *VCH Essex* iii 1963, 74

58 Summarized by Dr Warwick Rodwell in a note in *Brit* 3 (1972) 290–293

59 The large number of Claudian imitation coins is a possible pointer to this, as Michael Hammerson has suggested in an interesting survey of the coins of Southwark, showing that the losses of these coins occur in late Neronian-Flavian levels, rather than earlier ones (*Southwark Excavations* 1972–74 ii 1978, 587–600 and Fig 248

60 OS *Map of Southern Britain in the Iron Age* and Map 6; *Proc Camb Antiq Soc* 51 (1958) 19–29; 56 and 57 (1964) 123–124

61 Apart from a stray harness trapping said to be from the Lakenheath area in the Bury St Edmunds Museum. The presence of a piece of *lorica segmentata* from the Santon hoard of 1897 can be excluded as it is probably Icenian loot of the revolt period, as Dr Mansel Spratling has suggested; *Brit* 6 (1975) 206–207

62 *Proc Camb Antiq Soc* 58 (1965) 29–36

63 This road was carefully surveyed and described by I D Margary in his *Roman Ways in the Weald* 1948, 45–92

64 *Sussex Archaeol Coll* 64 (1922) 81–104; 65 (1923) 112–157

65 *Trans Birmingham and Warks Archaeol Soc* 86 (1974) 56–57

66 *Sussex Archaeol Coll* 68 (1927) 89–132

67 *Brit* 5 (1971) 458

68 His first report on this fascinating site was published as Research Report No 26 by the Soc of Antiquaries of London in 1971 *Excavations at Fishbourne 1961–1969* in two volumes. A more popular version by Professor Cunliffe has appeared in the New Aspects of Antiquity series of Thames and Hudson *Fishbourne, a Roman Palace and its Garden* 1971

69 Now in the Lewes Museum. It still has an oyster-shell attached to the crest-knob, a clear indication of its being lost in estuarine waters

70 By Dudley Waterman *Antiq J* 27 (1947) 151–171

71 M A Cotton and P W Gathercole *Excavations at Clausentum, Southampton 1951–1954* HMSO 1958; see also G Rogers and Lloyd R Laing *Gallo-Roman Pottery from Southampton* City Museum Pub No 6, 1966

72 1958 Report Fig 12 Nos 6 and 7 as at Hod Hill, Richborough, Aislingen, Saalburg, Zugmantel etc; in these two examples the iron points have corroded away or dropped out

73 The great German scholar Emil Hübner suggested that Plautius landed here and that the name was a contraction of 'Claudientum' (*Hermes* 16 (1881) 527–530), but this was shown to be highly unlikely by Bernard Henderson (*English Hist Rev* for Jan 1903, 6)

74 BM *Antiquities of Roman Britain* 1951, 46 and Fig 21 iii a2

75 The small amount of pottery recovered is now in Poole Museum but it includes a piece of Claudian samian

76 *Antiq J* 42 (1968) 309–311; S S Frere *Britannia* 1961, 72–74; *Dorset Nat Hist & Archaeol Soc* 93 (1971) 161

77 Which I directed but did not continue since a by-pass was planned to cross the site and a large-scale rescue excavation anticipated. This has also delayed the report, which will be integrated in the further work now being continued by Ian Horsey

78 *Proc Dorset Nat Hist & Archaeol Soc* 95 (1973) 86–87

79 *Proc Devon Archaeol Explor Soc* 2 (1935) 200; 3 (1938) 67; 4 (1949) 20; *Brit* 6 (1975) 276

80 *Brit* 9 (1978) 468; *The London Archaeologist* 3 (1978) 180–186

81 *ibid* 467

82 *Brit* 4 (1973) 317; 5 (1974) 213–216; 6 (1975) 278

83 A long series of interim reports have appeared in the *Antiq J*

84 *Winchester Excavations 1949–1960 I* 1964, ed Barry Cunliffe

85 When the army gave up a fort, all the buildings were dismantled, the usable timber recovered and the decayed and small pieces burnt. The clay infilling of the walls was spread over the site which was left as a levelled plateau

86 *Antiq J* 45 (1965) 234–235 and Pl LXVIII. The four-post structure looks like the foundations of a typical Iron Age granary and the possibility must remain that it has no connection with the hut, but is an earlier or later structure.

87 Barry Cunliffe *Iron Age Communities in Britain* 1974 Figs 3 : 5 and A 4–18; D W Harding *The Iron Age in Lowland Britain* 1974 Fig 68

88 Information kindly given to me by Professor Cunliffe

89 *Brit* 7 (1976) 280–283

90 Information kindly supplied by Mrs Vivien Swan. The excavations at Old Sarum have produced a harness trace-junction which is more Roman in style than Celtic and could have been military (*Antiq J* 17 (1937) 438)

91 *Excavations in Cranborne Chase 1881–5* i 1887; ii 1888

92 *ibid* ii Pl civ Nos 12 and 13

93 Thus echoing the compiler of *VCH Wilts* i 1973: ii 440 'hint at a passing contact'. There is also a complete scabbard binding (Pl C iii No 10) with very neat moulding which could be Roman, as it compares well with pieces of indisputable origin (cf. from *Rheingönheim Limesforschungen* 9 1969 Taf 43 Nos 12 and 21)

94 Now in the Corinium Museum. Some of these items have been published (*Archeol J* 115 (1960) 73–75 Nos 24–42) and those found in recent excavations will be described in the forthcoming report

95 See the annual summaries in *Antiq J* 42 (1962) 3–51; 43 (1963) 15–16; 45 (1965) 97–101; 47 (1967) 185–197; 49 (1969) 222–243; main report forthcoming

96 The pottery is not sufficient in quantity to be very helpful; see V Rigby 'The Gallo-Belgic pottery from Cirencester' in *Roman Pottery Studies in Britain and Beyond* eds J Dore and K Greene *BAR* 1977, 39

97 As revealed by rescue excavations: *Brit* 1 (1970) 300; 2 (1971) 282; 7 (1976) 362; 8 (1971) 416–417

98 *ibid* 8 (1977) 416

99 Suggested by Professor Frere who excavated here in 1962 (*Archeol J* 119 (1964) 128–129)

100 *Antiq J* 12 (1932) Pl xviii No 8 is a harness-clip and there is a baldric loop in the Ashmolean Museum (Acc No 1972, 2143) and Nick Griffiths tells me that there are also some military fragments in the Banbury Museum

101 *Archeologia* 102 (1969) 44–45 and Fig 5

102 *ibid* 39; but it could be later on the evidence of the 1939 excavation the south street of the unnumbered *insula* east of XXIV by the North Gate sealed a hut floor in which a coin of Domitian was found (*Archeologia* 92 (1947) 135–137) this means that the street plan cannot be earlier than the end of the first century

103 These include a barnacle pendant i.e. an amulet in the shape of half a barnacle-bit used for curbing unruly horses and four pieces of horse trapping typical of this period

104 Also known as Wylye Camp. The excavations of 1959–60 have not been published, but a summary of all the available evidence from this site has been collected by Collin Bowen (*Wilts Archeol Mag* 58 (1961) 32–34). The most puzzling features found by Reverend E H Steele were a carefully levelled strip, 15 feet wide, on the outer side of the inner (Iron Age) ditch and a 'rough trench' 6 feet, 6 inches by 1 foot, 6 inches on the inner side of the ditch and parallel to it. This could be better explained as the result of deliberate and systematic slighting by the army rather than as fort construction, but the matter remains much in doubt. The early Roman pottery does, however, suggest occupation of some kind.

105 *Wilts Archaeol Mag* 43 (1926) Pls i and ii; the pottery includes St Rémy and pre-Flavian imported colour-coated wares, so Mrs Vivien

Swan kindly informs me

106 Now in Devizes Museum, the mount is slightly curved and may not be military; Cold Kitchen Hill is the site of a settlement with a temple (*Wilts Archaeol Mag* 43 (1926) 327–332; 44 (1927) 138–142

107 *Proc Univ Bristol Spelaeol Soc* 13 (1974) 329; *Brit* 2 (1971) 277 and Fig 12. Peter Fowler had studied the photographs and suggested that there are two periods involving a change of axis (*The Roman West Country* 1976, 26). For pottery from the site see *Somerset Archaeol Nat Hist Soc* 118 (1974) 44–46

108 *CIL* xiii 3491; *Flints Hist Soc* 13 for 1952–53, 11

109 *CIL* vii 1201 and 1202; the latter appears to be dedicated to Britannicus the unfortunate son of Claudius who was poisoned by Nero as soon as he assumed the purple (Suet *Nero* 33). The cold-struck stamp reads VETP which may refer to the two consuls of 49 but there are other stamps which read VEB, probably the first part of the name of the district so VETP may be a blundered version of this.

110 Colt-Hoare gave it the name AD AXIVM after the river (*Ravenna Cosmography* 237). There is the place-name 'Borough Walls' which may be significant

111 The early coins include issues of Augustus to Nero (*Wilts Archaeol Mag* 41 (1921) 392) and brooches of Aucissa and other exotic types often associated with the army (*VCH Wilts* i; (1957) 104)

112 *Wilts Archaeol and Nat Hist Mag* 69 (1976) 176–179; another possible military object is recorded from Folly Farm (*ibid* 70/71 (1978) 126–127)

113 *JRS* 43 (1953) Pl XIII 2; see also *Small Towns of Roman Britain* 1975, 12, 34 and Pl VIII a

114 Ken Annable (*Wilts Archaeol and Nat Hist Mag* 61 (1966) 14). Mildenhall is a very difficult site to understand without more evidence. There are two different areas of occupation divided by the river, named Upper and Lower Cunetio by Colt Hoare (Plan between pp 90 and 91). The former includes Church and Butt Heys Fields, and the latter, Folly Farm and Black Field, includes the walled town and earlier defences. The road system is suggestive of alterations unless there were three different crossing points! There is also evidence of pre-Roman native occupation and a massacre placed in the 'Belgic' period, but this has not yet been published and deserves detailed study (*VCH Wilts* i pt i 87)

115 *Wilts Archaeol Mag* 36 (1909) 125–139; for similar pottery at Mildenhall see *ibid* 61 (1960) 13 and fn 14

116 *Brit* 6 (1975) 37–61

117 A much poorer example came from Hod Hill (i 1926 Fig 11 E 5). Mrs Elizabeth Fowler, I am informed, regards them as of Iberian origin and thinks that they were brought here by Spanish auxiliaries

118 *Proc Dorset Nat Hist and Archaeol Soc* 95 (1973) 87–88

119 The collection was published by John Brailsford for the BM in

1962 *(Hod Hill i Antiquities from Hod Hill in the Durden Collection)*
120 For the record I would like to add that I spent several summers with Sir Ian at this site to my great enjoyment and enlightenment when I was Curator of the Grosvenor Museum, Chester
121 Richmond calculated that the barrack accommodation was for seven *turmae* (234) men. The presence of the *praefectus* means that the HQ staff were also here and the other half of the unit on outpost duty elsewhere
122 Report pp 78–79 and Figs 43 and 44
123 There are later strays which have no connection with the fort
124 Very little is known about it, not even its precise location
125 It was found by means of a metal detector. I am most grateful to Ken Annable, the Curator of Devizes Museum for allowing me to use his drawing, it was taken there for examination, but remains in the hands of the finder
126 *JRS* 14 (1924) 232; *Trans Bristol and Glos Archaeol Soc* 61 (1939) 202; 65 (1944) 195; 66 (1945) 294; 68 (1949) 184; 71 (1954) 70; *Archaeol J* 105 (1960) 89. The excavations since these have been concentrated on the later civil settlement. There are also military objects from this site in the Spencer Percival Collection in the Downing Street Museum, Cambridge. I am grateful to Mary Cra'ster for allowing me to examine them
127 *Wilts Archaeol Mag* 38 (1913) 53–105
128 Report Pl 1 No 5; this object is probably published half-size and not full-size as stated; it has a concealed loop at the back through which a trace was threaded. The *terra rubra* plate stamped Attissus, wrongly ascribed by Mrs Swan to Oare (as she has kindly informed me) *Brit* 6 (1975) 58 has been considered above
129 It is in the Devizes Museum and I am grateful to Ken Annable for allowing me to examine and draw it
130 *Devizes Museum Cat* Pl LXI illustrates a *terra nigra* dish; see also *Wilts Archaeol Mag* 70/71 (1978) 135
131 *Antiq J* 37 (1957) Pl VI
132 i.e. a nielloed belt-plate from *Insula* XVII; *Archaeologia* 90 (1944); others in the Verulamium Museum are described in *Archaeol J* 115 (1960) Nos 203–209
133 *Verulamium I* Report of the Soc of Antiq No 28, 1972; included in the bronzes are two decorated bands probably from helmets (Nos 30 and 31 Fig 32) identified as bracelets; a cuirass loop (No 36) identified as an earring; belt or strap mounts (Nos 37–41); probably Nos 42 and 43 (Fig 33); an apron mount (No 49); a pendant (No 50); a harness loop (No 127 Fig 40); possibly a trumpet mount-piece (No 129), There is also the beautifully decorated scabbard-guard with a Celtic pattern (*Proc Soc Antiqs* 24 for 1911–12; 132 and *VCH Herts* 1914, 119)
134 By the Berkhampstead and Dist Archaeol Soc (*Brit* 6 (1975) 257; 7 (1976) 338–39; 8 (1971) 401; 9 (1978) 444). It is a strange site with at

least ten deep shafts for wells or iron smelting. Early metal working seems to have been a feature of this valley. I am indebted to Mr Eric Holland for this information

135 *Proc Soc Antiq* 5 for 1870–73; 362; *Vetusta Monumenta* v 1835 Pls 26 and 27; *VCH Herts* 1914, 158–9, Pl 1

136 *VCH Oxon* i 1939, 330–331; among the many finds over the years are military imitation coin issues of Claudius

137 An odd name as there is no river and therefore no bridge (*Brit* 1 (1970) 73)

138 I am indebted for this information, in advance of publication, to Mrs Charmian Woodfield

139 They include rich native burials; *JRS* 49 (1969), 221–222; *Brit* 1 (1970) 289; 2 (1972) 269; 3 (1973) 329; 4 (1974) 298; 7 (1976) 338; also *Archaeol Excavations 1971* HMSO 19

140 They have been studied by David Johnston *Beds Archaeol J* 9 (1975) 35–55

141 *Small Towns of Roman Britain* 1975, 225

142 Only a fragment of this road, east of Great Chesterford, has so far been identified

143 *Assoc Archaeol Socs Reports and Papers* 13 (1874) 110

144 *Antiquity* 4 (1930) 274; 13 (1939) 455

145 The three objects published in *Archaeol J* 115 (1960) Nos 230–232 are not helpful as they did not come from either site. No 232, the eagle head cart-fitting, is now in the Ashmolean Museum, Oxford

146 A fine scabbard mount was found in excavations at Dockwell Mill, Wood Burcote, a mile to the south of the town (*Brit* 6 (1975) 255); but in a shallow ditch with a coin of Vespasian and early Flavian pottery; I am grateful to M Turland for detailed information. Mrs Charmian Woodfield tells me that a fragment of *terra nigra* with part of a stamp has turned up in a builder's trench in the town.

147 *Brit* 3 (1972) 325; 4 (1973) 296; the rescue work was carried out by the Rugby Archaeol Soc and Steven Taylor (Reports forthcoming)

148 Now partly covered by a radio communication station

149 *Trans Birmingham Archaeol Soc* 81 (1966) 143–144 and Pl 30; it is now in the Warwick Museum

150 M Todd *The Roman Fort at Great Chesterton, Rutland* University of Nottingham 1968

151 *JRS* 47 (1957) 210; 56 (1966) 203; 57 (1967) 182; 58 (1968) 184; 59 (1969) 214

152 *Brit* 1 (1970) 284

153 By Malcolm Todd in *Roman Fort Defences to AD 117*, 1975, 127; details of any finds await full publication

154 *Brit* 8 (1977) 118–192

155 *JRS* 5 (1961) 171; 52 (1962) 167; for a brief summary see *Sleaford, South Lincs Archaeology No 3* 1979, 6

156 The existence of an anti-Roman faction may be indicated by the hoards of Coritanian coins found in Brigantia at Honley and Lightcliffe (D Allen *The Coins of the Coritani* 1963), which suggests a flight of refugees. Many of these coins are inscribed issues and include the name VOLISIOS linked with DVMNOCOVEROS, DVMNOVELLAV(NOS) and CARTIVEL(LAVNOS?) who may have been his sons or joint rulers (*ibid* Pls IV, V and VIII). The Honley hoard also includes two coins of Vespasian (AD 72–73) which indicates a deposition at the time of the Roman northern campaigns

157 There is a rectangular earthwork east of the Roman settlement still visible, *Sleaford* 1979, 28; (NGR TF 078458) but this is probably medieval

158 *Brit* 7 (1976) 334

159 *Milton Keynes J Archaeol Hist* 1 (1972) 7–9; 3 (1974) 9–10

160 There have been several suggestions as early as Haverfield, that the Nene Valley may have offered the Roman army a frontier in the early advance across the Midlands, especially if hostility was anticipated from the Coritani and neighbouring tribes. It could have marked a stage in the Plautian advance

161 D H Hall and N Nickerson 'Excavations at Irchester 1962–3' and J K Knight 'Excavations at the Roman Town of Irchester 1962–3' *Archaeol J* 124 (1966) 65–99 and 100–128

162 *The Small Towns of Roman Britain* ed Warwick Rodwell *BAR* 1975, 31a

163 *Brit* 3 (1972) 322 and 325

164 *Current Archaeol* 3 No 31 (1972) 204–205

165 N Thomas *Guide to Prehistoric England* 1976, 94–95

166 *Brit* 8 (1977) 107–148; this site produced some very strange timber buildings (Report Fig 6) which the excavator thought 'comparable to Roman army barrack-blocks'. What is shown could be the bottom of construction trenches in the military model (they are too wide for sill-beams) reduced by ploughing and erosion to this level, but the suggestion is not supported by any other evidence

167 It is, in a sense, already State property since it belongs to the Duchy of Lancaster

168 In the Salter and Norris Collections

169 *Proc Soc Antiq* 21 for 1908–1906, 135; *Proc Somerset Archaeol and Nat Hist Soc* 69 (1923) Pl xi; *VCH Somerset* i (1906) Fig 63; *Archaeol J* 115 (1960) 80–83 Nos 105–103 and Pl XI C

170 'A large V-shaped ditch' was observed in 1975, but no details given, *Proc Somerset Archaeol and Nat Hist Soc* 121 (1977) 98

171 *Archaeol Excavations* 1975 HMSO 126

172 W J Wedlake *Excavations at Camerton, Somerset* 1958

173 The 1978 edition of *Roman Britain*

174 Information kindly given by Mrs Swan (*Brit* 6 (1975) 45) who has published a baldric loop in Devizes Museum, from the earlier Priestley excavations of 1938–52; *Wilts Archaeol Mag* 65 (1970)

175 There is a sharp escarpment on the north side of the river and Roman occupation has been noted on the north side of the village. (I owe this information to Ted Price).

176 There is a pasture field about a mile along the Harbury-Whitnash road with the interesting name – Quinchester; it occupies a slight plateau which may repay further investigation

177 Later to become Mrs Brian Hartley; although it has a turf revetted rampart and V-ditch with possible internal timber buildings, no pottery or objects were found to prove military occupation; *Brit* 2 (1971) 258

178 The name indicates the presence of an important Celtic shrine; *Brit* 1 (1970) 80

179 Summaries of his work appeared in *JRS* 12 (1922) 249; 13 (1923) 114; 14 (1924) 255; 16 (1926) 36; 17 (1927) 195; 18 (1928) 198; 19 (1929) 193; 22 (1932) 206; 23 (1933) 196; 25 (1935) 77 and 210

180 Malcolm Todd's report of his excavations of 1966–68; *Trans Thoroton Soc* 73 for 1969–70, 17–38; for a useful summary see Alan McWhirr in his survey of the early military history of the East Midlands; *Leics Archaeol and Hist Soc* 45 for 1969, 6–7

181 This is clearly indicated by the name although no Roman road is known on either side of the river, one would at least expect military routes towards the north-west

182 *JRS* 43 (1953) 91; 48 (1958) 98 and Pl XV 1; also *The Civitas Capital of Roman Britain* 1968 ed J Wacher 28–29

183 Summarised by Alan McWhirr (*op cit* fn 180 above)

184 *JRS* 54 (1964) 159 Fig 12 and Pl XIIII I; 56 (1966) 203 Fig 10

185 *Archaeologia* 58 (1903) 573 and Pl lv

186 She is holding a twisted staff which has been identified by Anne Ross as a *cornucopia* (*Pagan Celtic Britain* 1967, 199 Fig 131) but its similarity with one on another cheek-piece from Gloucester suggests that they were both symbols of power possibly derived from Jupiter's thunderbolt

187 *JRS* 43 (1953) 91; 51 (1961) 132 and Pl x 2

188 Nor should it seem the place to rehearse all the evidence and argument but it would be pointed out that the Claudian date attributed to the legionary tombstones (*RIB* 255 and 257), based on the absence of the full *tria nomina*, is not conclusive

189 A site here would help to explain the presence of a military cemetery along the road approaching the river from the south, at least a mile from the late legionary fortress. Military tombstones have been found in the Manson Street area (e.g. *RIB* 249, 253, 254, 255, 257 and 258)

190 *Brit* 4 (1973) 286; the site also produced a *ballista* bolt-head (Christina Colyer *Lincoln*, a booklet published by the Archaeological Trust in 1975, 7) very similar to the one from Maiden Castle in the vertebrae of a native warrior in the war cemetery (*Maiden Castle* 1943

Fig 3 No 13)

191 *Brit* 3 (1974) 422

192 I M Stead *Excavations at Winterton Roman Villa* HMSO 1976, 18–19

193 Valerie Rigby, who has written a report on these wares, makes an interesting comparison between the two groups and concludes that there is a striking difference in the fabrics of the *terra nigra* wares, suggesting different sources. This could indicate that the Old Winteringham pottery had been brought there by the army and the other in the course of trade at the same time, or perhaps slightly earlier.

194 Unfortunately it is too wide and flat for the normal type (cf *Rheingönheim* Taf 31 No 20 etc)

195 *Archaeological Excavations* 1975 HMSO 64; 1976, 82–83; *Brit* 9 (1978) 433

196 *Lincs Hist and Archaeol* 1 No 1 Fig 4a and b

197 *Itinerarium Curiosum* ii 1776, 96; see also *VCH Notts* ii 1910, 19 ff

198 Information kindly supplied by the OS; a note based on information given by M Todd in M J Jones *Roman Fort Defences to* AD *117* 1975, *BAR* 161. Excavations near Littleborough have not produced any early material (*Brit* 1 (1970) 264)

199 They include a fine bronze saucepan; *Antiq J* 19 (1939) Pl 87; see also *E Midlands Archaeol Bull* No 8 (1965) 30

200 I am most grateful to Keith Scott for this information; he has been carrying out some small-scale excavations here, the results of which will be published shortly

201 It may be worthy of note that there is a *denarius* of Augustus (*RIC* 317) in the City Museum, Birmingham, found near here (Acc No 1535185–446; it is in the Scott Coll, but without any details of provenance)

202 Fully described by J A Stanford; *JRS* 27 (1937) 168–178

203 *Coventry Nat Hist and Scientific Soc* 2 No 5 (1951) 147

204 Although the Iron Age fort on Bredon Hill may have been deserted by the conquest (N Thomas *Guide to Prehistoric England* 1976, 145) there are many signs of occupation on the lower ground round the hill

205 Identified only as a 'substantial building' by the OS and given the name – Millhampost; it also goes by the name of Wycomb and according to the RCHM (England); *Monuments in the Gloucestershire Cotswolds* 1976, 124–126, it covers at least 28 acres and there are finds which indicate a late Iron Age occupation

206 *Bagendon: A Belgic Oppidum, 1961*; this may be resolved by further excavation now being undertaken by Dr Richard Reece

207 G B Dannell 'The Samian from Bagendon' in *Roman Pottery Studies in Britain and Beyond* eds J Dore and J Geene *BAR* 1977, 229–234

208 *Brit* 6 (1975) 59–61

209 *Brit* 6 (1975) 44–45

210 *Trans Bristol and Glos Archaeol Soc* 78 (1954) 24–43; a brief note on further pottery found in 1957, 83 (1964) 145–6

211 1976, 70–75

212 B N Eagles and Vivien Swan 'The Chessalls, a Romano-British Settlement at Kingscote' *Trans Bristol and Glos Archaeol Soc* 91 (1972) 60–89

213 *Brit* 8 (1977) 413; 9 (1978) 456; The area at present being excavated is on the north-west edge of the settlement adjacent to sites Nos 2 and 3 on Fig 1 in the above report; a likely site for a fort would be on the promontory on the 700 feet contour to the east of the settlement

214 *Proc Somerset Archaeol and Nat Hist Soc* 103 (1959) 81–91; the carefully planned nature of the defences and the selection of the site were given as indicative of Roman military work

215 I have been kindly informed by Dr Valerie Maxfield that a campaign camp has shown up here as a crop-mark on an aerial photograph

216 Aileen Fox and William Ravenhill 'The Stoke Hill Roman signal station' *Trans Devon Ass* 91 (1959) 71–82

217 *Brit* 3 (1972) Fig 17

7 The Claudian Celebrations and Departure of Plautius

1 I owe much of what follows to the valuable paper by my old colleague and collaborator, Donald Dudley; 'The Celebration of Claudius' British Victories', *Univ of Birmingham Hist J* No 1 (1958) 6–17

2 Dio lx 22, 1

3 Suet *Claud* 17

4 This was a covered two-wheeled carriage drawn by a pair of mules. It was a vehicle used by the Etruscans at their weddings, and so had a religious sanctuary from antiquity

5 D E Eichholz has taken much trouble to prove this to have been unlikely (*Brit* 3 (1972) 149–163), but it all depends on the date of the triumph, since it is not certain if it was late in 44 or later still. Under the year 47, Dio related an incident in Britain in which Vespasian was surrounded by barbarians and rescued by his son Titus. But as Titus would only have been eight at the time, it can hardly have happened in this year and the episode probably belongs to the Judaean Wars. In any case, Vespasian's three-year post as a legionary commander would have ended in 46

6 Pliny *Nat Hist* iii 1119; xvi 201

7 P Lond iii 1178 (this papyrus, now in the BM, is a second century copy); two of the envoys bringing the gifts had received their citizenship under Claudius and taken his name

8 Riese *Anthologia Latina* i 419–426

9 *coniunctum est, quod adhuc orbis et orbis erat* (the final line of No 426)

10 *CIL* iii 7061 = *ILS* 217

11 M P Charlesworth *Documents to illustrate the reigns of Claudius and Nero* 1939, 9

12 Suet *Claud* 24

13 *Aufstieg und Niedergang der Römishchen Welt* eds H Temporini and W Haase ii Principat 3rd Band 1975, 290–324

14 *Silchester, The Roman Town of Calleva* 1974, 40–42

Appendix 1
Translation of Cassius Dio lx 19–22, 2
by Mary Beard and Neil Wright

While these events were taking place in Rome, at the very same time Aulus Plautius, a most respected senator, led an expedition to Britain. A certain Bericus who had been exiled from that island as a result of a political dispute had persuaded Claudius to send a force there, and so Plautius assumed command. However, he had trouble taking the soldiers out of Gaul, as they were uneasy about serving beyond the boundaries of the inhabited world. They could not be induced to obey him until Narcissus, an ex-slave, who had been sent out by Claudius, tried to get up onto the rostrum of Plautius and make an address. They then became much more angry at Narcissus and did not allow him to speak; instead they shouted out the sarcastic comment 'O Saturnalia'[1] and immediately followed Plautius quite willingly. Because of these delays they made their departure somewhat late. The troops were divided into three groups so that they should not be prevented from making a landing, as they might have been, had they crossed in a single body. Early in the voyage they were disheartened when the wind turned against them, but they were later encouraged when a light rising from the east ran across the sky towards the west, the direction in which they were bound. They landed on the island with no opposition. For the Britons, from information they had received, had not expected the Romans to come and so had not assembled in readiness. In fact, even when they did assemble, they failed to engage the enemy in close combat but retreated to the marshland and the forests, for they hoped to wear out their foe by different means and force them to sail away unsuccessful, as had happened when Julius Caesar came.

Plautius encountered great difficulty in discovering them, but when he did come upon them he defeated first Caratacus then Togodumnus, both sons of Cunobelinus, now dead.[2] When they had fled he brought over by negotiation a part of the Bodunni, previously under the control of the Catevellaunian princes, and then, leaving a garrison, proceeded further. Eventually he came to a river which the natives thought he would be unable to cross without bridges. Consequently they had encamped somewhat carelessly on the bank opposite. Plautius sent over the German auxiliaries who were used to swimming easily across even the fastest flowing rivers without removing their equipment. These attacked the enemy unexpectedly and, instead of shooting at the men, wounded the horses drawing the chariots and threw them into such confusion that their occupants were unable to

200

reach safety. He also sent across Flavius Vespasianus[3] and his brother Sabinus, who was his subordinate. And so they managed to cross the river and kill many of the natives who were taken by surprise. However, the rest did not take flight but, attacking again on the next day, engaged in a struggle with the Romans that was not to be resolved until Gaias Hosidius Geta, after risking his own capture, inflicted such a severe defeat upon them that he was awarded triumphal ornaments, although he had never held the consulship. The Britons then retreated to the river Thames or, more precisely, to the mouth of that river, where it forms a lake at flood tide. This they forded with ease on account of their exact knowledge of the safe and accessible ground in the area. At first the Romans were confused by the ground in their attempt to follow but then the Germans managed to swim across again and other troops crossed on bridge a little further upstream. Once on the other side they attacked the natives from several directions simultaneously and slaughtered many of them. But, as they followed up the remainder without due care, they became entangled in the trackless marshland and lost many men.

However, at the death of Togodumnus, so far from surrendering, the Britons united all the more strongly against the Romans to avenge him. Worried by this and by the minor reverse they had suffered earlier, Plautius did not advance any further but consolidated his gains with garrisons and sent off for Claudius. He was under orders to do this if serious opposition was encountered, since many and varied supplies (along with elephants) had been prepared to reinforce the expedition.

On the arrival of the message, Claudius handed over to his colleague in the consulship, Lucius Vitellis, control of affairs at home, including command of the troops stationed in Italy.[4] Claudius himself left on campaign; he sailed down to Ostia and from there was conveyed round to Massilia, from which point, journeying partly on foot and partly on river transport, he arrived at the Atlantic coast. After he had made the crossing to Britain, he joined the army awaiting him in camps by the Thames and assumed overall command. Then, once having crossed the river, he engaged the natives who had gathered together to repel his attack and defeated them in a pitched battle. He also took Camulodunum, the royal seat of Cunobelinus. As a result of this victory he brought over many of the Britons, some by negotiation, others by force, and was therefore hail-*Imperator* many times, contrary to custom.[5] He proceeded to disarm these natives and entrusted them to Plautius whom he instructed to bring the remaining territory under Roman control. Claudius himself returned to Rome, sending his sons-in-law, Magnus and Silanus, ahead of him with news of the victory. When the Senate learnt of his success, they gave him the honorific title 'Britannicus' and allowed him to hold a triumph. They also voted him a yearly festival and two triumphal arches, one in Rome and one in Gaul, since it was from that country that he had crossed to

Britain. The same title, 'Britannicus', was conferred on his son, a title which by its habitual use came to be his regular name. Finally Messalina was granted the privilege of occupying a front seat in the theatre (as Livia had been before) and permission to use a carriage within the city of Rome.

Notes

1 At the Saturnalia (equivalent to our Christmas) slaves exchange places with their masters and have a holiday.

2 The Britons were not autonomous, but were divided into tribes under different kings.

3 This man was later to rule as emperor.

4 Thus he caused him to remain in the consulship for a whole six months, as he did himself.

5 It is not standard for any one man to be granted this title more than once in the same campaign.

Mary Beard, *Newnham Coll. Cambridge*
Neil Wright, *St John's Coll. Cambridge*

Appendix 2
The number of units in the army of Plautius

On the map of the suggested layout of forts (Map II), the sites of no less than 130 are indicated. The problem is the number of troops needed to occupy all these forts. It is reasonable to assume that the number of auxiliaries would have approximated to that of the legionaries. Four legions contained about 24,000 and this equates to about 48 auxiliary units of 500 each. It is likely that extra units would have been allocated to the invasion force, but once the major battles were over, they would have returned to their original bases. If there had been some uncertainty about the hostility of some of the tribes, Plautius may have been able to have retained some of the units as part of the initial garrison. Even if he had 60 units these would have accommodated only half the number of forts suggested. But it is clear from the few large-scale excavations of these early sites that the internal layouts were very unorthodox. If forts like Hod Hill are typical of the whole, it means that the four legions provided men for out-post garrison duties and if each contributed two cohorts, this would have given Plautius another eight units. But it is also certain from Hod Hill that both legionary and auxiliary cohorts and *alae* were divided. One could garrison more forts by splitting units, but in such a way that each remained an effective fighting force. In this way, legionaries could be found in 20 forts or more and only in areas of known hostility would the garrisons have been up to full strength. One has, therefore, to visualize a very uneven spread of Roman troops, thin in the territory of the allies, but strong in the areas of potential hostility or uncertainty. At the same time, Plautius would have been careful to provide adequate troops for the frontier zones and this would have been the function of the *Legiones* IX and XIV, while the XXth watched the potentially dangerous elements of the Catuvellauni and the Trinovantes, while the IInd *Aug* were ready for trouble in the south-west, with some of its men in forward positions, as at Hod Hill and probably Ham Hill.

Appendix 3
Abbreviations

Acc No	Accession number
Antiq	Antiquaries or Antiquarian
Archaeol	Archaeological
Ass	Association
BM	British Museum
Bull	Bulletin
Cat	Catalogue
ed	edited by
fn	foot-note
Hist	Historical
ibid	*ibidem* (the same)
Inst	Institute
J	Journal
Mag	Magazine
Nat Hist	Natural History
NGR	National Grid Reference
op cit	*opere citato* (work quoted)
OS	Ordnance Survey
Pap	Papers
Proc	Proceedings
Rec	Records
RCHM	Royal Commission on Historical Monuments
Soc	Society
Stud	Studies
Trans	Transactions

Appendix 4
Bibliographical references

Ancient Sources

Caesar	*de Bello Gallico*
Cassius Dio	*Historia Romana*
Frontinus	*Strategemata*
Pliny the Elder	*Naturalis Historia*
Seneca	*Apocolocyntosis*
Suetonius	*de vita Caesarum*
Tacitus	*Agricola*
	Annals
	Histories
Vegetius	*Epitoma rei militaris*

Modern Works

Barry Cunliffe *Iron Age Communities in Britain* (Routledge) 1974
Barry Cunliffe and Trevor Rowley ed *Oppida in Barbarian Europe* (Bar) 1976
S S Frere *Britannia* 3rd ed (Routledge) 1978
Kevin Greene *The Pre-Flavian Fine Wares, Report on the Excavations at Usk 1965–1976* (University of Wales) 1979
D W Harding *The Iron Age in Lowland Britain* (Routledge) 1974
Ordnance Survey *Map of Roman Britain* 4th ed 1978
Ordnance Survey *Map of Southern Britain in the Iron Age* 1962
John Wacher *The Coming of Rome* (Routledge) 1979
Graham Webster *The Roman Imperial Army* (Black) 2nd ed 1969
Graham Webster *Boudica* (Batsford) 1978

Appendix 5
Glossary of Latin terms

ala a cavalry unit usually at this period about 500 strong divided into squadrons (*turmae*) and commanded by a *praefectus*.

amphora a large pottery container for transporting commodities like wine, oil, fish sauce (*garum*) etc. to distant parts of the empire. It became a unit of liquid measure

annona the corn tax which provincials were obliged to pay in kind to maintain the frontier armies

aquila the eagle standard of the legions, considered to be a symbol of the legion and was in consequence its most precious possession; normally kept in the *sacellum* of the *principia*

aquilifer the officer who carried the *aquila*. He was the senior of the junior officers below the centurionate and responsible for the legionary pay-chest and *deposita*

auxilia the general term for the Roman allies who provided troops for the army to assist the legions. Satisfactory service led to citizenship on discharge

ballista a spring-gun of which there were several kinds and sizes used normally by legionaries. The small gun (*carro-ballista*) was mounted on a cart, was provided for each century and operated by ten men

centuria the smallest operational unit in a legion and auxiliary cohort consisting of 80 men commanded by a centurion and divided into eight *contuburnia* (mess or tent parties)

civitas a tribe and its territory

civium romanorum the award of Roman citizenship; when given to auxiliary units as a reward for outstanding services, it is denoted by the letters C R as part of the unit's title

classis Britannica the fleet based on Britannia

clientala clients owing allegiance to a patron who in turn undertook responsibility for them.

cognomen the third name of the *tria nomina* of a citizen, usually peculiar to the individual

cohort a military unit of about 500 men when it was known as *quingenarius*. Those 1000 strong were *milliarius*

cohors equitata a part-mounted auxiliary unit

colonia a settlement of retired army veterans who were usually given land allotments

comites literally companions, but used here as members of the imperial retinue of Claudius

consularia insignia decorations awarded to men of consular status, i.e. governors of imperial provinces

conubium the legal right to marry and legitimize offspring by the union. This was especially important for auxiliary soldiers (see G R Watson *The Roman Soldier* 1969, 134 – 138)

cos ord the title of the two senior magistrates of Rome who entered office on the 1st January, then names identifying the year

cos suff the title of the pairs of magistrates who became consuls after the *consulares ordinaries*, usually holding office for three months

damnatio the official condemnation of unpopular emperors after death, the approved ones were deified

dilectus one 'chosen' for military service

denarius the silver Roman coin, 25 of which were equivalent to the gold *aureau*

depinti lettering or numerals painted or written in ink on vessels giving information about capacity or content

deposita the money deposited in a military bank on behalf of soldiers

dolabra an iron tool with a pick at one end and hoe-like blade at the other, carried by legionaries and used for digging ditches

dominus noster our lord – a title taken by fourth-century emperors

duplicarius a junior commander in an auxiliary *ala* in charge of a *turma*, and so-called as he was given double pay

evocatus a soldier, often a praetorian, who continued to serve after normal service, with promotion.

garum a sauce made for the Mediterranean fish *garus*

gemina a title given to a legion when it was created by splitting one into two, as with *Legio XIV Gem*.

gladius the short stabbing sword used by legionaries

hiberna winter quarters where units spend the winter 'under canvas'

insula an island, but also used of town blocks in a street grid

legatus a man to whom the Emperor delegated responsibility, as with provincial governors

legatus legionis the commander of a legion

legio a legion comprising Roman citizens and consisting of 10 cohorts nine of which were quingenary (i.e. 500 strong) and the first milliary (i.e. 1000 strong)

limes originally a dividing path between fields, but later a name given to a frontier

lorica segmentata a cuirass made of horizontal strips of steel, held together by vertical leather bands, worn by legionaries

oppidum the Latin word for any native defended settlement, but it has been usually restricted by British archaeologists to an area protected by Gallo-Belgic dykes, as at Camulodunum

ornamenta triumphalia insignia awards to victorious commanders and consuls

pater familias literally father of his family, but also applied to a patron and his *clientela*, as with the emperor and his subjects

pater patriae father of his country, a title assumed by emperors

pietas duty towards the gods and to those to whom one has responsibility, as in the patron and his clients

pilum the javelin used by legionaries. It was seven feet long mostly consisting of a wood shaft. The iron shank was left flexible but the pyramidal point was hardened

podium a platform, as was normally constructed for a temple

praefectus a commander of an auxiliary unit at this period

praefectus equitatus a man with an unusual command of a force of cavalry as may have been given to Didius Gallus by Claudius in the invasion of Britain (*ILS 970; Epig Stud* 4 (1967) 65)

praefectus fabrorum an officer in charge of ordnance and workshops

praetorium the house of the commanding officer of a unit and normally adjacent to the *principia*

primus pilus literally 'first javelin', was the chief centurion of a legion, an office held for a year, after which he became an equestrian and he could enter a higher career structure as one of the *primipilares* (see Brian Dobson *Die Primpilares: Entwicklung und Bedeutung, Lauf-bahnen und Persönlich keiten eines römischen Offiziersranges* 1978)

princeps literally 'first', used by Augustus 'the first citizen'

principia the headquarters building in a fort or fortress and occupying the central position

publicanus a man, normally of the equestrian order, whom tax collecting was farmed out i.e. he returned an approved amount to the governor, but could retain for himself any extra he could squeeze out of the provincials

rex king

scutum a shield

statua triumphalis statuettes of precious metal presented as an award for military service

terra nigra pottery made in Gaul and imported into Britain in the Claudian-Neronian period. It was mainly in the form of platters and dishes in a grey ware with a highly polished surface and usually stamped with the maker's name. It was widely imitated in Britain

terra rubra pottery made in Gaul and imported into Britain in the Claudian-Neronian period. It was mainly in the form of cups and bowls in a red ware with a burnished finish and often stamped with the potter's name

tessera a small block of stone or tile laid in mortar to form a tessellated pavement or mosaic

testudo literally a 'tortoise', a technique developed by legionaries – a tight group holding their shield over their head to enable them to advance to a gateway or base of a wall with a battering ram

toga the garment reserved for citizens and worn with carefully arranged drapes on ceremonial and official occasions

tria nomina the three names 'praenomen, nomen and cognomen' normally adopted by a Roman citizen

turma a squadron of 32 mounted men in a quingenary *ala* and probably 30 in a *turma* of a *cohors equitata*

umbo the boss of a shield, usually in heavy metal and often decorated

vigiles literally 'the watch'; there were seven cohorts in Rome whose main duty was to keep the peace at night, but they also acted as the fire brigade. They were an important element in law and order in troubled times.

Appendix 6
Glossary of technical terms

Arretine pottery made at Arretium (Arezzo) in North Italy

barnacle bit a toothed bit used for curbing horses

campaign camp a camp enclosed by a ditch and bank in which the Roman army pitched their tents when on field duties

Claudian the period of the Emperor Claudius (AD 41–54)

Flavian the period of the Flavian emperors, Vespasian, Titus and Domitian (AD 69–96)

fort the word used for a pernament Roman establishment of up to about eight acres, normally for an auxiliary unit

fortress the word used for a permanent legionary establishment

hill-fort a banked or ditched enclosure of pre-Roman times usually on a hill, following the contours

intaglio a carved design on a gemstone or a paste, usually for a ring

mica-dusted a technique used by potters for covering the surface of vessels with flakes of mica to give it a bronze-like appearance

martingale a piece of harness with three holes for traces to be gathered together

niello a black coloured inlay applied to bronzes

pennannular a circular brooch with a gap through which the pin attached loosely to the circle passes

pontoon a floating bridge usually consisting of a line of boats carrying a timber road

samian a red slip pottery made mainly in Gaul, both in plain and decorated forms widely exported to Britain in the first two centuries AD

stater originally a Greek weight but later applied to classical gold coins

Appendix 7
Place names in the modern and Roman forms

Note The tribal affiliations are in brackets since at the period of the conquest none of these places had become tribal capitals – also in the pre-conquest sections of the book Celtic settlements such as CAMVLODONON and VERVLAMION are given the Celtic ending – ON, since they did not become Latinized until after the conquest

Roman name	Modern name
ABONA	Sea Mills
AD PONTEM	East Stoke
AQVAE SVLIS	Bath
BANNAVENTA	Whilton Lodge (Northants)
BANNOVALIVM	Horncastle
CAESAROMAGVS	Chelmsford
CALLEVA (ATREBATVM)	Silchester
CAMVLODVNVM	Colchester
CANONIVM	Kelvedon (Essex)
CAVSENNIS	Ancaster
COMBRETOVIVM	Baylham House (Suffolk)
CORINIVM (DOBVNNVRVM)	Cirencester
CROCOCALANA	Brough (Notts)
CVNETIO	Mildenhall (Wilts)
DVRNOVARIA	Dorchester (Dorset)
DVROBRIVAE	Water Newton (Cambs)
DVROBRIVAE	Rochester
DVROCOBRIVIS	Dunstable
DVROLIPONTE (?)	Cambridge
DVROVERNVM (CANTIACORVM)	Canterbury
DVROVIGVTVM (?)	Godmanchester
GLEVVM	Gloucester
ISCA (DVMNONIORVM)	Exeter
LACTODVRVM	Towcester
LEVCOMAGVS	near Andover
LINDINIS	Ilchester
LINDVM	Lincoln
LONDINIVM	London
MAGIOVINIVM	Dropshort (Bucks)
MANDVESSEDVM	Mancetter (Warks)

Roman name	Modern name
MARGIDVNVM	Castle Hill (Notts)
NOVIOMAGVS (REGNORVM)	Chichester
PONTES	Staines
PORTVS DVBRIS	Dover
RATAE (CORITANORVM)	Leicester
REGVLBIVM	Reculver
RVTVPIAE	Richborough
SABRINA FL.	R Severn
SORVIODVNVM	Old Sarum
SVLLONIACIS	Brockley Hill (Greater London)
TAMESIS FL.	R Thames
TRIPONTIVM	Caves Inn (Warks)
TRISANTONA FL.	R Trent
VECTIS INS.	Isle of Wight
VENONIS	High Cross
VENTA (BELGARVM)	Winchester
VENTA (ICENORVM)	Caistor St Edmunds (Norf)
VERLVCIO	Sandy Lane (Wilts)
VERNEMETVM	Willoughby (Notts)
VERVLAMIVM	St Albans
VINDOCLADIA	Badbury

Modern name	Roman name
Ancaster	CAVSENNIS
Andover (near)	LEVCOMAGVS
Badbury	VINDOCLADIA
Bath	AQVAE SVLIS
Baylham House (Suff)	COMBRETOVIVM
Brockley Hill (Greater London)	SVLLONIACIS
Brough (Notts)	CROCOCALANA
Caistor St Edmunds (Norf)	VENTA (ICENORVM)
Cambridge	DVROLIPONTE (?)
Canterbury	DVROVERNVM (CANTIACORVM)
Castle Hill (Notts)	MARGIDVNVM
Caves Inn (Warks)	TRIPONTIVM
Chelmsford	CAESAROMAGVS
Chichester	NOVIOMAGVS (REGNORVM)
Cirencester	CORINIVM (DOBVNNORVM)
Colchester	CAMVLODVNVM
Dorchester (Dorset)	DVRNOVARIA
Dover	PORTVS DVBRIS
Dropshort (Bucks)	MAGIOVINIVM
Dunstable	DVROCOBRIVIS
East Stoke (Notts)	AD PONTEM

Modern name	Roman name
Exeter	ISCA (DVMNONIORVM)
Gloucester	GLEVVM
Godmanchester	DVROVIGVTVM (?)
High Cross (Leics)	VENONAE
Horncastle	BANNOVALVIM
Ilchester	LINDINIS
Kelvedon (Essex)	CANONIVM
Leicester	RATAE (CORITANORVM)
Lincoln	LINDVM
London	LONDINIVM
Mancetter (Warks)	MANDVESSEDVM
Mildenhall (Wilts)	CVNETIO
Old Sarum	SORVIODVNVM
Reculver	REGVLBIVM
Richborough	RVTVPIAE
St Albans	VERVLAMIVM
Sandy Lane (Wilts)	VERLVCIO
Sea Mills	ABONA
Severn R	SABRINA FL.
Silchester	CALLEVA
Staines	PONTES
Thames R	TAMESIS FL.
Towcester	LACTODVRVM
Trent R	TRISANTONA FL.
Water Newton (Cambs)	DVROBRIVAE
Whilton Lodge (Northants)	BANNAVENTA
Wight, Isle of	VECTIS INS.
Willoughby (Notts)	VERNEMETVM
Winchester	VENTA (BELGARVM)

Index